THE
MANICURIST'S
DAUGHTER

THE MANICURIST'S DAUGHTER

A MEMOIR

Susan Lieu

CELADON
BOOKS
NEW YORK

AUTHOR'S NOTE: This is a true story, although some names have been changed and some characters merged to protect their privacy.

www.celadonbooks.com

All photographs courtesy of the author unless otherwise noted

The Library of Congress Cataloging-in-Publication Data is available upon request.

ISBN 978-1-250-83504-8 (hardcover)
ISBN 978-1-250-83506-2 (ebook)

Our books may be purchased in bulk for promotional, educational,
or business use. Please contact your local bookseller or the Macmillan Corporate
and Premium Sales Department at 1-800-221-7945, extension 5442,
or by email at MacmillanSpecialMarkets@macmillan.com.

First Edition: 2024

10 9 8 7 6 5 4 3 2 1

For Má, Ba, Art,
and every person who wishes to heal.
It's possible.

Contents

PART III: MÀ, *BUT*

PART IV: MÁ, *MOTHER*

PART V: MẠ, *NEWBORN RICE SEEDLING*

PART VI: MÃ, *HORSE*

THE
MANICURIST'S
DAUGHTER

Prologue

Your ovary is angry," the ER ultrasound technician told me. "We need to figure out if it's strangling itself." Was this guy serious? I knew I had self-destructive thoughts, but I had no idea my body was capable of punishing itself. I tried to keep quiet as he twisted the probe inside me, up and down and sideways like a competitive baton twirler. He captured image after image, his right hand touching a combination of six round buttons so fast he looked like a DJ at a rave. My entire pelvic region was tender, but when he touched the spot, I gripped the metal bed railing and howled.

"Right there! Please stop!" It was 10:00 p.m. on a mid-December evening, and I was in the emergency room.

Up until noon that day, I was at an idyllic artist residency on Vashon Island, a quick ferry ride from urban Seattle. The opportunity was a blessing from the Universe that fell into my lap. Seventeen days in a gorgeous waterfront house with three other artists: a paper cutter devoted to the shape of hands, an animator obsessed with a Russian mirror catalog and CGI fashion, and another writer who had a history with notorious stalkers. This would be like *The Real World*, but for artists, and I was the lucky one who got a detached cottage so

I could finally be alone. I could turn off the nonstop demands of being a wife and a mother of a toddler. No responsibility with a capital R. I couldn't wait, and frankly, I was running out of time.

I had promised my editor a "killer" draft in the new year. Originally, I'd said October, which was pushed from my August hope. My advance money dried up, so I took on some side hustles, which ate up more writing time. As if I didn't have enough typical writer angst, there was one constraint I could not wriggle my way out of. I wanted to publish this memoir when I was thirty-eight, the same age my mother was when she died from a tummy tuck. That meant I had to get a polished draft to my editor in January, which meant I had to perform a literary miracle with my manuscript. As a procrastinator, I needed deadlines with actual consequences. This was a real deadline.

I was ten days into my residency and finally in the flow when an electric shock drove up into my pelvic area. I attempted to stand from my computer chair, but I couldn't move. The pain was at a level ten with sharp pangs coming from every direction. I started yelling, but no one could hear me—I was in my prized cottage, separate from the rest of the house.

It was happening again. The first time was a little more than a month earlier. I couldn't stand, sit, or walk, so I spent a few hours on the floor in the happy baby pose after popping ibuprofen and a THC gummy. To get to my bed ten feet away, it took five minutes of very tiny shuffling fully supported by my husband. Thankfully, it went away the next day. In the morning, I called my doctor, but she wasn't that concerned. No referral, no nothing.

Now the pain was back, and I was on an island that didn't have a hospital. But none of this should be happening. I had been diligently journaling my morning pages, meditating with an app, and bathing myself in affirmations on YouTube with galactic background music. Plus, I was training for a marathon while listening to *Oprah's Master Class* podcast. I thought I had the whole self-care box checked off.

Plus, I couldn't afford time away from the residency. My deadline was just two weeks away.

I looked around for my phone. I thought I was being clever by putting it in different drawers so I could be less distracted. But now I couldn't reach it. I got another thirty-second shock, a cramping pain so severe it felt like I was in labor again. When the pain subsided, I knew this was my chance. I hobbled to my front door, but before I could twist the knob, the lightning came again, even deeper. I slipped slowly onto the cold granite tile and flopped over into a fetal position. Right when the pain faded again, I made what felt like a fifty-foot dash for the residency director's office. Instead, I moved like I had gunshot wounds, holding my stomach, dragging a leg, grunting to move a few feet. I looked like a mummy who had to go potty.

"Heather? I need help." I tried to be calm, but the pain came again, and then I grabbed onto her desk to break my fall, giving her all the relevant details as I crumbled onto the floor. Eventually, we sped away in her tiny Chinese electric car, which topped out at a whopping thirty-five miles per hour. After an excruciatingly painful fifty-minute wait for the ferry (where I called several urgent care facilities only to be informed that their next appointment was in four hours), we went to the closest emergency room.

After my insurance company reassured me there would be no multi-thousand-dollar surprise, I checked into the facility at 2:30 p.m., where they took my vitals and a blood sample. I waited. And then waited some more. After two hours of leaning on the sides of my thighs to relieve the abdominal pressure, I couldn't take it any longer. I asked if I could lie down somehow.

"We don't have any empty beds. Sorry," said the apathetic receptionist, who was mostly texting on her phone. Then I asked for a mat or a sheet so I could lie on the floor with legs up on a chair, my lazy happy baby pose. "That's not recommended" was all she said. I asked her again, but now smoke was flaring out of my nose like an angry dragon.

"Please!" I begged. Didn't she understand that I didn't come here to hang out for fun? This pain was nonstop, but she didn't seem to care. "Fine!" I threw down my coat and carefully moved my body to the ground so I could relieve the pressure buildup. It was then that the receptionist appeared with three sets of sheets.

"Here," she said, tossing them down on the ground. I looked at the twentysomething employee the way I look at my toddler when I'm upset, scowling. As I lay down on the worn sheets, I started to cry. I didn't like being vulnerable. I hated that I couldn't fix my way out of this. A woman sitting in the waiting room asked if she could be with me. I let her. She seemed like a mom. I emoted. She listened. Three hours in, two other women also commiserated about their health ailments until we all got wheeled away by different nurses, waving until the double doors closed.

I spent the next five hours on a hospital bed doing more waiting. I still had waves of pain, but they were at a pain level of four or five. This time, I had more comfort from cable television featuring a *Friends* marathon. When my ER doctor came in, he said he'd ordered an ultrasound.

"My triage nurse said CT scan. Are we doing that too?" I asked. The doctor thought about it and agreed, which surprised me. "Wait, I'm not the medical professional here. Could we do both, or what's the benefit of doing one before the other?" I was confused. How could I have swayed him so quickly? He said he forgot what he read on my chart. The CT scan would give us a more comprehensive picture, and if needed, the ultrasound would zoom in on the problem. The last time I checked, I was an artist and he was the doctor. I had always been a little skeptical of relying on just Western medicine, but this interaction made me feel even more nervous. Was there anything else he forgot to consider?

The CT scan revealed a burst cyst on my right ovary, which led me to the ultrasound technician. My blood flow was regular, which meant my ovary wasn't actually strangling itself—yet. I could grow another cyst, and if it was much bigger than the one I had now, it had the ability to double over and choke my ovaries. I was discharged with the recommendation to have a follow-up with my ob-gyn.

"But what if the pain comes back?" I asked. "What exactly do I do?" My only tool would be ibuprofen and returning to the ER. Western medicine could only confirm what they saw. I arrived home at midnight after an almost ten-hour hospital visit and six episodes of Ross and Rachel giving each other mixed signals. The next morning, I hopped on the 9:30 a.m. ferry to return to Vashon Island. Jill, the writer from my residency, picked me up from the ferry. She was kind, lanky, and spoke in whispers.

Back at the residency, I kept hitting a wall with revising my memoir, so I kept doing irrelevant tasks to feel productive—that is, until the Universe intervened. At 4:00 p.m., another knife up my entire midsection. My phone was on the shelf, and I had ibuprofen ready, but I couldn't move my body to reach it. When the first wave passed, I got my provisions and slid onto the bed in the fetal position. I called my ob-gyn triage nurse, and in between my yelling and crying, she told me to call 9-1-1.

"But what if the pain goes away?" I screamed. Clearly, it hadn't. She urged me to get help so someone could come check my vitals. Amid the stabbing pain, I managed to call Jill because it was Heather's day off. Then I called my husband, Marvin, and asked him how much the ambulance would cost with our insurance. When Jill arrived, I gave her my phone. I kept trying to call 9-1-1 but kept pressing 6-9-9. I was useless.

Firefighters came, and I was eventually wrapped in a series of sheets and carried to the icy gravel driveway. They put me on a gurney and wheeled me backward into an ambulance as my residency friends waved goodbye. The doors slammed shut, I got strapped in, and then it hit me. This is what my mother went through the day she went into a coma and never returned. Rushed into an ambulance without any loved ones riding with her, completely subject to an EMT stranger. The parallels made me weep.

My mother was in an ambulance all alone when she was thirty-eight. A botched plastic surgery from a negligent surgeon. She went without oxygen to her brain for fourteen minutes before he made the 9-1-1 call. Here I was, thirty-seven years old, about the same height and weight as she was, also alone. I wasn't ready to die. My son was almost three. My mother died when I was eleven.

I started talking to my Creator. *Give me until I'm sixty—wait, no, seventy-five. And I'm not ready yet. I have to publish this book!* That was my real answer. I didn't say *spare me because of my son.* I wanted more time so I could tell my family story. Guilt, then shame set in. Then it was the pain that shocked me back to the present moment. I had also been listening to Eckhart Tolle on my runs, where he said "the now" was all there was. The Universe had a sick sense of humor.

My EMT, Bridgette, who was an on-call volunteer (and in the middle of making a fettucine alfredo when the firefighter called her cell), took my vitals as the ambulance raced to the ferry dock. I called out "Pain!" every time it came, while she took note of time intervals. I was having body shocks every three to five minutes for thirty seconds. If my cyst had already burst, why was the pain back in full force? They said once it ruptured, I should feel better, but I was only feeling worse. When I arrived at the hospital in the city center, it was 6:30 p.m. Since I'd come in on a stretcher, I had to wait only thirty minutes instead of three hours to be admitted. My privilege made me feel conflicted, but I was so relieved when they started giving me care.

For the next four hours, I was on a bed in hallway 9, and it was bustling. There was a woman in her eighties who kept wandering outside her room saying it wasn't her fault she beat up the man. She kept insisting for a clock, because without knowing the time, she found everything disorienting. There was another elderly woman whose eye was completely swollen shut with a busted lip from a bad fall. Her son and husband took turns sitting next to her as doctors rolled different devices in to treat her. An unhoused man with no socks grumpily ate some hospital food and slept. A social worker reviewed his history with him, trying to figure out if he had anyone in his life who would pick up a call. There were two temporary health care workers just sitting around looking at their phones, trying to avoid getting moved to another facility late at night. Another worker sanitized a room in a full hazmat suit. Nurses and doctors walked briskly in Hoka shoes past the nurse's station lit with blue Christmas lights. Maybe a nod to code blue.

The first nurse to check my vitals asked me where I was from. Santa Rosa, California, the artery of the wine country, I liked to say. He told me, as a young boy, he frequented the town's small airport to meet his father, who was a pilot. Somehow knowing that he took the same highway exits I once did calmed me down. It was irrational, but aren't most things we use to comfort ourselves?

After much poking and prodding, the ER doctor gave me the same diagnosis as the day before. But this time, I was prepared. I looked down at my handwritten list of questions. Doctors were like celebrities. There was so much anticipation to talk to them that I knew I would instantly forget my laundry list of concerns. I would only be able to react to whatever they said.

I started rattling off my questions. *What activities should I avoid? Should I only eat anti-inflammatory foods? Should I get a colonoscopy? My blood test says I'm low on that thing I can't pronounce. When I keep clicking on links and cross-referencing that with where my pain is—do I have liver cancer? What causes have been eliminated? What aggravates it? If I have another episode, what do I do?* She told me to carry pain relievers and cautioned me not to get too paranoid from internet research. Then I asked to see the on-call ob-gyn from the Northwest Women's Clinic who delivered babies at the hospital, including my own the last time I was in this hospital. I wanted a second opinion.

"I have a follow-up with the group's nurse next week, but since I'm here, can I see the doctor instead?" I asked.

The ER doctor leaned in close. "She's just going to tell you the same thing I told you," she said without much compassion.

I knew she was probably right, but no one had solved my body's mystery. Could this happen tomorrow or never again? Was this about the cyst or something else? And what was her deal?

"It would just give me peace of mind since I'm already here." I held my ground and waited, but I was now feeling a little scared for even asking.

"I'll call, but she's not going to tell you anything different," she mumbled as she walked away.

Her behavior was so unsettling. Since I started telling my family story about my mother's medical malpractice death, I learned about patient advocate principles: make a list of questions, bring a person to help support, ask for what I need. But even knowing all of this, having to insist on talking to my ob-gyn felt extremely uncomfortable.

Then it hit me again. The frustration and confusion I was feeling was just a fraction of what my Vietnamese refugee father went through when my mother was in a coma after her plastic surgery. No way was he going to challenge authority or know what questions to ask. The person he conferred with on all the decisions was my nineteen-year-old brother. Here I was with my two Ivy League degrees, communicating in my native language, and eager to make requests. He didn't have a high school education and spoke broken English. Even with all my advantages, I still felt belittled and intimidated by my doctor. My father didn't stand a chance.

The gynecologist came, bringing comfort and new information. The cyst did burst, but the ongoing pain was unusual. She was confident it was not an issue related to my uterus and encouraged me to keep investigating with my physician. It felt reassuring that the behemoth medical system still had individuals who cared.

The next morning, I decided I would not return to Vashon Island and just focus on my health instead. Since no one actually had answers, I did what I do when Western medicine can't cure me—I scheduled acupuncture. After waiting on hold for far too long with my primary care team, I did the thing that would make me feel undeniably good. I made an appointment for a haircut. My split ends had been looking obnoxious for months and agitated me every time I looked in the mirror. My biannual haircut was long overdue. Even though I despised driving, I hopped in the car and roughed it through the rain and dense traffic to a salon across town because my girlfriend said the style was nice and the price was right. Plus it was owned by a Vietnamese single mom.

Once I arrived at Hiếu Organic Spa, I waited with two other customers who were getting their nails done. When the stylist called my name, I decided to treat myself with a shampoo. Soothing circles around my temples, feeling held at different acupressure points, being bathed like a baby with warm water. I felt like I could finally relax after the nonstop forty-eight-hour health scare.

When it was time for my cut, I did what I usually do in Vietnamese salons—I pretended I didn't understand Vietnamese. Eavesdropping was such a guilty pleasure, and I wanted to see if they talked smack about me. I made my guess at who the owner was, the power broker out of them. The one who answered the phone and triaged all the walk-in customers was also my hair stylist, which comforted me. Owners take pride in their work, so I felt like I would be in good hands. As she twirled the black haircut cape around my front, customers kept coming through asking how long the wait time would be for a pedicure. The shop was so busy, she had to turn people away.

Above her station mirror, I saw a picture of her toddler boy posing in a 1930s-era outfit with an antique train. Whenever I met mothers of young children, I felt an instant affinity. We spoke about the shape of my cut and settled on layers like Rachel's from *Friends*. Television can be so influential. Then my stylist asked if I'd heard about the winter light show at Tulalip Resort Casino, the one by the outlets. She was thinking about taking her seven-year-old son to see that and the headlining singer.

"Vietnamese?" I asked.

"Yes, how did you know?" she asked, a bit surprised.

"I'm Vietnamese." I smirked. And so began our intense conversation. Where was the newest phở place to try? Which bánh mì place had the best bread? Then I nonchalantly brought up my family story. I had to.

"I'm writing a book on nail salons. My mom had two, but she died. She was thirty-eight." The stylist stopped thinning my hair with a razor. "Tummy tuck," I explained. I told her everything. The plastic surgeon's probation, his lack of malpractice insurance, Má having four kids. My hair stylist simultaneously translated to all her nail workers: her niece, her husband's sister, and her sister.

"San Francisco! Nineteen ninety-six!" she exclaimed. Before I could finish my story, she pulled up her long white-sleeve shirt. "Look!" Her arm was covered in goose bumps. "I've been thinking about getting a tummy tuck for the last three months," she admitted. "People have been saying Florida, Korea, maybe even Bellevue. But now you come here and sit in my chair and tell me this! I shouldn't do it." I looked at the hair that stood straight up on her arm and then at her son's photo. Earlier she had said my Vietnamese was so bad, I sounded cute, like a toddler. That may be true, but the Vietnamese I did know was the Vietnamese she needed to hear.

"Rồi bây giờ chị còn muốn thử mạng nữa không?" I asked. *So now, do you still want to keep playing with your life?* She complained about her C-section scar. "Think about who you're doing it for," I urged. And then she answered how I think my mother would have answered.

"For me," she said confidently.

"But why?" I pressed.

She replied right back without hesitation. "I want to be pretty," she said unabashedly. An answer so honest, what could I say back? Didn't I also squeeze my own belly fat and wish things could be different? I tried to stay neutral.

"Just let me send you my show" was all I said, trying to keep the urgency I felt out of my voice. I had written and performed a one-woman show about my family's tragedy, where I played fifteen characters. My mother thought plastic surgery was safe. After all, everyone was doing it. I wanted my stylist to see how my family's unprocessed grief still impacted us two decades later. She went by Felicity on Zelle, but she was Út to her workers, meaning the *youngest*. I was the út in my family too. She obliged and gave me her cell phone number.

With my new freshly cut locks, I pushed open the door and headed to my car, marveling at the fortuitous encounter. There were plenty of salons in my neighborhood, but there was a reason why I came all this way to sit in her chair, on this day, at this moment. Maybe my mother had a hand in it. When I got home, I sent my show link and another Vietnamese saying. Hôm nay có duyên. *Today was serendipitous.*

The salon was named after her son. Hiếu, meaning *filial piety*, was the Confucian concept of a child demonstrating care and respect for one's parents, especially in their older years. But how could her young son fulfill this virtue if Felicity died an early death? If anything bad happened with her plastic surgery, she wouldn't be around to see him become a young man to execute his duty. This was all hitting too close to home.

I didn't see Felicity as weak or insecure. She was entrepreneurial and running a successful salon. In so many ways, she reminded me of my mother, which was why I was afraid for her.

After three days without pain, I returned to Vashon Island refreshed and ready to write. I didn't need the Universe intervening with any more surprises, and I was simply tired of waiting—in the hospital, in the salon, in the writing chair. Who knew how much grace I would be given to finish what I set out to do with this memoir. This book couldn't wait any longer—body's orders.

Vengeance

EVERYONE KNOWS THE TRAGEDY OF THE DEAD,

BUT LET'S TALK ABOUT THE TRAGEDY OF THE LIVING.

t all began the first day of solo performance class with the task to tell a five-minute story. I was there because I didn't want to be a coward anymore. As a budding stand-up comic, I was in my orbit onstage, but a heckler at a charity comedy show made fun of me so bad, I avoided the microphone for three years. Now married, I was getting nonstop pressure from my father and aunts to have children, but a part of me felt disappointed with the adult I thought I would be (a revolutionary stage performer) and the one I actually became (a thirty-two-year-old with a corporate desk job as a contractor at Microsoft, not even FTE status). How could I tell my future kid to pursue their dreams when I hid from my own?

It was 2017, and I was sitting in the basement of a small community theater with four white women all decades older than I was. I let them go first. A bohemian shaman recounted how a neighbor obnoxiously interrupted her drum circle and how she retaliated by bitching her out. A spunky woman in her eighties fawned over a legendary Miami hairdresser named Alfonso, who changed women's lives. A soccer mom sang a song about sorting through her estranged late father's possessions. I tried to be present, but I kept thinking about what I would say. I had been quiet about my family story for twenty-one years, shaking the details back and forth like a two-liter soda bottle. When Paul, the instructor, asked me to speak, I tried to unscrew the cap with control, but it flew off like a cannon.

On the last day of her life, Má, my Vietnamese refugee *mother* and proud owner of two nail salons, went in for plastic surgery—a tummy tuck, the narrowing of her nostrils, a chin implant—and figured she would be home the next day with her beautiful new body. Two hours into the operation, she lost oxygen to her brain. The human brain can go without oxygen for up to four minutes before permanent brain damage occurs. Fourteen minutes passed before the surgeon called 9-1-1. After five days in a coma, she flatlined. And when Má died, when my sun fell out of the sky, she was thirty-eight years old. I was eleven.

After that, my family was never the same. Ba, my *father*, stopped singing karaoke on Sunday mornings. My aunts and grandparents on my mom's side moved out, so we had all these rice bowls we never used anymore. And nobody ever talked about it. Every year, on her death anniversary, we would light incense for her. Then we ate in silence. My mother was dead, but in a sense, we were too, and I was powerless to change it.

It wasn't until I went to college that I learned words like "capitalism," "exploitation," and "intergenerational trauma." In grad school, far away from my family, I began to plot my revenge. I realized my mother's death wasn't just tragic, it was complex. It was the result of a negligent white man with a track record of preying on vulnerable Vietnamese refugees. It was classist and sexist, and he got away with it, never paying my family a dime. Prior to my mother's procedure, he had been sanctioned by the medical board on two separate occasions, and he didn't even carry malpractice insurance. This was not some shady back-alley operation. This happened in San Francisco, on Geary Boulevard in 1996.

I wanted to make him suffer. I wanted to sue him for all the money he had and give it to my dad because he didn't have a retirement fund—he did nails. I started fantasizing about a multipronged marketing campaign with targeted Facebook ads to the doctor, a billboard by his clinic, an exposé in his local paper. I wanted him to never mess with Vietnamese people ever again. This was how I would avenge my mother's death.

And right when I was going to launch my smear campaign, I found out he died a month prior. Parkinson's. Picking cherry tomatoes in his garden. The gall. The very person that would free me from my misery slipped like oil through my fingers, along with any hope to bring redemption to my family. I had hit a wall. I could not win without an enemy. It was a sign that I had to finally move on. But three years after the doctor's death, I still had so many questions about my mother. I couldn't stop searching for her, because the very people who knew her best—my family—wouldn't let me in.

When I finally let it all out, I looked up at my instructor, Paul, feeling like I just did something illegal. I tried to read the stoic light-skinned faces in the room. For some reason, I wanted to apologize for burdening them. What the fuck had I done? My instructor began to clap.

"Have you performed this story before?" he asked. No, I told him, a little worried I'd just betrayed my family. I was conditioned to them yelling at me to stop. But here, to my shock, no one made me feel bad for talking about Má. Instead, Paul said my story needed to be told. I heard his words, but I didn't believe him. Adrenaline was surging through my veins, and alarm bells were going off in my head. I had done the thing I was not supposed to do.

"It's dirty laundry," I muttered to my hands. "Only my husband knows." And he knew it all too well. Inside our Seattle apartment, there was a small den that had all the clues I had been collecting over the years hastily hung with torn blue painter's tape like a crime scene investigation. A newspaper article on Dr. Moglen and my mother. The addresses of his plastic surgery clinics. Medical board verdicts. His obituary. The name of the Vietnamese magazine where Má probably saw his ad. Normal people have hobbies like book club, a socially acceptable excuse to drink wine and get a night away from their husbands. I had an obsession that I was not allowed to talk about. So I would eat edibles at my dining table and go down internet rabbit holes late into the night, wondering if the doctor and his family suffered the way mine did. Contemplating why my mom did it when she had gotten the American dream and then some. Why was she willing to risk it all when everything she had was already picture-perfect?

After the solo performance course ended, I began doing more research on who Má was, taking my findings to the stage so I could make sense of it all in real time. As I sorted through the few pictures I had of Má, searching for a clue as to who she was, I was tickled by her poses. There was a time when Vietnamese women loved taking portraits with their eyes gazing off camera as their face graced a beautiful rose. The mood was soft, gentle, forlorn. Over an eight-year period from 1988 to 1996, there were five photos of her, a fashionable statue in the flesh looking right into the camera with her jade-green bracelet, impeccably polished nails, and an elegant hairdo. She stood in bright jumpers and chic dresses in matching heels, but on tall rocks. It was as if she knew she would be immortalized.

Má was the general of the house and the center of our livelihood, our nail salon. And since all her employees were our bà con, *our relatives*, both were one and the same. From her perch at the head table closest to the salon door, her word was truth. She did not plead with anyone, she commanded. Somehow, she always knew what to do, and we dutifully obeyed. She had the master plan, leading with the omniscience of Oz, the high expectations of Confucius, and the charm of Princess Diana.

Má never whined, she manifested. After arriving penniless to America as boat people, we moved from a small subsidized apartment in Emeryville, California, to a two-story house in San Pablo that we owned in just eight years. One day, five relatives showed up all the way from Việt Nam to help us build our nail salon empire. Then, we had a second nail salon, a third car.

Má had a hot temper. Sometimes she would start yelling at my father, and he never fought back. When that would happen, all of us kids would wait and watch, not sure what would happen next. When she found out my older brother, Kang, was smoking pot in college, she changed the locks on the front door. She didn't give him a new key until he made the dean's list again.

Even though Má was completely responsible for everyone's livelihood, she never seemed scared; she was just scary. When I was six, Lan, our Vietnamese neighbor friend, accidentally cracked my forehead with an aluminum baseball bat when I was trying to get his attention behind home plate. I teetered, walking backward in shock with blood dripping down my face. Instead of tending to me, Lan started freaking out to my brothers: "Oh, man! Your mom is gonna kill me!" She was that mom who frightened all the neighborhood children.

Má was at the epicenter of our thirteen-person household, which meant I rarely had alone time with her. I can only recount four memories when it was just the two of us, and only one of those memories is not filled with shame. I observed my mother more than I interacted with her. My idea of hanging out with her was spinning in the black leather swivel chair at her station when we weren't busy. It was a space where she gave her full attention to customers, a place where I wanted to get to know her, but she always had me on another chore: fill the cotton containers, confirm the next day's appointments, vacuum the floor. Even though I never had those heart-to-heart conversations I saw on *Full House* between the kids and adults, it was nice to be needed by her.

Since she vanished, every experience I have in life goes through the sieve of my mother's death. Even when I dress my body, I think about her. I know which pieces fit a little too snugly, the ones that make me feel too self-conscious to wear. This has made me feel especially guilty because that kind of thinking killed her. And after I got married at thirty, my motherhood journey became a group decision with Ba and my aunts on my mother's side pounding their fists and me freaking out inside.

My elders insisted I start as soon as possible. "You're not a kid anymore," reminded Dì Phương, *Aunt* Phương. She was Má's youngest sister of her ten siblings. I laughed it off and said I didn't want kids, citing climate change and saving money for an early retirement. But the real answer I could never say to their faces was that if the baby came and I didn't know what to do, who would I call? How could I become a mother if I never knew my own?

When I am with my family, we talk about three things: how to make money, how to save money, and what we are going to eat next. Whenever I brought up a conversation that had the slightest whiff of vulnerability, I would get a series of stonewalled faces—my elders and Americanized siblings alike. Innocent questions about Má's personality became land mines. Even on her death anniversary, when we huddled around her grave offering her favorite foods, talking about her was off-limits.

As the youngest of my four siblings, I was not allowed to challenge anyone older than I was, which was everyone. I had to save face, even at the expense of my own. I was supposed to shrink to make space for others to be comfortable. Even though I was a hojicha-latte-drinking, downward-dog-bending, Ivy League–educated American, I would be forever microchipped Vietnamese. I was not, under any circumstances, allowed to talk about our secrets, or else I would risk my relationship with my family.

Má was more mystery than mother. In Vietnamese, there are six tones that can change the definition of a word. The mid-level tone "ma" means *ghost*. The high-rising tone "má" means *mother* in the southern Vietnamese dialect we speak at home. The low-falling tone "mà" means *but*, the word I kept saying when my family kept dismissing my insistence to know more. The low-rising or questioning tone "mả" means *tomb*, the place where we think we buried just a body but many more things are buried there too. The high broken tone, that kind of sounds like a bleating sheep, "mã" means *horse* (a Sino-Vietnamese word), my father's zodiac sign. And finally the heavy glottal stop "mạ," which means *newborn rice seedling*, the quintessential ingredient to a Vietnamese meal—and sometimes, unfortunately, the only way my family shows they care.

With just another diacritic mark, the same root word takes on a different meaning. It has taken me years, but now I know how all their meanings tie together to help me understand what happened to Má and to my family after her sudden death. For over two decades, we didn't speak of her. It was as if she never existed, which was worse than becoming a myth. At least with a myth, you had details. Instead, I had fragmented, fading memories. Perhaps sharing details would force my family to relive the pain of the past. Perhaps there was too much shame tied to how she died. But avoiding her altogether, that's how she truly died for me.

As the youngest child, I felt like I never knew her, and no one would let me in. They accused me of being too much of a baby, too emotional.

"Bỏ qua đi," said Ba with exasperation. *Let it go.* The verb "bỏ" is also used when throwing away trash.

"Có gì để nói?" whispered Dì Phương. *What else is there to say?*

"Live in the now," insisted Kang, my oldest sibling.

"Go wash your face!" ordered Hang, my second-oldest sibling, whenever I started to cry.

"Can we talk about something else?" squirmed Wendy, the next in line.

Even though we were boat people who came to America in 1983, Má's awful death made us refugees a second time in 1996. We had to rebuild our lives all over again, but instead of doing it together as we had always done with Má at the helm, each of us did it alone in silence. I have tried to process her death with therapists over the years, but retelling the narrative over and over again wears down even the steadiest of treadmills. Without my family providing me with more memories of Má or joining me in processing the worst experience of our lives, I have been stuck running in place going nowhere. And that can make a person do crazy things, like join a cult, track down the killer's family, seek justice through the help of spirit channelers, and put on a touring one-woman show about my family tragedy. But I'll get to all of that later.

Two decades after we lost her, I was still trying to reconstruct who she was, but no one—not Ba, my siblings, or my mother's sisters—wanted to talk. On the brink of motherhood myself, I felt scared. How could I become a mother if I never knew my own? I still had so many questions. I wanted to know why my self-empowered feminist mother wanted plastic surgery. I wanted to know who she was and how I was like her. And most of all, I wanted to know if I could heal from this trauma when my family could not give me what I need. I was on the hunt for answers, and this was my attempt to resurrect her so I would never forget what my family is capable of and where we come from. Seeking the truth was how I would avenge my mother's death. I am the manicurist's daughter, and this is our story.

PART 1

MA

Ghost

Susan's Nails

Memories of Má are fleeting. I try to grasp them tightly, but they slip away, becoming murkier with every passing year. The setting where she was the most alive was at Susan's Nails, our family nail salon named after me, the first born in America. Má was our fearless leader calling all the shots, and we all admired her.

My family traveled to the salon in our black-and-white Previa, which looked like Shamu the whale from SeaWorld. At 9:00 a.m., we pulled open the side door and spilled out like a clown car. Nine people in a seven-seater van. Dì Phương and our family friend Cô Thảo were at the trunk pulling out two black garbage bags full of hand towels we washed at home. Dì Ngân and Dì Hiệp handled Bà Ngoại's carefully packed lunch stacked in silver tiffins and reused old pickle jars. Bà Ngoại, my *maternal grandmother*, sealed the brown paper bag with another plastic bag and tied a double knot. "Chắc ăn hơn," she liked to say. *Extra secure.* My older cousin Hằng was hovering over two gallon-size jugs of acetone and cuticle remover, ready to do a dead lift.

Once Má pushed the back door kickstand down, we were supposed to enter the salon in single file. But I pushed past everyone, leaping over the ankle-level laser beam like a hurdle. It beeped whenever anyone walked into the salon so we knew when customers arrived. I swung the creaky restroom door open to see if I had to restock toilet paper, flipped on five light switches, and started sprinting down the long, narrow hallway. I zoomed past all the pedicure chairs and manicurist tables and then did a long jump toward the front door, where I leaned my entire torso into the front display window and yanked the metal beaded string, turning the neon-pink Open sign on. We were officially in business.

"Đốt nhang đi con!" Má yelled to me. *Light incense, kid!* I walked to the hand sink area where a two-foot-tall golden Buddha watched over us. He was bald, fat, and laughing. His statue was located directly underneath the TV that was placed twenty feet up on a ledge by the tiled mirror ceiling that curved at the top like a grand archway. Wherever you were in the shop, your reflection could be seen. I knelt on the floor by our small red altar with a statue of a bearded Asian guy with bushy eyebrows, a fancy robe, and a long staff. I didn't know his name, but we offered fruit to him every week, and it was my job to ask him and our ancestors to help us make a ton of money. I didn't want it to be my fault if we didn't have customers, so I had to really believe every time I lit incense.

My thumb took a few painful pulls at the lighter. Once the incense started to glow on the mustard-brown stick, I waved out the small flame and put the joss stick by my forehead with my eyes closed. I began to talk inside my head.

Dear Buddha, I hope we make so much money that Má gives me and Wendy money to buy lunch at the mall and we have a little extra to get some stickers from the Hello Kitty store. Thank you so much . . . Have a nice day.

I planted the stick into the holder, finding stability in the uncooked jasmine rice grains. After three bows on the dusty linoleum floor, I opened the scary supply closet and quickly pulled out the vacuum cleaner so I wouldn't get trapped in there. I started at the first table, the vacuum emitting a crackling sound like a deep fryer as it sucked up flimsy pieces of silk wrap, rogue cotton balls underneath the table, and inches of fake nail clippings. There were six nail salon workers on the assembly line, and they sat in their order of hierarchy: Má, Dì Phương, Cô Thảo, Dì Ngân, Dì Hiệp, and Hằng.

Má commanded from the first table, welcoming customers and inquiring what they wanted. From there, she delegated. Má was the most skilled, mastering the latest nail salon trends. She was the first to do paraffin wax to soften feet calluses, learn body waxing, master silk wrap and gel fills. As the general, she had no patience nor preference for pedicures. As Bà Ngoại's ninth child, her given name was Hà Thị Phường, but all her customers knew her as Jennifer.

Dì Phương, the youngest of Má's ten siblings, went by Kim and was a sweet talker to her customers at the second table. When my aunt first arrived in America, she shadowed Má during the day and applied acrylic tips to a scary life-size silicone hand in her downtime. At home after dinner, she spent her evenings memorizing every line in the cosmetology manual for her impending license exam. Since there was absolutely no space in the house, she studied at the top of the stairs until 3:00 a.m., nodding off and getting an occasional rude whack from Má to wake up. On exam day, Dì Phương was trembling because failing wasn't an option. The testing fees were high, and Má needed her working in the shop immediately. Since then, Dì Phương ascended the ranks and now had the highest number of scheduled appointments after Má. My youngest aunt had Má's strategic eye and served as a deputy officer, offering carefully measured insights when appropriate. My aunt's name was spelled exactly the same as my mother with just one different diacritic mark. Má was Phường and my aunt was Phương. To make it easier, all the adults called Má by her nickname, Muội. With strikingly similar facial structures, the two sisters were close in age and sometimes wore matching black knit sweaters adorned with flowers. Dì Phương looked the most like Ông Ngoại, my *maternal grandfather*, with their high-bridge nose. She was one of the few people who challenged Má and Bà Ngoại, but in a sweet way. I liked her the most because she took the time to play with me.

Cô Thảo, or *Miss* Thảo, was Dì Phương's childhood best friend from our home village, who sat at the third table. She had a more masculine energy, matched with a boyish haircut. She led with wit and was gregarious with her American customers, who knew her as Amy. She frequently asked them for definitions of American slang so she could quickly improve her English. With her Vietnamese counterparts, she was daring, always inviting them to go gambling at the casino or egging them on to take a sip of Bud Light out of Bà Ngoại's sight line. And when she had a microphone in hand, she was as masterful as Ba singing karaoke on Sundays when we opened a few hours later. When she had criticism, she wasn't afraid to hold her tongue. Perhaps she was less filtered around Má because she didn't owe her anything, unlike my mother's sisters, who were sponsored over by her. Nevertheless, Cô Thảo was a fighter and she did acrylic fills fast, so Má happily kept her around.

Dì Ngân (Tina, seventh-born) and Dì Hiệp (Diana, tenth-born) were interchangeable at the fourth and fifth tables. Dì Ngân was super short at four feet tall—I was just as tall as she was at eight years old. She was the oldest of the four sisters in America, but you wouldn't know it because she was a wallflower, her bob swaying from side to side whenever she chuckled with her faint wheezy laugh. Dì Hiệp was a little taller with a short boyish haircut and plump cheeks. She was simple, predictable, and sometimes aloof.

Both of them were reliable workhorses who were faster at mani-pedis over the acrylic fills. Even though they were both older than Má, they completely trusted their younger sister and complied with all her requests. After all, Má was the one who had beaten the odds and made it to America so everyone else could come over. These two sisters were not aggressive or egotistical, but it wasn't that they weren't ambitious. They knew the nail salon would be built on persistent effort, so they fully dedicated themselves to the workhorse role—in the name of family.

Near the end of the line was my cousin Hằng, daughter of the first-born of Bà Ngoại's clan of children. She was the freshest off the boat, having arrived in 1995. Má facilitated the marriage between her niece and her friend's son, another Vietnamese refugee who'd arrived a decade earlier. Then a fortunate thing happened: the couple actually fell in love. Now in America, Hằng started at the bottom of the ladder, spending her days observing Dì Phương so that she could pass her manicurist exam. And once she did, she would have to choose an American name that spoke to her.

Finally, at the last table was Ba, the Airbrush King. He wasn't the lowest ranked; he was Má's wild card. Most of the time, he was nowhere to be found, running errands that took him to Costco, the hardware store, and an hour south to Oakland for salon supplies. When it was especially busy, Má would page him on his beeper and he would magically appear, slinging acrylic fills at lightning speed like a shoot-out in a Western. His table also held the airbrush machine, which sounded like a loud jackhammer when customers wanted stenciled images of leopard prints and floating hearts. He only did acrylic fills and manicures. Like Má, he had a disdain for feet and the authority to deny them.

The two people who didn't get a table were Wendy and me. When we started at the shop, I was six and Wendy was nine. Má had me on beverages, serving instant Folgers coffee and jasmine tea. I would walk these hot Styrofoam cups in slow, measured steps, terrified I would spill on the carpet, or worse, a precious customer. Once my sister and I finished our homework, there was always something more to do: arrange the nail polish in numerical order; carry the customers' purses to the hand-drying station; feed the parking meters; fold the hand towels; straighten the magazines.

Then one day, Má said I was ready. She wanted me to call customers to confirm their appointments for the next day. My heart started to pound because this was a high-stakes job. I could mess up by dialing the wrong number. I could leave the wrong callback number on their answering machine. Even worse, what if the customer actually picked up the phone and I had to talk to them? I told Má I was too scared. All she did was say what she always said.

"You have one mind and two hands like everyone else—figure it out!" My six-year-old hands wouldn't stop sweating on the first call. By the end of it, I was acting like the customers were my best friends and I was inviting them to a sleepover. Now nine years old, I spent more time at the front of the shop removing nail polish and hamming it up with customers when we were running behind.

After I was done with the morning vacuuming, I made my rounds placing fresh towels at each of the manicure and pedicure stations. When all the store opening chores were done and we were waiting for customers to arrive, Cô Thảo took out a deck of cards from her drawer. It was time to play a round of Tiến Lên, a Vietnamese card game known as "attack," "advance forward," or "continue onwards"— the very thing Vietnamese were conditioned to do after a millennia of invasion.

"Vô đi, bà con ơi!" she hollered as she moved like a casino dealer, a riffle shuffle with a fancy cascade finish. *Come in, family!* Everyone started to gather around the airbrush table as the cards slid across the acrylic-dusted surface into four separate piles. We all pulled in chairs to watch or play, but the only player who would make the game truly exciting was Má.

When Má finished counting the petty cash, she walked over and sorted her cards with the same scrutiny as when she waxed eyebrows. She popped in a fresh stick of Wrigley's spearmint gum, her whole face totally focused on her first move. I slipped behind her and excitedly pointed to a top card. She hushed me, so I shut my mouth, but my knees kept wiggling, barely able to contain my excitement.

The lowest card, the three of spades, went first. Then the cards started to fly, and the shit-talking began. The most powerful card and star of the game were the twos, which were known as "pigs."

"Chết cho mầy biết!" Dì Phương exclaimed with a black two. *Now you know death!* It was early in the game, and she thought she was going to win the round—until it was Má's turn. She laid down three consecutive pairs, which trumped a two.

"I've slaughtered your pig!" said Má with a smirk. Now in control of the hand, Má was soon holding two cards while everyone still had a handful. She put down the highest card of the game, a two of hearts, which made everyone pass. Then a lone eight fell down right afterward, and Má showed her empty hands to everyone. The other players groaned.

"Đủ chưa?" Má teased. *Have you had enough?* Quarters landed with a thud in the center, and Má pocketed her winnings. Somehow Má always had the right amount of strategy and luck on her side.

"Rác không!" complained Dì Phương. *All I had was garbage!*

Má started mixing up the deck, and before she could deal herself the first card, the front door opened, setting off the laser and a dreamy soundscape from the pink horse wind chimes above the door. Immediately, we all stopped speaking Vietnamese. I flipped the switch on the stereo playing cải lương, sorrowful *Vietnamese opera* mourning war and love. Now it was time for Top 40 hits. It was time for the production line to begin.

Customers came into the shop from both entrances. Career women with big-shoulder-pad blazers, middle-aged women with their elderly mothers, bridal parties. They came in waves, some with appointments and some without. The game was to take every customer without having to turn any away. Throughout the day, Má would keep yelling out, "Ten minute! Pick a color!" Those five words were a clarion call. But her incantation was part blessing and part curse.

We were lucky to be so busy that someone had to wait, but we were also running behind, so we had to hurry. Má would direct the customers to a table while I acted as Má's right hand, hurriedly completing tasks to shave off time other customers spent waiting. I prepared the pedicure water with the right amount of spa powder, brought over the tray of gold nail charms, handled payment, and shuttled customers to the UV drying station and out the door. When we were especially behind, I ran around the hundred-space parking lot trying to find a customer's car to feed her meter so she wouldn't get a ticket. This was how I spent many of my Saturdays growing up, helping the family. And when there was downtime, Wendy and I got to walk to the mall and window-shop.

But there were three things I dreaded at the salon. The first was when I had to take off red nail polish—Candy Apple Red, to be exact. For most colors, two hands would take one or two cotton balls. But this color required four or five balls and repeated trips back to Má's station for more acetone. I would stand there holding the woman's hand, scrubbing the dripping cotton all over her finger, wondering if it would ever come off. By the end of it, the customer's acrylic nails would be a blushy pink and my skin a grayish white from all the chemicals.

The second thing that brought me anxiety were customers who made us feel bad. Usually when Má spoke in Vietnamese, it would be about the next task or helpful tidbits about the customer to help with conversation and service. This Sarah just got divorced (so don't ask about her husband), this Mary has two boys in high school and just came back from a vacation in Europe, this Beverly had a bunion and preferred to air-dry her toes while she read magazines. But sometimes, Má used our Vietnamese to heed a warning. That unstable curly-haired woman always came blaming us for a few broken nails even though she was long overdue for a fill. Give her the tips for free and get her out of here before she makes too much of a scene. That Patty was cheap, so when she impatiently walked off in a huff, know you didn't miss out on a tip. Even though all my relatives had a limited grasp of English, they were adept to how their customers felt. If anything ever blew up, we used our secret language to help process the awkwardness that ensued.

The final thing I couldn't stand at the shop was actually doing nails, because I was so clumsy. Once, when I was ten, I got handed an eight-year-old girl to polish her nails. Usually, Wendy could do it, but she was busy with a pedicure and all the waiting chairs were full. Mình bị kẹt. *We were stuck.*

A part of me envied my tiny customer. She probably spent her Saturdays dressing up as a princess, eating buttery popcorn at a sleepover her mother helped her host. I nervously unscrewed the bottle of polish and began to paint with my trembling hands. I kept messing up, getting polish on her cuticles and skin. Using my thumbnail, I cleaned off my mistakes. But before I finished, Dì Hiệp tapped me twice to get out of my seat. That was the only chance I ever got to bring in actual money, and I blew it. Feeling a little ashamed, I threw myself into all the other tasks that didn't require hand-eye coordination. I felt just awful knowing I messed up when money was on the line.

Once our first shop, Susan's Nails, was established, Má set her sights on moving up north for the better schools and wealthier customers. She bought a second shop called Today's Nails in Santa Rosa, California, smack in the middle of wine country. The family team split in half, overlapping with the previous owner to learn all the quirks of the clientele. When Má was ready, she sold off the old shop and then moved the clan to the north, where everyone was mostly white, some Mexican, and a minority of Asians. Soon, our new shop had such a great reputation, Hollywood stars got their nails done there when they were filming in our sleepy city. Within two years, Má opened Today's Nails #2, which Ba managed.

Even though business was booming, there was always an undercurrent of anxiety at the shop. The scariest day of the year was when health inspectors made their annual surprise visit. At ten years old, I was trying to decipher sex secrets from *Cosmo* when the front door beeped and two serious-looking men in plain clothes entered. Usually, if the rare man came into the shop, it was for a manicure. Wendy glanced up from her issue of *Seventeen*. I had a sinking feeling these guys were health inspectors from enemy number one: the California Board of Barbering and Cosmetology. Their job was to find something wrong, justifying their grievances by pointing at dense small-print manuals. After scribbling onto their clipboards, we would owe them money or they would force us to act grateful when they let us off with a warning. They had no idea how hard it was to turn a profit in a nail salon, let alone adhere to every obscure health code written in Má's second language.

"Hello. How can I help you?" Má asked through her face mask. She was on her nail drill giving an acrylic fill with Peggy, one of our longtime customers, a blond woman in her early forties. She was one of the loudest customers we had, always laughing and showing us pictures of her two dogs, who wore holiday sweaters. We called her "the lady with big eyes who's married to a lawyer."

They wanted to speak with the manager. They had issue with the Dooney & Bourke purses we were selling in our front display case. Má looked up with her drill zinging in midair, acrylic dust forming a small cloud and assured them she would give them a good price. They claimed they were counterfeit. That's when Má turned off her machine and had Dì Phương take over her customer. Má went outside to speak with them, and I started to count all her products. Six big bags, four small ones, and eight wallets. She had gotten her fake bags from San Jose, and they had been selling steadily for months now. The whole shop got quiet with worry.

After a breath-holding fifteen minutes, Má returned and had Dì Ngân gather the goods in a black trash bag. The officers left with the confiscated accessories, and Má returned to her chair telling Peggy everything was fine. Once her customer left, Má gave us every heart-stopping detail.

"Thằng chó đẻ!" she started. *That son of a bitch!* Each one of us was on the edge of our swivel chairs. Má got off with a warning this time, but if they caught her again, it could be a few thousand dollars in fines.

"Hết hồn hết vía, mày ơi!" exclaimed Dì Phương. *Oh, man, I wasn't even in my body anymore!* When Má was outside, my aunt kept imagining the worst, that all their nail licenses would get taken away.

Cô Thảo pretended to be a chiding officer. "Mười bóp, mười năm!"

Ten purses, ten years! Everyone kept laughing along. Má shook her head, smiling. It was a close one. All the adults kept joking about what happened. They did it during closing chores. They did it on the car ride home. Over dinner, Bà Ngoại relived Má's brush with prison. Each time the story was told, Má became slicker, cleverer. And each time the story was told, I became less surprised and more proud of Má. She was always in charge of the situation. She had a cool about her reserved for movie stars that played gangsters. I never doubted for a second that she would ever get into real trouble. So of course she got rid of the cops. I was as certain about her as she was about herself.

Má was even-keeled at the shop. She never got particularly flustered at anything, but one thing did make her excited. She always had her sights on making the rare thousand dollars in one day, meaning doing nails on sixty customers. I wanted this with all my heart because Má made me a deal. If it happened, she promised me a trip to the holy grail of American restaurants: Sizzler. I thought about it every Sunday night when we watched the sketch show *In Living Color* with Jim Carrey. That's when I would see commercials of char-grilled steaks, shrimp bouncing from the pan onto a plate, and steaming baked potatoes with overflowing dripping butter. There was a Sizzler just two blocks down from the shop. Whenever we drove by its pointy green roof, I daydreamed about the toppings I would stuff in my foil-wrapped potato and all the trips back to the kids' all-you-can-eat buffet bar. At eight years old, I became obsessed.

I had been asking every Saturday for months now, but this day, I was determined. Má said our dead relatives were powerful, so I marched into the shop and had a heart-to-heart with our ancestors. I told them I needed this miracle to happen, just like how my family screamed at Joe Montana to throw a winning touchdown with ten seconds left on the clock. This had to be the day. I could wait no longer.

Hi, guys. It's me. Please, please, please help us make more than a thousand dollars so I can finally go to Sizzler. If you make this happen, I promise to always get straight As. Also, I want proof to know you are actually listening. Thank you.

I hesitated. I had to let them know I was serious. I had to make concessions that mattered. I pressed the incense sticks harder against my forehead and kept going.

I'll brush my teeth every night. And I'm going to stop peeing in bed.

I put my incense stick in the holder in front of the bearded Chinese god and then knelt, tapping my head and palms lightly on the salon floor, bowing three times. I was embarrassed I still wet the bed, but nobody was perfect, I bet not even the ancestors. But I could try to change, especially if it meant we could go to Sizzler.

Then the door alarms beeped from both entrances, and female chatter began to fill our shop. It was late May, the few weeks that prom and wedding season overlapped, throwing us into a busy flurry. The filing and buffing moved at a quick tempo. All the manicurists were now doing less sweet-talking and more focused on speed.

"Square or round?" asked Cô Thảo in a muffled voice through her mask.

"Long or short?" asked Dì Ngân hastily.

"Ten minute! Pick a color!" hollered Má.

I had never worked so hard in my life, urgently moving from task to task. Má's instructions started to blur with customers' words. A few hours in, I forgot what I was supposed to do and then felt light-headed. Má excused me to the lunchroom. I managed to fill my cup of instant noodles with hot water and finally sat down, so tired I didn't know I was dizzy. After my ten-minute break, I was back at it while others rotated out to eat. By the end of the day, the magazines were a mess, polish was scattered at all the stations, and everyone was exhausted.

As we started to pack up, Má made her big announcement. For the first time ever, we made a thousand dollars in one day! She was so giddy, she jogged over to me, pinched my cheek so hard it hurt, and then pressed her nose against my cheek, giving me a sniff kiss on each side like her nostrils were suctions. Both sides so one cheek wouldn't be flatter than the other, she cried out! She gave me a playful slap on my cheek and then gave me a big pinch again, biting her lower lip. I had never seen her so happy before. She declared it was time to celebrate at Sizzler. Energy crept back into each person's face. I looked over to the small red altar. My ancestors *were* powerful.

After we shut off the salon lights, we drove the two blocks over to Sizzler. This was the moment I had been hoping for. Má held the glass door open, and we walked into their narrow hallway, looking up at the grand menu on the wall. Ba, Kang, Hang, and my grandparents were already there in awe of all the choices. My family began to talk about the strategy to split entrées. Dì Ngân was so short she could just do the kids' buffet. My other two aunts would share an entrée, and so would my grandparents.

"Thôi mà!" Má said. *No, come on!* "Hôm nay ăn chung cho vui đi!" *Today we eat with indulgence!* She was firm that each person would get their own meal. Dì Phương reminded Má of sending remittances back home to their siblings in Việt Nam. Má told her to stop worrying and order what she actually wanted. That meant everyone, including me, could have our own baked potato. Má stepped forward to the dopey teenage cashier and slid him a stack of neatly cut Buy One Get One Free coupons. One by one, each person ordered, not having to accommodate their tastes for the greater whole.

My family was so big, we had to scoot into two separate booths. Má looked smug as she ate her buffet salad of iceberg lettuce piled high with tomatoes, sprouts, sunflower seeds, Bac'n bits, and creamy ranch dressing. Then the kitchen door was kicked open by a Reba McEntire look-alike named Barbara carrying a giant oval tray over her shoulder. Each steak was the size of what our entire family would share in a night. But tonight, each person got their *own* portion. I did a small wiggle dance until my plate was placed in front of me.

I couldn't believe my praying worked. Our entire family, living and dead, made this special night possible, and I was in heaven. I carefully dabbed my meat in the tangy A1 steak sauce. I basked in the steam of the baked potato like I was giving myself a facial. I ate my cheesy toast extra slowly to savor it. I skipped back to the kids' buffet cart for more dino nuggets and red jiggly Jell-O. My aunts and grandparents kept exclaiming how the meal was completely over-the-top.

"Đây là nước Mỹ mà!" Má beamed with pride. *Come on, this is America!* In that moment, everything felt right. Má and I each got our special wish. Every family member got their meal deal. We were dog-tired, but we finally did it. At the shop, we labored hand and foot, serving Americans. And tonight, even if it was just for two hours, we weren't the servers, we were the served.

Squid and Chives

My first memory of Má was when she made Ba stop the car while we drove across the Bay Bridge. She screamed that if he didn't stop, she would just jump out. I was five years old and sitting on the car mat by my brother's worn shoes since we were six in a five-seater. I had to hide so we didn't get pulled over by the cops. He slowed down, and then the passenger door swung open. All I could see was the back of Má's head, her black hair flying like Medusa's snakes. Ba yelled after her, telling her she was crazy and to get back into the car. The bridge did not have a passenger walkway, and nothing protected her from the 220-foot drop into the Pacific Ocean. Wendy and I were crying for her to come back, but she had slammed the door shut. Cars were honking behind us, so Ba drove onward, without her. No one had any idea what she would do on the bridge or how she would get home. All night, I kept hoping for my bedroom door to crack open, but it never did.

The next morning, Má was standing by the stove making eggs over easy. She didn't apologize or reassure me that that would never happen again. She just slid a plate of food in front of me and told me to eat. I wasn't mad, I was just grateful she came back. That day on the bridge, Má made it clear she didn't follow anyone else's rules but her own.

For years, I have tried to come up with theories to explain her erratic behavior. She could have had an undiagnosed bipolar disorder. Then again, Má and Ba used to argue a lot. Maybe they would have eventually divorced if she didn't die when she did. Or maybe she just never got to process the trauma from her refugee escape. As the caretaker of four children and her now eight living siblings back in Việt Nam, self-reflection was a luxury requiring space and time she just didn't have.

A part of me wanted her to have a mental illness so I could have an answer to explain her unstable behavior and my own. If she was bipolar, and that was genetic, then I could blame the emotional episodes I experienced as a teen and well into adulthood on someone or something else. Whenever I cried in front of my family, they would blame me for it, calling me too sensitive, too weak, as if I could reverse course if I just tried harder. I never had the words to defend myself, so I would just cry harder at the table or hide in my room.

Throughout high school and college, I would experience anxiety attacks so overwhelming they would shut down my executive function capability, leaving me unable to shower or eat, sometimes covering my body in full hives. I would call Kang, and he would take me to the doctor or let me do nothing on his couch. He gave me *An Unquiet Mind* as a birthday gift once. We never talked about me getting therapy, but he always picked up my calls. And twice a year, these episodes would be so bad I would have suicidal ideation but never acted on it. It was usually a boyfriend who eased me back to reality.

In college, I was diagnosed with bipolar II disorder, a milder version of the mental illness. Over the years, I·tried to cope with therapy, exercise, meditation, and supplements, but my family's judgmental comments still rattled me and sent me spiraling. They saw me as weak, not as someone struggling to be better because of the mess we all made. I wasn't trying to be difficult. I had a chemical imbalance beyond my control. But because of the stigma mental illness carried, it was just easier for my family to say I wanted attention. Perhaps both Má and I were not inherently flawed people; we were just products of our circumstance.

Má, the ninth of eleven children, grew up with war in her backyard in southern Việt Nam, the province of Sóc Trăng by the Mekong Delta. In the 1970s, Má's brother, the fourth sibling in line, had a post as a guard protecting a building during the civil war. On his day off, he helped cover a friend's shift. He was mistaken for the other man and killed at gunpoint. He was just at the wrong place at the wrong time, a completely disposable civilian.

Six years after the fall of Sài Gòn, Má escaped in 1981 with Ba and my two brothers, promising to come back for her impoverished clan. After ten years in America, Má pivoted from seamstress to manicurist, successfully getting off welfare so her sponsorship paperwork could be approved. Her parents and three sisters were coming just like she'd promised. But she wasn't just helping them, they were helping us. Her sisters would help at the nail salon, and her parents would take care of everything at the house—cooking, cleaning, and children. Any extra money would be sent back to Việt Nam to her struggling siblings, who had to choose between school fees and eating.

While America had its opportunities, it also came with its own set of silent struggles. My family's Vietnamese names were inconvenient eyesores that had to be repeated, only to be mispronounced again. Má thought blending in would make everyone's lives easier; it would be a guaranteed way to be a little less othered. So on the day my family became naturalized citizens, Má gave my siblings one hour to come up with their American names on the BART ride over to the immigration office. Kang chose Anthony, named after his cool friend at school. Hang chose Kevin, based on the most All-American boy on cable television, Kevin Arnold from *The Wonder Years*. My sister Tú Uyên already knew she would be Wendy, the girl in *Peter Pan*. After all, "Uyên" and "Wen" sounded similar enough.

Then our Vietnamese got lazy. It started when Kang got us siblings all kicked out of Saturday Vietnamese language school. We eagerly traded in those composition books for Michael Jordan jerseys and Polly Pockets. Us siblings lost our ear for accuracy and began to speak a Vietnamese that was just more *convenient*. Kang's real name was actually Khánh, but I thought it was easier if both of my brothers' names rhymed, and then it stuck. My siblings and I called him "Kang," and all the adults in the family called him by his Chinese nickname, Khện. Hang's actual Vietnamese name was written as Hưng, but with our Chinese Vietnamese roots, everyone correctly pronounced it as "Hang." I had been misspelling my own brother's name for decades, and simply never knew.

Má saw the writing on the wall. She didn't want us to get too Americanized and forget our heritage, so she made sure our bà con, *our relatives*, would Vietnamize us back by any means necessary. Of course, none of this context was explained to me as an eight-year-old. When our extended family came, my privacy fell away along with any little time I ever had with Má.

The night our bà con marched in all the way from Việt Nam, our big house became small, and the rules began to change. We had to play musical chairs with the rooms in the four-bedroom house. Suddenly, our six-person family ballooned to eleven. Kang left his room to join Hang's. Wendy and I moved out of ours so our grandparents could move in. Kang's old room was now the official girls' room, with beds touching each of the three walls. Dì Ngân and Dì Hiệp took over our bunk beds. Wendy, Dì Phương, and I slept on two twin-size beds pushed together, with me usually sleeping on the crack. With five people in one room, we didn't have enough space for individual dressers, so each person had one cabinet in the hallway to stack their things.

Bà Ngoại was usually in the kitchen cooking and taking menthol hits of green Eagle oil from her front pajama pocket. She wasn't exactly the freshly baked cookies and milk kind of grandma. When I got a runny nose, she would scratch my back skin off with the edge of a quarter, leaving pink lines all over my body. And if I got really sick, she would scoop out some black liquid from a five-gallon glass jar she had at the top of the pantry that housed a giant dead black cobra. Tracing the smoke from a burning-hot incense stick up and down my back, she would spit the black mystery juice all over me as I lay face-down on an old ragged towel. After that, I much preferred taking a teaspoon of thick cough syrup, even if it made me gag.

Most days, Bà Ngoại was correcting me, forcing me to cross my arms and say an obedient formal "dạ" instead of a casual "ừ" whenever I wanted to say *yes*. Every time I forgot, she went ballistic with a dramatic sigh and an agonized face. She never did that to my older brothers. Ông Ngoại, my *maternal grandfather*, spent a lot of time in the garden taking care of the herbs, fruit trees, and the three new chicken pets clucking freely in the backyard. The free-range chickens reminded him of Việt Nam, he said.

"Ăn cơm! Ăn cơm!" Bà Ngoại hollered into the open garage. *Time to eat! Time to eat!* I was hunched over, crammed sitting in a red-and-yellow Little Tikes toy car three years too young for me, holding an umbrella out one window. I had been trying to turn it into a time machine for the last hour. I kept tinkering with Ba's big wrench I found in the garage.

"Bà con ơi! Vô đi, vô đi!" echoed Bà Ngoại with a higher sense of urgency. *Oh, family! Come in, come in!* I sighed and slowly crawled out of the car I had outgrown. On my way in, I pressed the garage door button, sealing off our Vietnamese microclimate from our cul-de-sac with a mechanical boom.

Dinnertime also required an adjustment. More chairs were added to the dining table so there was barely any elbow space to raise my rice bowl to my mouth. Bà Ngoại ran the kitchen, so we had to follow her rules, but the problem was she would change them all the time. I never knew when I was going to make her mad. I could see how Má took after her.

Inside the kitchen, I pulled open the newspaper drawer and then lined the dining table with a few pages of classifieds and colored ads. As I was counting out the chopsticks and soup spoons, Bà Ngoại started shouting like an umpire.

"Nước sôi! Nước sôi!" she shouted as she walked over with a big bowl of soup from the stove. *Boiling water! Boiling water!* She wanted to make sure I didn't run into her and spill everything. At the rice cooker on the kitchen island, Dì Phương formed bowls of jasmine rice that looked like perfectly curved rising suns. Wendy and I shuttled them over to the table. I used to scoop the rice, but Bà Ngoại didn't like how I flattened the rice with the paddle. She gave me one chance to correct my technique, and I messed it up. That's why Dì Phương was now on rice duty. When the table was fully set, I climbed up on a chair and waited.

Canh chua cá bông lau was already on the table with its tangy aroma beckoning me. The clear *catfish sour soup* was made from tamarind pulp and loaded with okra, pineapples, tomatoes, bean sprouts, and my favorite vegetable in the entire world, bạc hà. It was known as the *giant elephant ear* for its spongy and porous texture, soaking up the umami flavors of the soup. There were never enough of those pieces, and as much as I wanted all of them, food was distributed based on power, gender, and age. Má and Ba got first choice since they were the head of the family. Then it was Hang and Kang because they were growing teenage boys. Next were the aunts, then Wendy and me. My grandparents ate the previous day's leftovers before we came home so they would be ready to help with anything in the kitchen while the rest of us ate.

On top of the soup floated garnishes of fried garlic, sawtooth coriander (which felt like a scratchy weed down my throat), and rice paddy herbs Bà Ngoại threw like dice right before serving. The soup itself was sour and sweet, but a salty, spicy zing came from the freshly scissored red Thai chilies in the communal fish sauce plate, which was taken up by a catfish steak. Dipping a small piece of meat into the fish sauce was a bold thunderclap in my mouth. Canh chua was the soup we ate twice a month, and it had to be served with a clay pot of caramelized pork or fish. One dish would be naked without the other.

Bà Ngoại rushed back to the table with her gold-thread slippers slapping loudly against the floor. With dishrags in each hand, she was carrying a wired clay pot, which she placed on a straw trivet in the center of the table. She lifted the lid, and I got a whiff of black pepper making my nostrils sweat from the spice. Thịt kho tiêu! *Caramelized clay pot pork loin with fresh ground black pepper.* It was still bubbling, and I was ready to eat.

Bà Ngoại dashed back to the table with the final dish of giá hẹ xào mực, *sautéed squid with Chinese chives and bean sprouts,* the dish I hated the most in the world, and it was right in front of me. The squid pieces were either shaped like curled-up Tootsie Rolls or mini headless octopuses with stringy legs hanging out. I hated this dish because the chives were like thick, bitter blades of grass. No matter how much I worked at it, the chives always ended up as a ball of green yarn in my mouth. Any attempt to swallow triggered my gag reflex as I coughed it back up. Má insisted these chives helped remove toxins out of our system. With all the chemicals we were exposed to in the nail salon, we needed to eat them. She said the same thing about pig blood cubes, which I also protested. I looked up and saw Bà Ngoại watching us from the kitchen as we started to eat.

I happily reached for everything except the chives. I dipped vegetables from the soup into the fish sauce, alternating bites with the pepper pork. I spooned a little clay pot caramel sauce onto my rice, coating every bite with even fierier flavor. When we ate, we sounded like a symphony, the sound of chopsticks tapping against rice bowls, the praising of each dish to Bà Ngoại, and the measured slurping of the soup. When the broth level dropped halfway, Bà Ngoại was right back at the table ladling in more canh chua, which she kept on a simmer while we ate. No bite should ever go cold. Once I was done, I asked for Má's permission to go play. But she wouldn't let me because

I hadn't eaten the chives yet. I had been caught. How did she even notice?

"I don't like it," I whispered to her. Má calmly put her bowl down, but her eyes glowed like red lasers. Maybe that was the wrong choice of words.

"Bà Ngoại làm, mày phải ăn!" said Má with a stern voice. *Grandma made it, so you have to eat it!* But instead of calling me the little kid pronoun of "con," she used "mày," which meant I was really in trouble. I tried to shake my head just a little bit to Má so Bà Ngoại couldn't see. Má continued eating without looking at me.

Panicked, I searched for help, but no one defended me. They just looked down, picking at food with their chopsticks like chickens eating freshly thrown grain. No one was going to challenge either matriarch. Bà Ngoại was standing by the kitchen counter, wiping it with an old T-shirt rag so fervently, you'd have thought she was sanding it down. I wasn't sure what Bà Ngoại had against me, but she was always nagging me about how I was messing up.

The old woman was adamant about me not pointing with the index finger. The middle finger was more polite. When I put on a white headband to match my white jumper, Bà Ngoại gripped her heart and said, "Mô Phật!," which was the same as *oh my god*, but to Buddha. She pulled the headband out of my hair, saying it was bad luck. I heard her tell on me to Má. Something about how I was inviting death to come to our family.

When I ate, I had to eat everything in my rice bowl. Otherwise, I would go to hell. For every leftover grain of rice, I would have to eat one worm in hell before I could go to heaven, which was confusing, because we were Buddhists who believed in reincarnation. I was not taught to listen to my body, I was taught to listen to my elders. Even if I was too full, I had to finish it. This was further complicated by the fact that eating a lot was a way of showing the cook appreciation. At the same time, Bà Ngoại would make comments if I went to the rice cooker for seconds. I could never win.

And tonight was one of those nights where I was sure to lose. Má said I couldn't go to sleep until I ate all the chives. Bà Ngoại had consolidated the rest of the dish, which now looked like a towering impossible task. My aunts crumpled up the soiled newspaper and pushed in their chairs. Everyone else was done eating. The kitchen emptied out, and the only light on was the hot lamp hanging above my head. The entire dining table was clean except for my rice bowl and the now cold squid and chives. If I couldn't go to sleep, then I would be tired at school. And if I was tired at school, how was I supposed to get good grades? I laid my head down on the table, my cheek pressing against the glass. I started to whine like an injured animal, hoping someone would come excuse me. Minutes passed, and no one came. All the house lights were turned off except for the one above me at the dining room table.

I grabbed some squid and chives with my chopsticks and forced myself to eat. The chives were slimy, and the squid was tough. The squid went down, but the chives didn't. I pulled the green string out, feeling a few inches scratch the lining of my throat on the way up. I put the regurgitated mess of strangled chives in the shadow of my bowl on the newspaper print.

Wait, no one saw that, right? I checked all the possible entry points: the kitchen hallway to the garage, the doorway to the living room, and the backyard sliding door. All dark and all clear. I quickly gobbled up the squid pieces and then rolled up the greens with newspaper. I flipped open the trash can lid, lifted up some junk mail, and pressed the evidence down to the bottom where no one could find it.

This wasn't the first time Má used food as punishment. When I was six, Má, Wendy, and I were at Viễn Hương, our family's favorite noodle house. Má placed an order for the dish I loved the most, fried fish cake and bowls of hủ tiếu Triều Châu, the house specialty. The owners were a Vietnamese-Chinese family, with roots that traced all the way back to Guangdong, just like ours. In the giant world that was America, that connection made us almost related. Má was busy wiping the chopsticks and soup spoons with the paper napkins from the silver two-sided dispenser. They could be dirty, she said.

Má poured soy sauce into a small dish, adding slices of pickled green jalapeños and drops of chili sa tế oil. Wendy and I played a game of kicking each other's legs under the table. Then a short man with white eyebrows walked briskly over to us, slid a red plastic tray a few inches onto the table, and called out sizes.

"Lớn! Nhỏ!" he yelled, carefully handing out the hot bowls of steaming goodness. *Big! Small!* The last to land was a small oval dish with five pieces of fish cake, nestled among small slices of pickled cabbage, carrots, and daikon. Soy milks and an iced coffee in clear glasses scattered onto the table. The waiter pulled the tray away, wiping a few spots of broth with a hand towel he pulled quickly from his shoulder and snapped right back on. Then he was off.

"Ăn đi! Ăn đi!" Má encouraged, gesturing us to eat with both of her hands. *Come on, eat!* I dipped the half-inch-thick fish cake in my soy sauce and took a small bite, breathing out the just-fried heat. The spongy texture bounced around my mouth, leaving a trace of sesame oil and honey on my lips. A carrot crunch cleaned the grease from my palate, my tongue ready for more flavor.

Now it was time for the main course. I started by slurping a spoonful of the clear, sweet pork bone broth, feeling the warmth move from my lips down my throat and then into my belly. Submerging my spoon in the broth, I started arranging one long piece of the wide white hủ tiếu noodle, a tail-on shrimp, and a little ground pork to make the most epic bite. I blew at the soup spoon and then inhaled a mouthful of the slippery noodle soup. Chewy, firm, and tender to the bite. Since there were only two pieces of shrimp and two fish balls in each bowl, I started the meal with one of each and saved the rest for last.

I alternated wet with dry bites, constructing an elaborate spoon of meat and noodle combinations and then dipping solo pieces of meat into soy sauce as its own savory bite. Just beef meatball. Poached shredded chicken, bean sprouts, and noodle. Fish ball and noodle.

During the sacred communion with noodle soup, all conversation at the table had stopped, which meant it was delicious. Eating too slowly would render your noodles too expanded from all the broth absorption, a terrible situation. Chatting too much would render your broth lukewarm. My upper lip started to sweat, and the soup level began to drop. Soon I was left with just two meat choices and a big pile of noodles. My least favorite, the dry bland pork kidney slashed with crisscrosses, and my most favorite protein ever, the smooth white fish ball. But at this point, I felt stuffed.

"Ăn hết đi con," said Má, encouraging me to finish. *Eat all of it.*

"But, Má, I'm full," I whispered.

"Đừng bỏ mứa con, có tội," said Má. *Don't waste food, or else you'll get sins.* I was so full I found it hard to breathe, but I obliged. I made another spoonful of noodles and topped it with the kidney. Two big bites and I would be done. Kidney and then fish ball. Work, then reward. I spent a whole minute painstakingly grinding the rubbery organ to a pulp. I washed it all down with a few gulps of the now warm soy milk, the liquid candy forming a rim around my lips.

A hot swirl churned in my stomach. A sourness crept up my throat, and saliva started to pool in my mouth. I peered down to my prized floating fish ball and then it was all over. I couldn't keep anything down, and in front of the entire restaurant, I vomited the meal I had been looking forward to all week.

I looked up at the shocked eyes of Má and Wendy. Faces at every table looked over, horrified. I wasted the soup. Was I supposed to tell everyone I was sorry? I looked down at my bowl and my eyes glazed over and started to burn. Má pushed her chair back and dragged me to the bathroom.

"Con hư quá," Má scolded while pumping electric-pink soap into my hands, which were being blasted by hot water. *You're so naughty.* "Không ai cưng mày đâu." *No one cares for you.* Her words stung me like no one else's could. She wiped the throw-up unsympathetically from my lips with a stiff brown paper towel and then walked out of the bathroom without me. I wondered if she only cleaned me up so the bystanders would judge her less, not because she was concerned about me. I looked down at my shoes and followed her. Like usual, everything was always my fault.

I spent the rest of the car ride home trying to be invisible so I couldn't mess up again. I didn't speak for the rest of the day and just did as I was told. A part of me wanted to scream at Má and blame her for everything. I was too full, and she forced me to keep eating. If I wanted to belong, I had to obey Má, which meant I had to abandon my own inner knowing. If I stood up for myself, I would have been seen as ungrateful and whooped real good. I walked out of the restaurant that day believing I would continue to ruin everything else if I didn't obey my elders. So I sulked and said nothing.

That was the day I disowned my own body. I stopped listening to my needs so I could keep trying to get the approval of someone impossible to please. Eating, my favorite activity in the world, became complicated. What and how much I put in my body became about accommodating other people's wishes. As a girl and as the youngest, I had to center other people's comfort. In Confucianism, there was an emphasis on preserving group harmony by prioritizing the collective over the individual, which had its nuances. As a young girl, I interpreted this as my needs didn't matter—that I didn't matter.

I daydreamed about a mother who would actually listen and coddle me. I never admitted this out loud, but sometimes I wished my mother didn't exist.

Fighting Words

When I turned eleven, my rift with Má deepened. I was on the toilet in Má's master bathroom, my arms on my knees like I was bracing for an airplane crash. It felt like knives were stabbing me in the stomach. There was a dark brown stain on my underwear, and faint red drops kept dripping into the toilet bowl. I thought I was dying. Every few minutes, I mustered a big yell for help and then would wait. Eventually, my sister came to nonchalantly deliver the news that I had just gotten my first period. I had learned about menstruation at school, but nobody said how frightening it would be. I knew there was a box of pads Wendy and the aunts used, but I never asked about it—it was all grown-up stuff.

I kept whimpering from the cramps, and Wendy just shrugged. As she turned to leave, I felt the garage door hum below my feet. The Previa was home from the nail salon. I moaned for her to get Má. Minutes later, I could hear someone coming and felt relief. When Má came over, she looked unconcerned. I frantically pointed to my underwear.

"Tưởng gì!" she said, dismissing my pain. *I thought something had happened!* My heart sank. I was in pain, and the thing that would officially make me a woman was happening! Her face was blank. She was in another world, but I needed her in this one. I pleaded for her help. All she did was squat down by her double sink and reach into the lower cabinet. She pulled out a light green pad and tossed it at my feet. Then she walked out. I didn't know how to put it on. I didn't know how to make the cramps stop. I just sat there keeled over, waiting to die.

Finally, Wendy came back with clean underwear. She showed me how to position the pad and fold the wing flaps underneath. When I came downstairs for dinner, everyone was almost done eating. I knew they knew what happened, but we all pretended that it hadn't.

I thought becoming a woman was supposed to be special. I had imagined a ceremony where all the women in the house would form a circle, slather my hand with lotion, and force on a jade bracelet, hugging me and welcoming me into the Feminine Order. But when Má found out, there were no comforting words or space to ask questions. The only thing she seemed concerned about was making sure I didn't stain the white dining room chairs. My period was now a task I had to manage on my own. She didn't make my coming-of-age moment a big deal, so I took after her attitude. I started to see my body as a burden, a thing that needed to be dealt with rather than celebrated. I wished Má could have supported me in a different way, but I didn't bring it up, because that would make me a nuisance. After that, I tried to emotionally distance myself from Má. When I didn't care as much, I didn't feel so let down.

The following school year, I entered the sixth grade. On the first day of school, I walked past all the first graders on the first day like I owned the place. I was very quickly put in my place when the name-calling began again: four eyes, flat nose, Ching Chong. My crush asked me why I ate carpet (which was actually pork floss) in my bánh mì sandwich. I had deep envy for all the popular girls who were on the school volleyball team and wished I could be the same as everyone else, meaning, I wished I could be white.

The next week, I forced my parents to trade my clunky Bugle Boy glasses for contacts and snuck white bread and deli meat into our grocery shopping cart. I couldn't do anything about my face, so I became obsessed with trying out for the volleyball team. But there was one big problem. Má was firmly against it.

We had already clashed on language. She was livid I was speaking too much English at home, so she grounded me one day for every English word I spoke. I had racked up a whole month of house arrest in one afternoon and protested by not speaking to her for a week until she dropped the rule altogether. I had already floated the volleyball idea to her, and she was not giving in. She wanted me to focus on my studies and complained the sport was too expensive with its twenty-dollar jersey. And since she wasn't going to change her mind, I convinced myself it would be easier for everyone if I just did it behind her back.

On the morning of tryouts, there was an optional practice before school. I woke up at 6:00 a.m., made myself a ham and cheese sandwich, and was about to head to school when I bumped into Má in the kitchen. We were both surprised to see each other so early. I usually left the house at 7:30 a.m., and she would leave at 8:30 a.m.

One look from her, and I fessed up right away. I could sneak around her, but I couldn't lie to her face. Má was clear that volleyball was forbidden. I told her I was the top student in class. She said we didn't have money for the uniform. I told her all my friends were going to be there.

"Má, please," I said, tugging on her sleeve. Má turned around from making her French chicory coffee with condensed milk.

"Má nói no!" she snarled. *I said no!*

I backed away and locked my jaw, ready to fight.

"Well, fine, then . . . I hate you!" I shot daggers into her eyes, shocked that I actually said it out loud. She looked shocked too, but didn't respond. Our stare-down continued until I heard Ba's voice come from the garage. It was time for them to go wherever they were headed. I followed her to the garage and slammed the door as their car backed out of our driveway. I would show her. I stomped the whole way to school practicing my underhand volleyball serve. Hell or high water, I was going to make the team.

When I came home after tryouts in the late afternoon, Hang's car was in the driveway. He went to college at UC Berkeley an hour away and usually came home on the weekends, not Fridays. When I found him inside the house, his eyes looked rabid. He told me to pack my things because Má was in a coma in San Francisco.

A flood of questions came rushing in. What happened to her? What was she doing in San Francisco? How many days would we be gone? I was stunned. I asked a half question to my brother, but he was barking the same information over and over again. He was leaving in ten minutes, so I needed to hurry if I wanted to go with him. I ran up the stairs in a daze. Wendy was in our room putting her things into her prized Adidas soccer bag. Her eyes looked puffy.

"I just don't know how many underwear to bring," I said quietly.

"I don't know. Five? Figure it out." She went to the bathroom to pack her toiletries. I found an empty backpack and started stuffing my days-of-the-week underwear into it. I lost Saturday and Thursday, so now I just wore the underwear any day of the week. I threw in pajamas, a few shirts, and *The Grapes of Wrath* (for extra credit).

After Hang tried starting his car a few times, the engine took, and we puttered away in his old silver Honda with magenta velvet seats. Hang was quiet, so we listened to rap on the staticky radio the whole way there. I kept replaying what he'd said over and over again. "Má is in a coma in San Francisco." I never knew anyone in a coma before except for the people in soap operas we watched at the salon. The news was so surreal, I didn't feel scared; I became numb. I reassured myself that Má always figured out a way. For all we knew, Má would be awake by the time we got there. We crossed the Golden Gate Bridge, strong winds beating the sides of Hang's flimsy car. We drove through dense fog, which felt like clouds, making the journey to the hospital feel even more like a dream.

An hour and a half later, we reached UCSF Mount Zion Medical

Center. We weaved through a maze of sick patients, gloomy visitors, and medical staff in scrubs. Then I saw Ba and Kang in the waiting area. Ba barely looked at us. Kang saw us and got up.

"Come with me," Kang said. We followed him down a hallway as wheelchairs and gurneys moved past us. Everywhere smelled like urine. Kang turned in to a room and we filed right behind him, oldest to youngest. And then, I saw her. Her skin was an abnormal puffy yellow, so swollen, I could barely see her cheekbones. She looked so eerie, I didn't take another step. She had tubes coming out of her arms and nose. She was wearing a hospital gown, and a white sheet covered her up to her chest. Her eyes were closed, and she was expressionless, which was so unlike her. Machines were beeping everywhere. Wendy covered her mouth and nose and looked away. An oxygen machine sucked in air through a pump, stopped for a second, and then pushed it out super loud. The machine worked nonstop, just like Má always did. Kang and Hang stood right by her bedside, their stoic faces making this moment even grimmer.

"Talk to her," Kang said softly, his hand touching hers. Wendy walked closer to her body, but I didn't. Hang nudged me, but I resisted. I didn't want to get too close. When I felt ready, I leaned up against the metal railing on the hospital bed, and then I felt a bag by my waist. It was a hanging bag of yellow liquid connected to a knot of tubes, attached to more machines. As I glanced up from her bag to her, I caught a flash of red. Her nails. Freshly polished in Candy Apple Red. Her mouth was slightly open, her hair wild by her side. The oxygen machine sounded exhausted, sighing loudly as it released a big push of air.

Má was just lying there. She didn't open her eyes. She hadn't yelled at me yet, which was so not like her. Where was Má, and whose body was this really? In soap operas, it could take a few months or even a few years until the person woke up. Not one of my siblings said anything. I wasn't sure what to do or say. I just kept hearing the crunching sound of Wendy's windbreaker as she raised her arm to wipe her nose.

"Come on, let's go eat," said Kang gently. He took Wendy and me downstairs to the hospital café, where we ate prepackaged soggy tuna and egg salad sandwiches on cold, stiff chairs. I wasn't allowed to waste food, so I tried my best to finish the sad meal. I asked my brother why Má was in a coma and if the doctors could fix the problem.

"We don't know yet, but I hope so." This only raised more questions.

Visiting hours were over, so Kang dropped us off at a motel near the hospital so we could do our homework. The door clicked shut, and I started snooping around, sliding open all the drawers while Wendy worked on a problem set.

"Wendy, look! Someone forgot their Bible!"

"They come in all motels, duh," said Wendy without looking up. Even though we were Buddhist, Má could use all the help she could get. Whenever we watched wrestling, Stone Cold Steve Austin always made a big deal about John 3:16, so I looked for that passage and then clasped my hands together to pray like I saw people do on television.

Hey, Má, I know we're not Christian or anything, but if God is any-where near you, say you believe in him so you can have everlasting life down here. You know . . . alive. Amen?

The next morning, I found Dì Phương, Dì Hiệp, Bà Ngoại, and Ông Ngoại in the waiting room, sitting by my checked-out father. He still had a blank stare, hands folded, thumbs rubbing back and forth. After years of not taking a vacation day besides a federal holiday, our shops were closed. All the women were dabbing their eyes, blowing their noses. They kept shaking their heads and saying "mổ bụng," which meant *stomach surgery*. Did Má have appendicitis?

When Dì Phương saw me, she grabbed my hand and started heading toward the patient rooms. I kept pulling back to stay behind. I didn't want to go. She dragged me all the way to Má's room. When we arrived, Dì Ngân looked up, both hands clutching Má's left hand, sitting on a chair scooted close to Má's body. Her eyes were bloodshot.

"Lại đi con. Nói chuyện với Má đi." *Come here, child. Speak with your mother.* I walked over to Dì Ngân. She grabbed my wrist hard and swapped places with me. Dì Ngân left for the restroom, and Dì Phương was standing by Má's bedside. I heard the gentle beeping of the machines. The sighing oxygen compressor. Unfortunately, Má looked the same as yesterday.

"I don't know what to say," I told Dì Phương, who was now sobbing into a folded paper towel.

"Nói đi con. Xin cho Má về đi." *Say it, child. Make a wish for her to return.* Dì Phương dabbed her eyes firmly and snorted snot back up into her nose. "Nói đi con." *Say it, child.* Then she got up and left me alone—with *her*. She left too quickly before I could insist for her to stay. I bit my lower lip and then mustered all my courage to pick up Má's hand. I dropped it suddenly and scooted back in my chair. Her hand was icy cold.

"Hey, Dì Phương, can you tell the nurses to turn the heat up in here?" I tried to yell it out to her in the hallway, but it just came as a soft mumble. After thirty seconds of staring, I picked up her lifeless hand again and held it with both of my own.

"Hey, Má, it's me, Susan. Um, I'm really sorry I told you I hated you. I—I didn't mean it." I looked up at her face. No change. I tried to rub warmth into her hands. I had to try another way.

"And remember how you used to say that when I go to college, you'd come with me? Well, could you come back? Because I don't want to go to college alone." My tears started to hit her sheet like raindrops at the beginning of a monsoon. Drip, drop, then they poured down heavily and quicker with every passing second.

"And if you come back, I'll never go to volleyball ever again, and I'll always listen to you. But you have to come back. You hear me? Okay, Má?" Mucus dribbled from my nose into my mouth. I looked at her face. Still no change. I pinched all the snot away with my two fingers and then smeared it on my jeans. I stared at my scuffed-up shoes dangling above the hospital room floor. I picked up her hands again.

"I messed up. I'm sorry, Má!" I pleaded. "And if you come back, I'll always be a good girl and I'll always listen, but you have to come back, okay? Okay?!" I was choking out my words in between sniffles.

"I don't want to be alone, Má! I don't want to be alone!" I cried out, now hyperventilating in between words. When my body finally calmed down, there was nowhere else to wipe on my damp jeans. And there was no one to tell me it was all going to be okay.

"Come back," I whispered, unsure if she heard any of it. I snuck one more look. Nothing. No change on her face. No change on the vitals monitor. The only thing that responded were the machines that beeped back. I left Má's room and found a distraught Dì Phương in the hallway. I tagged her back in and stood by the doorway, eavesdropping on her concessions. My aunt pleaded for Má to come back so they could take one last trip to gamble at Reno and binge at the all-you-can-eat buffet. Má was always inviting the aunts to go when the shop closed on holidays, but they always wanted to stay back to save money. This time, Dì Phương would go, but only if her older sister regained consciousness.

On my way back to the waiting room, four monks paraded by me with their brown robes, shaved heads, and socks in Velcro-strapped Teva sandals. Inside her room, they chanted monotone words that seemed rooted in Vietnamese but were from another era. They kept to a rhythm, tapping on their gourds, calling to her for hours. It was the only thing that felt steady that day.

The days started to melt into one another. I couldn't admit this out loud, but I hated visiting hours. I didn't like seeing Má so weak, so vulnerable, so helpless. I would pass the time reading every article from wrinkled *Country Living* and *National Geographic* magazines scattered about the waiting room. Sometimes Wendy and I would go to the vending machines to get snacks or go downstairs to the cafeteria to get Ba a coffee. Any excuse to get out of there was a welcome relief. It became draining to hear Bà Ngoại or one of the aunts cry.

They were contagious. Right when one quieted down, another would start again.

When visiting hours were over, Ba drove us across the Bay Bridge to his sister's house in Albany. We called her Tùa Cô. My aunts and grandparents on Má's side were following in another car, and my brothers went somewhere else.

"Vô đi," grumbled Tïa, my uncle, with his cigarette voice as he opened the door. *Come in.* He gruffly patted Ba on the back two times. He never did that. We crammed into the doorway and removed our shoes while standing up. Wendy and I greeted the elders with half-hearted bows and crossed arms. No one asked about Má. Ba's aunt Lầu Ý got up from her La-Z-Boy recliner and shuffled to the dining table to present the food. She lifted the neon-orange plastic dome to reveal a feast to care for our broken hearts.

"Ăn đi, ăn đi," said Tùa Cô as she ushered us to her long oval table. *Eat, eat.* At the table, I saw a clay pot of teeny-tiny fish and rau muống xào chao, long stalks of *water spinach sautéed with a fermented tofu sauce.* Slices of glistening garlic on one of my favorite dishes. Lầu Ý returned from the kitchen with a piping-hot soup bowl of canh khoai mỡ, *creamy purple taro soup* with shrimp, scallions, and fresh-ground white pepper on top.

All the adults took a seat around the oblong table. Wendy and I got small foldable stools that were wedged into the curves of the oval edges. The warm rice was so much more comforting than the sterile hospital food we ate all day. No one spoke, because there were no updates. No small indications to stay hopeful. Just the sound of chop-sticks softly tapping our rice bowls and the slurping of soup. We were in the second movement of a symphony, the slow and quiet andante, the part where you don't know how the song will end. Without Má here as the conductor, we were aimless.

After we were done eating, all the women and girls cleared the ta-ble while the men headed to the couch to watch a Chinese soap opera.

Wendy and I went down to the basement level with our girl cousins to play the Game of Life, a board game we didn't have. But once all the cars were set up with stick figure people at the wheel, I heard a creepy laugh come from upstairs. We all sprinted up the stairs. The family shih tzu was going crazy, barking nonstop at Ba. All of the elders surrounded him on the floor in a circle. Tùa Cô was shouting in Ba's ear.

"Ai đó?" *Who's there?* Ba was rocking back and forth, wailing. He was spirit channeling, as he had done my entire childhood, which meant he was possessed and now a portal to the spiritual world. Tùa Cô kept repeating the question. Both Dì Phương and Dì Ngân were leaning forward on their knees, grabbing each of his hands, hoping to get a lifeline to their sister.

"Muội à? Muội à?" Dì Phương kept calling for Má by her child-hood nickname. I was on the outside, eyeing the phone in case we had to call 9-1-1. Then Ba's mouth puckered, and he started violently shaking his head.

"Tôi cũng tên là Thu!" he shouted, spitting with every word. *My name is also Thu.* If the ghost had the same name as Ba, what could that mean? Ba's head moved up and down, side to side, tracing the shape of an infinity sign.

"Trễ quá! Không vào được." *It's too late! I can't come back in.* Ba rocked back and forth with his eyes closed, his voice starting to rise to a high-pitched, banshee scream.

"Trễ quá! Trễ quá!" *Too late! Too late!* And then Ba collapsed onto the floor. Tùa Cô lifted his head into her lap. Lầu Ý was by Ba's side, trying to give him bottled water. Dì Phương started tapping his hands to revive him. Ba ever so slowly opened his eyes. He was in a daze.

"Có . . . sao không?" he asked. *Is there . . . anything wrong?* Lầu Ý urged him to take a few sips. If everything he said was true, then that meant Má wasn't coming back. Dì Phương started to cry that the kids were still too young. The rest of my maternal side fell like dominoes, all weeping together. Wendy and I just sat on the floor cross-legged, watching the adults cry. Lầu Ý approached me and pressed into my hand a piece of White Rabbit candy, the sticky condensed milk taffy that got stuck in my molars. In my other hand, she gave me something that felt like wadded-up cash and then folded my fingers into a tight fist. She announced to everyone that she was tired, and then her house slippers carried her away, her hunched back propelling her forward to her bedroom.

I climbed onto Tùa Cô's white leather couch and sank into the coldness, while the rice paper around the candy dissolved in my mouth. I lay on my side and closed my eyes, just wanting to wake up from the nightmare. All I wanted was for everything to go back to normal. A jacket landed across my back. Underneath the jacket, I peeked at the bill inside my fist. She'd given me a twenty.

My thoughts kept going back to Ba's spirit channeling. Was that seriously Má? Sometimes we didn't know the wandering spirits that came into him. But tonight, everything the spirit said was so specific, so spot-on. It *had* to have been Má. And if it was she, then what was all that "too late" stuff she was talking about? In soap operas, you were supposed to hold on to hope, even if the doctor said there was a one-in-a-million chance of coming back. If I prayed hard enough, she had to come back. It couldn't be too late. Má was always in control— she always figured it out. She had to come back.

That night, I heard my aunts and Bà Ngoại talking about Má's stomach surgery, blaming a friend who convinced Má it was safe. The friend was married to a doctor and was confident nothing could go wrong. Everyone was doing plastic surgery, she said. She also told Má that her favorite dress, the fuchsia mandarin collar one with the white-sequined peacock, fit too tight. My aunts were livid. Then they all started blaming themselves, wishing they could have stopped her. I started to blame myself too. All I could think about were my last words to her. I was the awful one.

That night, I rode with my aunts and grandparents back to the house. Ba stayed back. There was something he needed to do. The next day, Ba came home and said we needed to start making preparations.

"For what?" I asked.

"For Má's funeral," he said with a face too tired to fight, now too tired to live. Then he walked up the stairs to their bedroom, which became just his bedroom.

Goodbye

Dì Hiệp pulled up to Sunset View Cemetery and Mortuary in El Cerrito, a mile away from our first nail salon, Susan's Nails. The main building of the funeral home was a sharp, pointy triangle, just like the *Star Trek* symbol, making Má's funeral day feel celestial, even further removed from reality. Once Wendy and I were out of the car, Dì Phương gave each of us a thin white mourning robe that looked like a medical gown with the tie in back. Then she tied a long white strip around my forehead, making me look like the Karate Kid. I looked in the rearview mirror and smirked but quickly wiped it off my face. I couldn't be caught smiling.

Inside the funeral home, the nonstop sound of a beating gourd and the smoky haze of incense led us to Má's open casket. She was on an elevated platform, waiting for us in a cherrywood box. The entire room was lined with two dozen flower stands mostly made with yellow mums. Má used to love flowers. From this point forward, talking about Má would be in the past tense: she used to, she was.

The monks were in the front row chanting indecipherable words as women sniffled and occasionally wailed. Dì Phương pushed me down the center aisle straight to Má's casket. I wanted to see her, but I was afraid of what I would see. I had never seen a dead person before.

Three joss sticks landed in my hands, the tips glowing red, the smoke rising to the afterlife. The lines were open for her to hear.

All the other times I was forced to talk to my ancestors, I did it with a little reluctance and sometimes a little doubt. I used to ask for high marks, fruit snacks, and attention from my crush. But now, all I wanted was for Má to come back. What was the point of asking for something impossible? A few burning sticks were supposedly my only direct line to Má now.

As Dì Phương and Wendy took their turns saying goodbye, I closed my eyes, pressed the incense stick against my forehead, and spoke to her.

Hey, Má. I . . . I hope you're in a better place now . . . and that you're not mad at me. I'm really sorry about everything. You probably already know this, but I made the volleyball team. Let me know if you want me to quit.

I placed the incense stick in the holder, bowed, and then inched my way toward her casket to get a look. I peered in and then looked away. It was actually Má. Her face was swollen, making everything but her nose one level. The makeup was much heavier than anything she would ever put on, but maybe they had to cover up the embalming chemicals that had been pumped into her body. She seemed like a fake version of herself in a wax museum. Má wore her favorite gray angora cardigan with fake pearls sewn on the sleeves. Whenever she wore it, I thought she looked like a snow princess. Her hands were clasped on top of her stomach, showing off her jade bracelet gleaming on one wrist, a thin set of gold bangles on the other, and her vibrant red nails. Má was looking fabulous considering the circumstances.

I held my ground and kept waiting for her to scare me—open up her eyes with a big "Boo!" Wouldn't it be great if it was all just a big joke? It would be so easy to go back to how things were. I waited for her to say something, anything—but she didn't move. Then I felt a tug at my hand. Dì Phương escorted me back to the middle row of pews, where Wendy sat with our day's provisions: tissues, water bottles, and a six-pack of Oreo cookies. Crying women surrounded me. But my own tears didn't come, which made me feel even more anxious. I was a bad daughter on her last day, and now I couldn't even give her a proper goodbye.

I watched each person slowly approach the casket with reverence to pay their respects. Then they would move at the same pace to Ba sitting in the front row, patting his back. No hugs, just two pats. One person missing from the room was Hang. The fortune-teller said it would be bad luck given his zodiac sign and birth year. The clairvoyant barred Dì Phương from helping dress Má's corpse for the same reason. There were so many rules we had to follow, I just didn't get it. Couldn't we ease up on these superstitions? Wasn't it terrible enough that she'd died?

After eight hours of friends and relatives passing through, an usher closed her casket. There were no eulogies, no remembering of the good times. Instead, we all got into cars and drove up a big hill to Sunset Lawn, a small green hillside overlooking the Bay Bridge. A white tent on wheels covered Má's tombstone and a big rectangular hole in the ground. On her brown-red marble tombstone was Má's face from Hang's high school graduation. You could even see his honors gold cord over her shoulder. She looked neutral with a small smile, which meant she was beaming inside.

The rest of the procession continued to feel surreal. Má's hearse arrived, and all the men in my family, along with an uncle and some cousins, carried her casket to the big boxy hole lined with a green carpet and a metal railing. Cemetery employees used canvas straps to lower her casket. I took a white carnation from a bucket and tossed it to Má, now ten feet in the ground. I kept wondering if this was a nightmare and if I would wake up any moment. I kept waiting for everyone to say the joke was on me. But she was being buried. She was really gone.

As we stood around her grave site, I started to hear murmurings about how she'd died. Something related to anesthesia and her stomach surgery that had gone wrong. I still didn't know exactly what had happened. No one would tell me. And everyone couldn't believe how young she was. "Thirty-eight with four kids," they kept repeating.

Vietnamese elders kept approaching me, reminding me to always be on my best behavior and focus on school. Then they would pat my back two times and walk away. I wasn't a dog, I was eleven.

After the funeral, we returned home permanently without her. Only essential lights were turned on and then immediately turned off. Even the house was grieving. As I was choosing my school clothes for the next day, Ba came in and let me know I didn't have to go. He insisted that I rest, and then he disappeared to his room. Even though Wendy and I weren't particularly close to Ba, we decided it was best that we slept in his room that night. It just felt like the right thing to do. We dragged our comforters to Ba's room, laying the blankets on the floor next to his bed, facing the TV. He didn't say anything. He just turned out the light. I replayed Má's funeral over and over again in my head. None of it felt real, but I had to tell myself it was.

When I woke up in the morning, I was alone. Ba and the aunts had gone to the nail salon, and Wendy was nowhere to be found. I scrounged the leftovers to see what I could eat. I walked into Bà Ngoại's room to make sure I had permission.

"Bà Ngoại?" No answer. She was lying on top of her blanket, hands folded over her stomach like she was in her own casket. She shooed me away. I heated up some food and then spent the morning watching cartoons and game shows. But boredom had a way of amplifying this new aching loneliness. I went to look for Bà Ngoại, and when I found her, she still didn't greet me. She just sat at the dining room table with a mug of jasmine tea, staring out the window. It was so strange not to see her up at the stove. I closed my bedroom door and disappeared into the safe and predictable world of *The Baby-Sitters Club* and *Goosebumps*. Sometimes I read issues of *The Economist*, which Kang subscribed to and suggested I read. I zeroed in on hurricanes in Central America that wiped out homes and left children orphaned. I started to feel disgusted with all my self-pity. At least I had one parent still alive. Maybe my situation wasn't that bad.

During the day, it didn't feel like Má was dead, because she would have been at work anyway. It was when the garage door opened at the end of the day that things fell apart. At dinner, no one made eye contact or even had much of an appetite. Without Má there, we lost the person always scheming the next big trip, meal, or party. But now no one was looking forward to anything. It was just eat, sleep, work, repeat.

After a week of puttering around the house, I noticed the smaller flower arrangements had wilted. When Ông Ngoại threw them out, I decided it was time to go back to school. Nature had moved on. It was time for me to move forward.

On the school playground, I sat on a stone bench facing the entire blacktop. Kids battled at the ball wall, girls played hopscotch, and boys played a vicious game with their Pogs and slammers. But no part of me wanted to play. I saw it as meaningless.

"Hey, flat nose!" My thoughts were interrupted by Jessica, the tomboy in my class always getting into trouble. I barely glanced at her. I used to be scared of her, but now I didn't care about anything. "What's wrong with you? Your mom die or something?" I bit my upper lip and started to stare at the faded four-square lines like they were the most interesting thing in the world. How did she know? Did my teacher make an announcement or something? Tears started to well up in my eyes. I bolted to the safest place on the playground, the yard duty lady.

"Come on, chill out! I'm just playing! God!" trailed off Jessica. I raced to the blurry giant woman. When I reached her long plaid dress and whistle, I lunged for her.

"Oh, honey, what's wrong?" She bent down, and I got a big whiff of her perfume. I was trying to speak, but nothing was coming out. My throat felt strangled. Instead of pushing out a sound, I started hyperventilating, mumbling half words to this stranger. She pulled me close to her squishy bosom. In the two weeks since Má's coma and her funeral, no one had hugged me.

"My—my—my . . . mom . . . died," I mumbled into her chest. I kept wiping snot on my sleeve, and now I was bawling into her sweater. The morning bell rang, and then the whole playground got quiet. I tried to not make a sound, but I couldn't control my hyperventilating.

"Hold on a second, honey," she said gently. She kept her hand on my back as she blew her whistle, motioning for all the kids to line up. I hid in the folds of her clothes even though everyone could plainly see that there was something wrong with me. Once the kids started filing away, the yard duty lady wrapped her arms around me again. I clenched her fabric with both fists. All the tears I had been holding back released like an opened dam. I cried until there was nothing left and finally let go when my breathing evened out.

She walked me to the nurse's office, where I was given an ice pack wrapped in a coarse brown paper towel. I lay down in a fetal position on the bed covered in crinkly thin paper, blowing my nose on one-ply toilet paper until I rubbed my upper lip raw. After an hour of just lying there, I washed my face and returned to class. When I handed my teacher the pink hall pass, I could feel my classmates' eyes on me. My cheeks were burning, and the only thing I could do was pretend none of it happened. Not the coma, not the funeral, and not the yard duty lady.

My family never did grief counseling, nor did anyone ever ask me if I was okay. My life was out of control, so I started to obsess about the two things I could control: my grades and my body. I spent the rest of sixth grade getting A-pluses and tracking my weight with a diet and exercise journal. I was tired of elders nitpicking my body. I wanted their judgment to stop. I wished someone would give me affection and reassure me that I was enough. I wanted to be loved. So I wrote down every piece of food I ate and every mile I ran, daydreaming for a prince-like boyfriend to save me.

Exodus

Two years after Má's death, a bomb dropped on the family again. Wendy and I were getting ready for bed, brushing our teeth in the bathroom that separated the aunts' room from our room. We had reconfigured our sleeping situation when we moved up to Santa Rosa a few years prior. Our sliding bathroom door was hanging crooked at a diagonal. Ba hadn't fixed anything in the house in a long time.

Dì Phương was on the toilet and rustled her *Báo Mõ*, the free Vietnamese weekly magazine we picked up on our Sunday trips to the Vietnamese grocer and nail salon supply store an hour away. She cleared her throat and casually told us Ba would remarry someone else. My aunts and grandparents were planning to move out, and we had a choice to come with them. She didn't even look at us when she said this—she just kept reading her magazine.

I was brushing my teeth and started to cough toothpaste suds all over the sink, staring at her in disbelief through the mirror. Ba hadn't mentioned a thing.

"But why do you have to leave?" I asked.

"You two are old enough now. People need freedom," she said simply. She flushed the toilet and then shut her bedroom door, ending the discussion. Wendy was sixteen, and I was thirteen. I finally joined Wendy as a teenager, but I didn't feel ready for more change.

Snuggled in my bottom bunk bed, I whispered up to Wendy to figure out what we would do.

"I don't know, dude, but that was gross—she had the door open!"

I laughed softly and agreed. As Wendy dozed off, I kept playing out the scenario of staying or leaving. Either way would hurt someone. Either way just wasn't fair.

When Má first died, all the regular customers asked where Jennifer was, and each of her sisters had to give an explanation, reliving the trauma over and over again for two straight months. Má's shoes were too big to fill, so we had to all work harder without her. The previous joy of being busy morphed into a nihilistic grind. Every day at the shop was a reminder that she was gone.

Dì Phương took over Má's table as the new manager of Today's Nails #1. Her English was not as steady, but everyone who worked at the shop fell in line. Ba was still managing Today's Nails #2 in the next town over in Windsor. Since #1 was busier, Wendy and I were expected to show up to help when we could.

The Saturday after Dì Phương's big news, I was at our flagship shop. When the afternoon rush died down, I headed to the back for lunch. I found Dì Phương there with a bowl of just microwaved Mama instant noodle soup. The steam rose from the tom yum broth. She pushed over thinly cut chả lụa, Vietnamese ham, and a small saucer of lemon juice with salt and pepper. Elders were supposed to eat first, but she made it just for me. I eagerly began sucking up the noodles, feeling special because of her gesture.

As I ate, she reviewed all my favorite dishes, asking if I enjoyed eating them. I nodded while I blew on my noodles. Then she asked me if I loved Bà Ngoại. Even though the woman terrified me, of course I had to say yes. With her clever logic, Dì Phương invited me again to move out with them.

"I'm not sure," I said in between bites. I didn't want to disappoint her, but I didn't know what else to say. She seemed hurt and left the break room in a huff. I put down my chopsticks and stared at my bowl until the broth became cold. I completely lost my appetite but couldn't throw out the food. Bà Ngoại always said to eat the meat, even if I wasn't hungry. I force-fed myself and felt terrible. No matter what I did, it was the wrong choice.

That week, dinner became increasingly tense. Ba quickly ate first and then went up to his room. Then the aunts, Wendy, and I would eat. Dì Phương picked bones out of the fish and put meaty pieces into my bowl. Everyone was acting so strangely but pretending everything was normal. Now the whole family was playing my game of pretend. After dinner, I went to Ba's room. He was sitting in front of Má's vanity mirror, sorting through a pile of salon service tickets and punching into the adding machine. That used to be Má's job.

"Um, Ba. How come the aunts want to leave?" I asked.

He looked annoyed at me. "Sao mày hỏi nhiều quá vậy? Không quan trọng. Ngu quá!" *How come you ask so many questions? It's not important. You're so stupid!* He tsked and shooed me off. My throat tightened, and I backed away, closing the door softly behind me. I didn't mean to upset him. I went to my room and pulled the covers up even though I hadn't changed into my pajamas. If I stayed with Ba, would he keep being mean to me? Were the aunts mad at him because he actually had a secret girlfriend, or was that all made up?

That night, I called my brothers at college to see what I should do. Hang saw the aunts' actions as betrayal. They were abandoning the family when we needed them most. They were traitors in his eyes. When I called Kang, he said he would keep staying in touch with them because family was family. Both of them told me to stay with Ba, so I did. But my brothers' disagreement meant they stopped talking to each other. Somehow things just kept getting worse.

A week later, I woke up on Sunday morning and heard a steady clunking sound on the stairs. It was Dì Phương moving down a giant black suitcase. I stuck my head in the aunts' doorway. Everything was cleared out except for swaying hangers in the closet. Nothing in their medicine cabinet mirror. No tall stacks of magazines by the toilet. I raced down to the garage. The shoe shelves Ông Ngoại and Ba built on the garage back wall just had Ba's, Wendy's, and my shoes remaining. There used to be a hundred shoes there. Now there were just a dozen. The garage was open, and Ông Ngoại was shoving boxes into the trunk of Cô Thảo's car. I grabbed the first pair of shoes I saw and shuffled out wearing Ba's colossal sneakers.

"Where are you going?" I demanded of Dì Phương.

"Ba mày không muốn mình ở đây." *Your father doesn't want us here.* What? I had to change his mind. I tried to run back into the house with my oversize shoes flopping behind me. I dashed up the stairs and jiggled Ba's bedroom door, but it was locked. I raced back down to the car. Wendy was standing by the car window. Bà Ngoại sat in the passenger seat with the window up. She shook her palm goodbye a few times and then looked away.

Through the crack in the window, I heard Ông Ngoại say, "Bà ơi, rồi mọi chuyện sẽ qua thôi." *Old woman, all of this will pass.* Dì Ngân and Dì Phương sniff-kissed us both and then dabbed at their eyes with their palms.

"Nhớ gọi điện thoại nha," said Dì Phương. *Remember to call.* She reminded us they weren't far, just the next town over. Ten hands waved inside the cars, and then they drove away. Inside the house, I walked by Bà Ngoại's room. Their large bed frame was gone, and the only thing left was a trace of her menthol smell. All the kitchen supplies were still there, but Bà Ngoại's giant glass jar with the black cobra was gone. Nothing was on the stove. I didn't realize the house could feel even emptier than it had when we lost Má. I made a bowl of cereal and then turned on the TV to break this new silence. Má would have never let this happen.

An hour later, Ba emerged downstairs and opened the garage door. With clippers in hand, he started pruning Má's roses. Our front yard had eight rose trees that dotted the triangle front yard of our American dream home. Má had picked trees with the most fragrant smell, and Ba helped them take root into the earth. Back when she was alive, he would alternate his Sunday mornings singing ballads on his karaoke machine with wearing industrial earmuffs to take care of the front yard. After pulling the choke on the lawn mower a few times, he would cut the lawn, using the Weedwacker to trim the edges around the base of the rose trees, and then finish with the blower, leaving the yard pristine. He would smell like gasoline when he came in for breakfast. For as long as we lived in that house, he tended those roses like they were his church. I asked him if he wanted anything, but he just waved me off, dropping wilted flowers into a soap bucket.

For the past five years, Bà Ngoại had cooked every meal for us, but now we were on our own. For lunch, we ate canned clam chowder. Then I was deserted for a second time in one day. Wendy moved all her things into the aunts' room. For dinner, we got a take-and-bake pizza. At every meal, I thought Ba would talk about what happened. Acknowledge that they had moved out. Give us a pep talk that everything was going to be okay. But he didn't. We just ate our food, washed the dishes, and then went to our separate rooms.

Ba was forced to play a role he never wanted. A widow with four children and now the owner of two nail salons with no employees. He was forced to become the glue that only Má could be. It was only inevitable that everything would fall apart.

PART II

MẢ

Tomb

Severance

With Má's family out of the house, Ba, the man who had always been there but never in the forefront, was forced to take over. Bà Ngoại's elaborate four-dish dinners became Ba's Spam fried rice. Whenever I started feeling sick, regardless of my symptoms, Ba made me drink a cup of Theraflu. A few months after the rest of the family left, Ba decided it was time for me to get braces. He insisted that I get a perfect smile.

"If you don't, then people will judge you," he warned. For two years, Ba was always at our meeting spot at my middle school with the car running, shuttling me to the orthodontist. We didn't talk much in the car; we just listened to radio commercials to pass the time.

Even though Ba's snoring vibrated the walls in our two-story house, his major decisions were hushed. Three years after Má's death, he went to Việt Nam for a two-week trip. He came back with a spring in his step and six eleven-by-seventeen-inch portraits of him and his new wife framed in black lacquer. As he was hammering nails into his bedroom wall, he cheerily announced she would come to America by the end of the year. I would call her Dì Nhung, *Aunt* Nhưng. I stood there staring at the wall decorations, stunned. He didn't bother to ask me about how I felt. Instead, he sent me to the library to get a name dictionary so he could choose a meaningful English name for her and, two years later, for their new baby girl. I wouldn't be the youngest anymore.

A family friend had introduced them. Over the phone, she was taken by Ba's commitment to his children. He needed help raising them and running the nail salon. She was game. The only caveat was her family could not know he had children, because a widower remarrying was considered taboo. And so the pile of family secrets continued to grow.

When she arrived, she traded her calculator for a nail file. In Việt Nam, she was a white-collared accountant, college-educated, and one of the few Vietnamese adults I knew with a diploma. She was earnest about helping Ba at the shop and always saw the positive, even in sour moments. When gossip about her floated back to us, Ba was visibly distressed. Dì Nhung held her head high, reminding us that character was based on everyday actions, not on what others said. When Ba forbade me from going to prom, I retaliated by chipping dishes as I washed them. Dì Nhung worked her diplomatic magic and gave me some money to buy a dress.

Unlike Má, Ba was not a natural businessperson. He sold our second nail salon, but things began to crumble on his watch. He was at the first table now. For some reason, he had a *Playboy*-like calendar right by his nail station that customers saw when they walked into the shop. As a fifteen-year-old, I confronted him about it, and he reminded me who was in charge.

"Mầy không biết gì về bus-i-ness đâu!" *You don't know anything about business!* After that, I kept my mouth shut even though the shop barely ever had customers sitting in the waiting chairs. During the summer, he would have my stepmother apply dollar sign decals on his big toe so we would attract more customers. He paid his other two employees a day wage instead of commission, which disincentivized them to help build the business. Even though he was a kind employer, this meant most of the time, our family made less than his workers.

His parenting was just as confusing. For my first car, he insisted on a four-by-four. He was convinced I needed one even though we lived in a flat suburb in the California wine country. My dream car was a fuel-efficient Toyota Echo.

"Safe-tee quan trọng. Đừng hỏi nữa!" *Safety is important. Don't ask any more [questions]!* On my sixteenth birthday, a used Isuzu Rodeo appeared in the driveway. I felt good, but I also felt bad. I knew things weren't going well at the shop. I didn't want to be a burden, and I didn't want a gas-guzzling SUV. Ba said he was tired of driving me around and put the keys in my palm.

By the time I graduated high school, we weren't communicating much. Ba recited his expectations regularly: get good grades, get into a good college, get a master's degree, and *then* get a boyfriend. If I didn't follow his plan, I was giving him the Vietnamese middle finger because I lacked hiếu, *filial piety*. I kept going to the registrar's office to show Ba proof I was ranked number one, but he didn't care. He was enraged that I did community service and student government. He thought extracurriculars were distracting me from getting into the best college possible, even though it was my competitive edge. I tried to explain that college admissions in the U.S. was different from Communist Việt Nam. I neglected to say that all the adult advisors in my extracurriculars actually made me feel like I mattered, unlike him.

Ba also had a sixth sense whenever I did have a boyfriend and would threaten to kick me out of the house.

"Do you want to become homeless?" he would growl. I would run up to my room and slam the door, trying to make the yelling stop. He saw me as a rebellious daughter who disobeyed his wishes. I saw him as a paranoid father who didn't trust me. I just wanted to be with someone who cared for me. There was so much I couldn't communicate with my broken Vietnamese, so I just didn't, and neither did he.

When I found out I got into Harvard, I reread the acceptance email three times before I called Ba at the nail salon. I couldn't wait for his praise. But his only response was "Why didn't you get into Stanford?" His words were crushing. There were no congratulations or

I-am-proud-of-yous. He said he was busy with a customer and hung up. Suddenly this joyful moment turned dark. *Whatever*, I thought. Maybe a customer would talk some sense into him.

My graduation party was the nail in the coffin. I wore a thrift store royal-purple pleated skirt and tied myself in a beautiful iridescent ribbon with a bow over my chest like I was a gift, hugging all the people who helped me get to this next step. I was showered with presents and well-wishes. I had always been hard on myself, but that day, I allowed myself to feel good. After all the guests left, Ba stared me down.

"You think they all like you?" he scoffed. "They're lying to your face. They're faking it." The giddy smile I'd had the entire party sagged. My eyes started to sting. I didn't know what to say. Was he jealous? Or worse, was he right? Was I actually the fool?

I grabbed my car keys and slammed the front door so hard the frame shook. I was tired of being his disappointment. There was never a resolve about the past. We couldn't communicate about the present. And with me about to move across the country for college, it was unclear if there would even be a future with both of us in it.

The Cult

Going to college would be my way of starting over. I couldn't wait to leave my judgmental father, who didn't understand me. But I didn't exactly fit in at Harvard. During the first month in the dining hall, someone asked what our parents did, so we went around the table.

"Professor at University of Hawai'i."

"Neurologist and lawyer."

"They're both on the Hill."

"My dad does nails," I said without much thought.

Then the skepticism came.

"You're kidding."

"No, seriously, what does he actually do?"

"He's a man-i-curist," I said, fully enunciating.

A nice girl from Maine leaned over and touched my arm. "Wow, that's amazing. *Seriously*," she emphasized.

I didn't know if she was being genuine or patronizing. I just wanted to run far away with my tray of food and never speak to these people ever again.

"And what about your mother?" she probed.

"Oh, she does nails too," I lied. I kept looking for an easy exit. The dining hall dish carousel was in sight. Maine girl smoothly changed the topic to classifying each of the final clubs on campus, sussing out which of the boys at the table were going to get into Harvard's equivalent of a Greek fraternity. Legacy was the number one factor. That's when each person revealed if their parents went to Harvard too. Neither of my parents finished high school. My shame turned to fury. I wanted to tackle these elitist brats. I got in fully on my own merit, but I couldn't help but wonder: Was I the admissions office's mistake?

Many of my classmates wore popped J.Crew collars and had attended elite boarding schools. I, on the other hand, applied to Harvard on a whim after watching Reese Witherspoon get admitted in *Legally Blonde*. I went to a public school, and my high school counselor looked annoyed when I asked her to sign twenty-one fee waivers for elite colleges. She wanted me to apply to safety schools like Chico State instead. Fortunately, I didn't listen, but the disparity at Harvard was stark. I was "the low-income kid" on a 90 percent scholarship.

I tried to join the Harvard Vietnamese Association, but my clumsy attempts at conical hat dancing, broken Vietlish, and lack of interest in premed made me feel like an outcast even though these classmates all looked like I did. I thought I would find my tribe in college, but now I was three thousand miles away from home and lonelier than when I left.

All I wanted to do was run back home. But now my face was full of pus-filled acne, and none of the clothes I came with fit anymore. I didn't just gain the freshman fifteen, I put on a whole twenty pounds from the dining hall buffet. I tried to hide it with big sweatshirts and elastic waistbands, but I knew my family would take jabs at me during the holiday break. I started pounding SlimFast strawberry shakes the week before coming home to drop the weight. When I arrived home, Ba and my siblings kept the criticism coming. Ba had made a wonderful spread of Vietnamese food I had been craving for months. But now with them gawking, I didn't enjoy a single bite. I returned back to campus and felt emotionally unstable, trying anything that would help me feel more sure of myself.

During my first three years at college, I became a spiritual seeker. I cried with strangers at personal growth workshops, spent my sophomore spring break at a ten-day silent meditation retreat (a monk scribbled the name of the center while we were at a Japanese grocery store conveyor belt), splurged on self-help books, took mushrooms in a sweat lodge to reconnect with my mother's womb, and even went to Burning Man by myself, catching a ride with a man named Eric in a Prius whom I found on Craigslist.

But then, on a brisk February evening my junior year, I attended a free yoga class at the Harvard Divinity School Andover Chapel. I came in fully expecting to do cat, cow, and child's pose. Our instructor, Nicholas, who was also a graduate student there, had us on our backs with taut abs, legs held in the air in a ninety-degree position, neck lifted off the ground, hands stretched above our heads. I had become the sleeping dragon. One minute in, my body was trembling. *You can't.* I told myself I could. *You can't.* I opened my eyes and saw everyone else peacefully holding their pose. This voice yelling at me wasn't my own. So where was it coming from? *You can't.* It was Hang telling me to dump my elementary school best friends who still played with toy horses at thirteen. He said I needed to be more strategic about my social ranking. *You can't be friends with them.* My sister excluding me from her life when we became teenagers. *You can't hang out with us.* Ba calling me pathetic when I told him I wasn't pursuing med school. *You can't even try because you're too dumb.* I screamed, *You can't,* right back inside of my head, telling all of them what I never had the courage to say. My body shuddered as the rage escaped my body like bats flying out from a cave. Hot tears fell from the sides of my eyes into the chapel carpet floor.

And then I heard a clear voice inside of me speak. It was not mine, it was someone else's.

"All those times you've felt unloved or alone, you weren't. God, through the presence of the body, has always been there for you." Who was this voice? And how could my body be the key to loving myself? My body was always something I had seen as an inconvenience, a detached thing I had to fix. But tonight, I felt welcome to get to know my body. After two more yoga classes, I was hooked. That's when Nicholas invited me to Shim Song, a weekend yoga workshop in a Boston hotel.

I was standing in a large circle with a hundred people of all ages, from college students to people in their sixties, wearing a white canvas uniform with bottoms that ballooned out like MC Hammer pants. We were all eager participants following instructions from the short Korean instructor onstage. She had us close our eyes and tap our fists against our stomachs, which she called a "dahn-jon." Our bodies had three dahn-jons that served as energy centers, and the one at the abdomen powered the physical body energy. Once we could ground ourselves there, we were one step closer to establishing a balance with our emotional and spiritual bodies.

We bounced in long lines facing the teacher on the stage. "Dahn-jon, dahn-jon, feel your dahn-jon!" she hollered at us. At first I thought it was a little silly, but when I peeked, I saw everyone pounding their stomachs with big smiles on their faces. I adopted the same expression.

Then a Caucasian woman who looked like a modern-day Snow White with fair skin and black hair took the stage. She softly introduced herself as Michelle-nim and then instructed us to hold sleeping dragon. "Nim" is a formal Korean honorific used to show respect. Her intonation was a little strange. It was as if she were a Korean person speaking English with pauses in funny places—but she was white. Ten minutes in, my legs began to convulse, which she explained was stagnant energy leaving the body. Michelle-nim had us ask ourselves over and over again, "What do I want? What do I want?" My mind started to wonder why I had become such a self-help junkie over the years. Did I still not have closure from Má's death? Could I live a life where I wasn't so sensitive about what my family thought of me?

Next up was the energy tunnel, where we formed two straight

lines facing one another. We were instructed to go through with 100 percent effort. When it was my turn, I spun and danced, twisting my body as everyone chanted. Even though I wasn't trying to be performative, I did take note of what the people did who got the loudest cheers. After everyone went through, Michelle-nim encouraged us to *really* do it with 100 percent if we didn't think we did. I ran to the front of the line and started somersaulting through the tunnel, not giving a damn about my inner critic. The crowd roared, making me feel celebrated. It was as if I'd just crossed the finish line of my first spiritual marathon. I just got my first medal.

During lunchtime, I sized up the sandwich boxes. Roast beef, chicken Waldorf salad, caprese. This type of decision-making always made my cortisol levels go haywire because I didn't ever want to miss out on the best one.

"I love your energy," said a voice to my left. I looked up and saw a handsome man in his late twenties with dark brown hair, glasses, and an ambiguous skin tone I couldn't quite pinpoint. Armenian? "I'm JJ-nim," he introduced himself. He was gorgeous.

I struggled to remember my own name. "I'm . . . Susan."

He invited me to eat with him, so I grabbed a random lunchbox and followed him. We sat knee to knee, and he told me that he was a Sabin-nim, a master and teacher for Dahn Yoga. He was also the national president of the Body & Brain Club and YEHA, short for Young Earth Human Alliance, the college arm for Dahn. When he was a college student, he felt his studies were so removed from actually helping humanity. He wanted to dedicate his life to social change, so he'd joined Dahn three years earlier and hadn't looked back ever since. His idealism and vision for a better world made me instantly smitten. He was an Aries, which meant we could be compatible as friends and lovers. I always wanted to find my soulmate, and there he was, eating kettle chips right in front of me.

Michelle-nim's closing talk was about the "freedom flea." If a flea was stuck inside a box, it adapted to the lid and learned to jump only as high as the lid. Once the lid was removed, it could only then realize it had been trapped all along and finally could be free. She said what we experienced today was the removal of that lid. I couldn't wait to see what more training would bring.

That evening, I hopped back onto the T, sending loving energy to all the late-night passengers on my ride back to Harvard Square. As the doors opened, I twirled out onto the platform, dancing up the station steps. Back in my dorm room, I gazed in the mirror and admired my face and body with soft eyes. Usually, I was ashamed of my appearance, but tonight was different.

"You're beautiful," I promised. I pressed my lips one inch away from my reflection, fogging up the glass, looking straight into my soul. "I'm sorry. I love you," I said, carefully following Michelle-nim's instructions. "I forgive you."

After the weekend was over, I found myself crying in Michelle-nim's arms. I felt so seen and safe with her. I asked if she would become my spiritual guide and show me the way. She hugged me even tighter.

I started training with Michelle-nim at the Dahn Cambridge yoga studio she managed right across the street from campus. Sometimes after yoga class, I would follow her to the studio's back room, where this white woman fed me Korean food with dishes of mackerel, burdock root, and teeny-tiny crispy anchovies with salted peanuts. We ate on a table a few inches off the floor, sitting on bamboo mats. Holding a small rice bowl up to my mouth, I felt an admiration for Michelle-nim that I felt once for Má.

One of the few times I was alone with my mother, I was eight and we were driving back from a nail salon–scouting trip. Má had just visited the women at Today's Nails in Santa Rosa. Once the meeting was done, we walked out to a charming farmers market that was nothing like the San Jose flea market. That one sold churros, knockoff Bart Simpson tank tops, and secondhand appliances on blue tarps. This place had exotic tastes like white peaches, black Mission figs, fire-roasted aubergine spread, and jumbo turkey legs. After we walked the whole market, Má started to backtrack to our car. I pulled at her sleeve and pointed at the stand that sold chicken wings, to share with Wendy, I insisted. I waited for her to say no, but to my delight, she peeled off a ten-dollar bill from the rolled-up wad of cash in her pocket.

Once we were in the car, the wings were in a brown paper bag on the car floor mat. Má just bought a brand-new sky-blue 1993 Toyota Cressida with leather seats, a CD player, and automatic windows that went up and down with the touch of a button. It was such a hot summer day that my skin below my shorts started to melt against the smoking-hot leather. I scooted all the way to the edge, stretching my seat belt as far as it would allow, waiting for the blasting AC to make things better.

As Má pulled onto the highway, I peeked my head in the bag and looked at my new precious specimens. The wings were a golden caramel brown with crispy edges. They smelled delicious. I bet they wouldn't be as good later when they cooled down. And Má said we had a whole hour before we got back to Susan's Nails.

I looked back down at those cute morsels. I mean, I bought ten whole pieces. If I tried just one, then there would be nine pieces left to share with Wendy. I just wanted a taste. I would give her five, and then I would have four. Perfect.

"Ăn đi con," encouraged Má. *Eat it, child.*

I guided my hand carefully into the bag so the sauce touched just my two fingers. The chicken wing glistened in the sunny afternoon light. I offered it to Má, but she said it would be too messy. I started to lick the wing like it was an ice cream cone, feeling the tiny ridges of gooey garlic scratch my tongue. I scraped the bone clean with my teeth, joyfully crunching at the cartilage. With nothing edible left, I tucked the bone into a napkin and set it on my lap.

I rolled up the bag and gazed at the wide-open green pastures dotted with cows. But all I could think about was those wings! I shouldn't actually—and then just like that, my hands were back in the bag, searching for the smallest piece so I could save Wendy the bigger ones. I tried to eat slowly, but my mouth could not be stopped.

I looked down at the remaining eight pieces. Four each was still a good share—even three each would do! I could have just two more and then there would be plenty left. One wing past my limit, I rolled up the bag again and put it on the car mat far out of reach. I started sucking on my fingers and reminiscing about the first piece. It tasted so much better fresh. Maybe sharing two each would still be good. If I didn't tell Wendy I'd started with ten wings, she wouldn't know the difference. I kept rehearsing the perfect line in my head to explain my predicament to Má. After five minutes, I clumsily outlined my painful problem. My cheeks felt red-hot. I was terrified she would accuse me of being a troublemaker.

"Đừng lo con" was all she said. *Don't worry.* With her blessing, I lost all willpower. My greedy little hands went at it. Wendy didn't have to know. I didn't have to share *everything* with my sister. With just four wings left, I finished off another two and felt stuffed. The wings were tasty, but now I didn't want them as much. I looked back inside the bag. I had more bones in my lap than what was left in the bag. The two wings looked pitiful, lonely even. Sharing food with others should be inviting, plentiful, a gesture to show we were always considering them. Looking at the remaining pieces, I started to stress about my grand plan. If I was going to share with Wendy, I should have kept the whole bag intact. I didn't want Wendy to feel left out, but I also couldn't waste food. I gave in to the only option I had left. I force-fed myself the last two chicken wings with disgust. I was an inconsiderate sister.

I crumpled the bag shut one last time and looked over to Má. Her sunglasses stared straight ahead. I pressed the CD button on the audio console of the car, and Madonna's "Lucky Star" from her *Immaculate Collection* took me to another place of hope, a place where everything was okay, where I was absolved of my chicken wing sin. I placed my arm on the window's edge and leaned my chin on it, feeling the wind slap my bangs against my forehead. The wind howled through the car as we cruised down the freeway. I kept worrying Wendy would find out and she would resent me forever.

When we arrived back at the Susan's Nails parking lot, I got up on my tiptoes and opened the giant gray dumpster, throwing the bag of evidence away. On the walk to the front door, Má told me to wash my hands with a wink. When she entered the salon, she made a big show of the white peaches she got from the farmers market, praising their subtle sweet taste without a peep about my scandal. I made a beeline for the sink so Wendy wouldn't smell my guilt. With Má as my accomplice, I felt worthy of her time and attention. I relished that afternoon, replaying our blissful car ride on a loop, savoring it as much as the first chicken wing.

At Dahn, I felt the same type of trust I felt with Michelle-nim as I did with my mother. Whenever I felt overwhelmed about school or life, I called Michelle-nim. Her voice was so disarming and encouraging. She helped me feel confident and capable. She became the mother I always needed.

After one month, Michelle-nim said my spiritual growth would intensify with a "big action." She said I was ready to go to Sedona to attend the national YEHA summit. There were hundreds of other college students like me who were committed to the Young Earth Human Alliance mission, a vision for inner and outer peace. I was a little hesitant to spend $250, but that changed after my heartthrob JJ-nim called. My cheeks were burning as he explained he would be facilitating the whole weekend and really wanted me there. I gave Dahn my registration fee and booked my flight immediately.

During the last night of the YEHA summit, we had a completely sober four-hour dance rager. As I started getting blisters, I had visions. I saw myself birthing out all my demons that have made me feel so crippled. One by one, the darkness left my body. Then the bass dropped and JJ-nim had everyone screaming their lungs out. I yelled until I had nothing left, making me feel light-headed, pure. Sweat dripped down my back, and I felt my old skin falling away, a new self emerging. The volume faded, and then JJ-nim had us all lie down.

"What does your true self want?" he asked into the microphone. A part of me just wanted to have his babies. And the other part of me wanted to treat myself like a baby. I wanted to be my own mother. For years, I kept expecting someone else to save me, but now it was time to take care of myself. If I wanted to work toward world peace, I needed to work on myself. I was scared shitless, but the answer was clear. To do this, I had to become a Sabin-nim and dedicate my life to Dahn.

I regularly went to see Michelle-nim at her training center. But after tens of thousands of dahn-jon pats, I started to feel skeptical about Dahn Yoga. The time I spent with Michelle-nim left me feeling refreshed and calm, but the conversation always went back to buying more programs. I had been carefully logging how much I was spending on Dahn and trying to save in other ways. Instead of buying course pack readings for class, I would borrow a friend's and make an illegal copy. Whenever a friend invited me out for bubble tea, I suggested the dining hall instead. I skipped out on trips with friends to make sure I wouldn't get an overdraft fee at my bank.

In my heart, I knew charging high prices for peace was unfair. I had been filling out scholarship forms since I was nine, which allowed me to explore the world beyond the walls of our nail salon. Shouldn't programs like Dahn be more accessible? When I brought this up, Michelle-nim just laughed.

"Dahn attracts people on a higher vibration. So much mind energy! Move the energy down," she emphasized by poking at my pudgy tummy. "Money is just energy. Your dahn-jon is getting stronger. People who say they cannot pay live on a lower vibration. When you show them Dahn, they will do their money training too. Trust your heart. Right now, too much fear." My heart sank. Michelle-nim's explanation reduced poverty to a lack of will, not circumstance. My family worked their asses off just to survive. She was starting to make me feel uneasy. I felt a tightness in my dahn-jon.

I felt conflicted. I had processed more emotional trauma in the last month with Dahn than I had with my therapist in the last three years. Michelle-nim said I was ready for healing sessions. Fifteen of them for $3,000. I didn't actually have the money, so she encouraged me to get a student loan to pay for it; that had worked for her other members. When the financial aid office said no, I opened a credit card with 14 percent interest. Money was just energy anyway, she reminded me.

First it was the healing sessions where she would massage my stomach meridian lines and then I would pass out. Then she wanted me to change my senior thesis topic. I threw out studying HIV/AIDS prevention programs for sex workers in Việt Nam to focus on measuring the impact of mind-body programs, a.k.a. Dahn Yoga, on leadership development. Then it was $5,500 on Healer School, where apparently I could become a healer in six days. When I said I was concerned about the price, she had me try my family.

I called up Dì Ngân. It had been eight years since I'd last spoken to her. After the aunts moved out when I was in seventh grade, they just disappeared from my life. During my freshman year at college, I received an envelope from them addressed in flawless italic penmanship, identical to Má's handwriting. Inside was a glorious hundred-dollar check with the memo line "birthday." I really wanted to deposit it. With that money, I could finally pay for a round of crab rangoon and scorpion bowls from the Kong, a greasy Chinese restaurant and nightclub across the street from campus. But I knew I needed to honor my father. I tore the check up into confetti and sent it right back to their nail salon. So it wasn't much of a surprise when Dì Ngân turned me down for a loan.

"Why do you need money for school if you are about to finish school?" she asked.

The next day, Ba somehow knew to call to join the pileup.

"You need to follow my plan for you," he said.

"I *am*, Ba! I'm studying for the LSAT . . . And I'm really sad right now, and Healer School is going to make me happy." There was no way I could articulate the monumental transformation I was going through with my basic Vietlish. He called me ungrateful and stupid, twisting a knife into my gut. I tried to tap into feeling compassion for him, but my nervous system was going haywire. I hung up without saying goodbye, and then I spiraled. I felt worthless and didn't know what to do.

I didn't want to tap my dahn-jon. I didn't want to go to a lecture. I didn't want to meet my friends. I just wanted to hide out in my dorm room away from everyone. I felt broken, and I didn't want to get rejected by anyone else. This went on for three days until I ran out of clean underwear. I had flipped a few inside out, but now the only clean thing left was my swimsuit. I kept telling myself to get out of bed before breakfast service was over at the dining hall, but the hours just melted into one another.

As I lay under the covers, I finally gathered the motivation to call Michelle-nim. By the afternoon, I was back in the Dahn studio learning new moves with a bow staff. She said I was ready for Dahn Mu Do school, focusing on learning martial arts, and a lifetime gold membership, where I could go to yoga classes for the rest of my life for "free." All in with Healer School, I owed them $14,000. And for some reason, I had to make a decision within the next five days. I opened another credit card.

I confided in my college friend Senait, and she tried to point me to other spiritual organizations that were free or low-cost. Then I started reading up on ex-Dahn members who wrote scathing critiques. There was the woman who died in the desert while she was training to become a master. They made her hike uphill for miles with rocks in her backpack and wouldn't give her water, as a form of "training," they said. I freaked out. I scheduled a meeting with Michelle-nim to say goodbye. When I arrived, she looked up from the reception desk.

"Come here," she said, trying to soothe me. She held me tightly, and I started to sob into her chest.

"I . . . need . . . to quit." As I told her my concerns, she handed me a tissue. Dahn exploited people for money. This was some kind of pyramid scheme, not truly about world peace. She rubbed my back in slow, big circles. A tear cascaded down her cheek with Hollywood timing.

"Dear, sweet Suzen, how can you understand if you have not gone to the end?"

I felt torn. Since I'd come back from the first YEHA summit, I had changed my name from Susan to Suzen, the z-e-n underscoring my dedication to the spiritual path. I didn't want to forget all the truth and wisdom I'd realized in the desert. But now I was giving up because I felt like I was being manipulated. Was my intuition right, or did Michelle-nim know something that I did not?

"I want my money back," I said in a hushed voice. Michelle-nim opened up her arms again, and I collapsed right back into her. I cried because she had been like a mother to me. I cried because I had to go back to my old life where my family pretended everything was normal even though we were emotionally bankrupt. No one ever asked or cared to know how I was really doing except for Michelle-nim. I filled out the withdrawal form and stepped back into the elevator. She stood across the threshold with tears trickling down her face, waving to me as the doors closed. After a week, I was back, and she ran the charges again. Even though Dahn was dysfunctional, I felt more love from them than my own family.

And so this cycle continued, painfully, for another two months. My family even agreed to go to a Dahn class with me when they visited for my pretend graduation. I had taken a semester off to run an NGO focused on enrichment programs in Zambian refugee camps. Because of that, I participated in all the pomp and circumstance with my classmates, but I didn't actually have my diploma yet.

No one in my family knew how much money I had been spending. They seemed to finally be accepting my choices—even Ba, who was smiling serenely as he thumped his dahn-jon. As we were leaving class, Michelle-nim bowed deeply from her waist, and each of my family members bowed right back to her. The elevator shut tightly, and then my entire family burst into laughter except for Ba. Hang began to beat his stomach like he was King Kong. Everyone else was bending over and clutching their stomachs from laughing so hard. I felt deceived, but I played along, reminding myself to be grateful they even showed up.

On our final night, I stayed up with my siblings and their partners watching the stunt show *Jackass* and drinking Heinekens in their hotel room. Kang lowered the volume.

"Susan, we need to talk."

I looked over at him as he was sipping his beer, staring at the TV. Everyone else had their eyes glued to the TV. I braced myself.

"I'm trying to wrap my head around this yoga stuff, you know? Like, why do you need it?" Kang still wasn't making eye contact. His face was locked on the screen. I thought back to the last four months with Dahn and tried to distill the essence of why it had been so life-changing.

"I know this sounds crazy, but it helps me feel fearless."

"That's cool. Exercise is cool. But why do you need to be a teacher for them?"

Then Hang chimed in. "Just—don't let your emotions overcome you," he said harshly.

Overcome me? I felt more in touch with my emotions than I ever had. I was starting to feel attacked. Was this an intervention?

"Be confident in your outer image," piled on Kang. I looked down at my seashell dress I'd found in a free bin. I was happy with how I looked.

"And move back to California to be around nice people," added Wendy.

I felt like I was shrinking in the room. I felt small, insignificant. I nodded to the TV a few times and then walked toward the door.

"Go wash your face," commanded Hang.

It was an order he had said to me all my life when I got emotional. Every cell in my body wanted to leave, but Dahn training had prepared me for this moment. I knew that it was just my mind and that I was not my mind. I let go of the handle. I didn't want to give up on them. In the bathroom, I splashed cold water on my face for a whole minute, diluting my tears with fresh water. All I wanted was Michelle-nim's protection.

"I see you," I said to my defeated face in the mirror. I forced a smile and showed all my teeth. "I'm fine," I lied to myself. I just needed to get through this. When I returned, we pretended like the conversation never happened, just like old times. When it got late, I got up to go, but then Hang called after me.

"You're in a fucking cult, Susan."

I felt too defeated to fight back. I opened the door and walked right back to Dahn, even if it was a cult. At least I felt welcome there.

After my family left, I had a week to kill before my summer thesis research began on a Dahn program called the Phoenix Project. I crashed with my college friend Senait, but I started getting weird vibes from her. She had always been concerned about Dahn, and she was surprised I was continuing my research with them.

When I arrived, she gave me icy one-word answers for everything. The next morning, we agreed it was best if I left. Since all my other friends stopped talking to me, I had nowhere to go except for a Dahn studio. Michelle-nim connected me with a Jewish woman who was a mother of two Sabin-nims. Even though I had never met her, she invited me to stay with her for the rest of the week. I was immensely grateful. Another testament to the sincerity of Dahn people.

Admittedly, when I was with Dahn, I felt loved even though I knew I was being manipulated. This was better than with my family, where I felt indirectly loved out of obligation, but also manipulated. But the constant flip-flopping was wearing on me. I needed someone to talk some sense into me.

I met with my thesis advisor, and he couldn't believe everything I told him. He absolutely thought it was a cult. My research was supposed to explore the linkages between the mind-body connection and leadership development, specifically how Dahn as a yoga and martial arts program improved the development of self-efficacy, self-awareness, and emotional intelligence. I had quantitative and qualitative measures in place. But it became quite obvious that Dahn was training an army of program-selling followers, and I had been brainwashed to spread the good word. I was on the inside, which gave me a unique vantage point to expose them. If I could complete my research, maybe I could help others. I left that meeting feeling hesitant but relieved. Someone validated my doubts about Dahn without shutting me down.

That night, I got an email from Hang, which was odd because he never emailed me. It was just two lines long.

Hey, if you truly believe in the ways of the law of attraction, then you would move forward instead of perpetuating your problems.

I recently pushed *The Secret* book onto him, which detailed the law of attraction, positive thinking as the key to getting what you want. Reading his cryptic email, I still felt like he was blaming me instead of trying to understand me. Of course I wanted to move on from Má's death, but I couldn't do it alone. I saw his message as avoidant of the greater issue at hand. My unresolved grief about Má weren't just my problems, they were our family problems. I didn't know how to respond, so I didn't.

The next day, I was on the T to go to a healing session with Michelle-nim. Instead of getting off at Copley, her new studio location, I got off at the next stop. I called her to quit. She said I had heart blockages. I asked for a refund. When I hung up, all I wanted to do was go home to California. But I needed to collect the data for my thesis. What was I going to do now? Call up Harvard and say I was in a cult and needed to change my thesis topic *again*?

As I headed back to the T, someone handed me a flyer. *Psychic Reading by Helena. SHE CAN HELP WHERE OTHERS HAVE FAILED. $5.00 OFF with this coupon.* I looked up and saw a dark purple glow from a window lined with a shimmering beaded curtain. I believed in signs, so I pushed open the door to jingling bells. The room was decorated with two gaudy purple velvet armchairs and chakra posters. A display case had multicolored geodes and a dozen potion bottles. Rows of pink, white, purple, and amber stones lined a crystal sound bowl.

"Hello?" I asked into the empty space. I heard a door creak above me, and then a white woman in her fifties hobbled down the squeaky stairs, holding the railing steady as she came down.

"Dear, please, have a seat," she gestured. I chose one of the giant armchairs and then handed her the coupon for a tarot reading. As she flipped each card face up, she described my past with such vague detail I started to think I had been conned. She told me that I really loved my soulmate, but he didn't realize it yet. Her claim was too generic. What woman doesn't feel that way? After more dramatic declarations, she offered a spiritual cleansing for $280 with a money-back guarantee. I banged my head against the velvet cushion. I didn't know who to trust anymore. I went outside to a nearby ATM and stood in line. I started scanning through my journal. *I'm tired of paying for enlightenment* caught my eye. Fuck Helena. Fuck Dahn.

I caught the free M2 shuttle back to Harvard Square to pay for what would actually make me feel good—pizza from Veggie Planet. Over a slice of butternut squash pizza with asiago cheese and caramelized onions, I had a real talk with myself. I didn't want to help Dahn expand from six hundred to thirty-six thousand yoga centers in three years. I didn't want to exploit people or be exploited. Michelle-nim said that fear and anger would always be my issue no matter where I went. She could be right, *and* I could live a purpose-driven life outside of Dahn. My $14,000 lesson was that my spiritual home was inside me all along, inside my body. No one could take that away from me, and I didn't have to pay another goddamn dollar to access it either.

Even though I quit the cult, I had to spend the next three weeks researching Dahn working alongside JJ-nim because of my thesis obligations. I wished I could say I held my ground, but the temptation was always there. Sometimes when his hand grazed my back or, heaven forbid, he talked to me directly, every ounce of me wanted to go back. I wanted a future with him, and if I did exactly what Michelle-nim said, I could ascend the ranks. I flip-flopped three more times after this.

My saving grace that finally got me out was a high school ex-boyfriend who started calling me again. He would listen to me talk for hours when I was in and when I was out of Dahn. Most importantly, he never made me feel judged. And when I was ready and asked for help, he gave me links to articles written by ex-instructors who claimed they were subjected to sexual manipulation and labor exploitation. He was gentle with me, helping me learn how to trust myself again. Michelle-nim wasn't giving me unconditional love; only I could give that to myself. My phone kept vibrating with texts from JJ-nim and her, but I didn't respond. I was afraid I would go back, just like all the times before.

In a moment of strength, I deleted both of their numbers from my phone and then set up a payment plan for all the credit card debt. I needed to finish my thesis, so I flew back home to my family. They were dysfunctional, but at least they weren't bleeding me dry.

Packing

Back at Ba's house, I helped him pack up his life. He had decided to sell the nail salon and move to Texas because the cost of living was so much lower than in California. The nail salon had been declining, and he was sinking deeper into debt. As I taped up the boxes, I realized this was the end of a chapter for our family. After he moved, I wouldn't ever have a reason to come back to Santa Rosa, because none of my siblings lived in the North Bay anymore. I couldn't remember the last time I'd raced down that narrow hallway at Today's Nails or pleaded with Má for money to buy lunch at the mall. I didn't think that the nail salon meant so much to me until that moment.

Once Ba left, I wouldn't be able to go back to the shop to feel Má's spirit there. Her manicurist chair, the case with her counterfeit purses, the altar where I prayed for thousand-dollar days. When I was in high school, I used to hate spending my Saturdays there. But now with Ba moving, the salon that was Má's fiefdom, and one of her last remaining artifacts, would be gone.

Ba and I took a break from packing to walk around Spring Lake, a 320-acre public park a few blocks away. We walked, listening to our sneakers crunch against loose rocks on the path. Ba's bleach-white Court Classic sneakers from Costco got a little dust on them. His jade

Buddha necklace peeked through his short-sleeved collared shirt, revealing a gold chain. The weather was a perfect seventy-five degrees, and the sun was shining. I missed California so much. A half mile in, I gathered courage. I didn't know when I would see Ba again.

"I'm going to miss you, Ba," I said, managing to finish the sentence.

He sighed. "Don't forget law school."

I reminded him there were two types of lawyers, corporate and public interest, and I would probably pursue the one that made less money. Ba pointed to a bench by the edge of the lake and started fanning his face with his hand. He sat down and offered me a water bottle from his cargo shorts. He pulled out a bottle of his own from his other pocket and took a big swig. I pretended to be fascinated by the ducks on the water. A yellow kayak glided by.

"You just need to graduate," he said.

We became silent again. I wished he would ask why I'd run to the cult instead of to him. I wished I could apologize for both of our mistakes. Make a pact to start over from a place of deep listening and love for each other. I inhaled the honey-sweet licorice smell of the madrone trees that gave us shade. When Má was alive, we lived on Madrone Court when we still had Susan's Nails. Coincidences like these made me feel like she was here, like she'd never left.

"Don't work so hard. We get to experience life on earth because of the heavens. When you live a life always resisting, life becomes a struggle," he said.

His advice surprised me. I never took him for much of a philosopher, but I was intrigued. Which moment in his life made him realize this?

Ba pulled out a granola bar and placed it in my hand. He kept watch on the ducks, and then he began to tell me a story about money. Not how to make it or save it but his own struggle with it. He had found one of my old high school spiral notebooks and used the blank pages to keep track of his income and expenses.

"After paying our workers, our bills, our mortgage, our insurance, and then giving all you kids money, we had just three hundred left. Every month." He and Dì Nhung had been working themselves to the bone, living paycheck to paycheck for years. I had been spending the allowance he so carefully saved to feel loved in a cult because I didn't feel it from him. We were so disconnected, we couldn't actually hear when the other spoke. "You need to be more careful with your money. You kids used to be so excited to eat McDonald's hamburgers on the weekends. Back then, they were just a quarter or two."

I choked up a little. I felt so indebted to him. I didn't know what to say, so I said nothing.

On the way home, we stopped by an ATM to deposit my last allowance of $300. Like all the other times, I insisted he shouldn't. The money wasn't free; it came with guilt. He gave it to me anyway, but this time it was different. Ba had sold the shop and was moving out of state. After this, he wasn't on the hook to support me anymore. He needed to be free too.

"Kiếm đường đi con," said Ba. *Go find a way.* Whenever I faced an obstacle, he would say this. That's what he always had to do as a refugee. Self-reliance was his only option, which I needed to figure out fast.

I was about to graduate but didn't have a job lined up. Ba was still breathing down my neck to become a lawyer, but what I actually wanted was to get rid of this turmoil I felt about Má. It made me do dumb things like join a cult. If I couldn't resolve this now, what else would I do in my life because I was projecting or triggered by her loss? I didn't want her death to continue to bind me.

Maybe there would be answers in Việt Nam, but that wouldn't come without its own share of challenges. My Vietnamese was functional but not great. I didn't really have a relationship with Má's relatives who were still there. The last time I'd visited, I was in high school, traveling with Wendy. We didn't reach out to them because our college-age brothers got accosted for money from our cousins the last time they visited. Even though I felt a little terrified about going back, I knew that also meant I was onto something. That meant there was something at stake for me, and I would much prefer to see where that took me than take a job I didn't care about. I could never have this kind of time and access again. Returning to the motherland would be complicated, but I knew I had to do it because I was scared.

I convinced myself this trip back to Việt Nam would be this all-in-one solution to deal with all my baggage: I would be reunited with my dead mother; I would feel secure with my Vietnamese identity; and I would know what to do with my life. In true type A form, I treated my existential crisis like a grocery shopping list. I arranged a human rights legal internship and booked my plane ticket.

Ba was furious. Why would I willingly choose to go to the very country he risked his life to escape? I tried to reassure him that this was my path to take just like he advised. This was me trying to find a way. I tried to patch things up before I left by visiting him in Texas for a few days. Naturally, we spent most of the time eating. One night over dinner, I told him my grand plan.

"Mày không biết sợ là gì!" sneered Ba. *You have never felt fear!* I didn't flinch. The Việt Nam War had ended more than three decades earlier. The U.S. and Việt Nam normalized relations in 1995. Even though my internship was based in Hà Nội, the epicenter of Communism, the U.S. embassy would be there to protect me if something went wrong. I didn't get why Ba was being so uptight. I was a U.S. citizen.

I tried to convince him that my human rights law internship in Việt Nam would give me an edge with law school applications. He just had to trust me. Ba shook his head and wagged his finger at me.

"Ba không tin!" *I don't believe you!* Ba was always doubting my ability to do anything, but I would figure out how to get into a top-ten law school. I would show him.

We continued to eat, now in silence. My stepmother kept insisting I eat. Even though I felt pretty full, I kept eating to show my appreciation for her. Finally, Ba broke the ice.

"You need to be careful there, and you need to flatten your stomach."

I became enraged at Ba, at Má's life-ending tummy tuck, at the pure misogyny of needing to have a flat stomach to find a good husband or be beautiful.

"You know what, Ba?" I said, raising my voice. I pushed my chair back and stood up. "Không." *No.* I stomped over to the living room couch, picked up Wendy's prized three-foot-long Hello Kitty doll, and slammed her onto the couch, throwing punches, beating the shit out of her.

"This is what you do to me when you say I'm too fat!" I was a size six at that point. I knocked her right where her mouth was supposed to be. She was one of the most famous icons in the world and yet had no way to speak. The audacity of the patriarchy. But before I could destroy her, my stepmother ran over to save Hello Kitty.

"Thôi con," said Dì Nhung. *Enough, child.* She held Hello Kitty protectively and then disappeared into her bedroom. I wasn't done with Ba yet.

"Ba có hiểu không? You do that to me!" My lower fangs were showing, and my voice was quivering. My body was shuddering, but I was ready to keep fighting. I wasn't scared of him anymore. Ba looked through me and then cleared his plate to the sink. He just stood there, cleaning, looking out the window straight into the brick wall of the house next door.

"Fine," I said quietly. I turned my back on him and retreated up to the guest bedroom. I was done living in Ba's tiny world where he dictated everything I could and couldn't do. He was too suffocating, and I completely lost my sense of self around him. No matter. Tomorrow I would be leaving for Việt Nam and would be thousands of miles away from his bullshit anyway.

Motherland

The first time I went to Việt Nam, I was nine years old. Má led the way with Ba pushing our squeaky cart stacked high with suitcases out of the Tân Sơn Nhất international airport. We four siblings stuck close behind, wary of this foreign land. Once the glass doors jiggled open, I felt the humidity outside smack my face. Suddenly, I was underwater, forcing my will against gravity just to take a few steps. I saw the mouths of hundreds of people opening and closing like hungry fish, leaning over both sides of the railing, eight people deep, searching for Việt Kiều, their *overseas Vietnamese relative*. Everyone was yelling like they had bets on us, roosters in the cockfight. So this was Việt Nam.

At the curb, our family was surrounded by rings of strangers grabbing at our luggage and pulling at my head from every direction, planting a set of nostrils on my cheek. Tiny women, no taller than I was, kept saying I looked like Ba and exclaiming that I had a crooked smile. Those same women, all of Má's relatives, kept praising Wendy's similarity to Má, such good looks. Then we all crammed into a minibus without seat belts and drove on a road that had no lanes, bicycles and scooters zipping around us, our driver punching the high-pitched horn nonstop. My jaw was clenched the whole ride, but Má seemed chipper, so I didn't expect the worst, though I sure imagined it.

Our first stop was to see one of Má's older sisters, Dì Châu. The van didn't fit through the alleyway, so we walked through a tiny street with all of our relatives parading in with our luggage. Immediately, the hẻm hawkers of the *hamlet* started squawking at us. "Việt Kiều! Việt Kiều!" *Overseas Vietnamese! Overseas Vietnamese!* I felt embarrassed. Did people want us here or not?

At our relatives' house, Má squatted down and opened each piece of luggage one by one, handing out boxes of Irish Spring soap, blue tins of Danish cookies, and tubes of Crest toothpaste to overjoyed relatives.

Everyone did a round of introductions, pointing to their chests and saying their names slowly and loudly like I was an idiot. Tài Dì, Dì Ngọc, Chương, Dì Châu, and then some in-laws of those relatives. And then my cousins said their names from oldest to youngest in rapid fire. Hia Lóc, Chế Ái, Chế Thanh, Chế Minh Tâm, Chế Tâm. My brothers chimed in their Vietnamese names, and Wendy codeswitched back to Tú Uyên with ease. When it was my turn, I casually said my name with American pronunciation, and all the cousins shook their heads and giggled.

"Tên lạ quá đi!" said my cousin Ái. *What a strange name!* It was only then and there that I realized every single person in my family had a Vietnamese name but me. I needed to Vietnamese myself so everyone else could say my name too.

"Sú Sàn," I decided.

I had never encountered so many Vietnamese names before; our clan just in Sài Gòn could have filled an entire soccer roster with a second string. When I told Má the problem, she laughed and renamed all the aunts and uncles with numbers based on their birth order. Not to further complicate things, but the eldest sibling was number two. It was believed that if the others correctly called the eldest as the firstborn, demons would try to kill that child. It was a safer bet to confuse them by starting count with the number two. Má explained my confusion and our newfound system for me to cope with all the names. Everyone else thought it was hilarious, but I didn't.

When I spoke with my cousins, I kept calling myself the pronoun "con," which meant *child*. Instead of calling them older or younger sibling, I was addressing myself like I was their kid and they were my parent. Ái tried to explain this to me in between cackling to herself. I was mortified. Up until this point, I only spoke Vietnamese with my elders and English with my siblings. I never had to actively change my pronoun based on hierarchy. But now, I had to remember if the relative was on my mother's or father's side and if they were older or younger than my parent—otherwise I was using the wrong pronoun. With the growing web of cousins that raced around and the new rules that nameless elders kept lecturing to me, I started to shut down. I didn't know how to correctly speak or behave. To stop people from laughing at me again, I decided it would be easier not to speak Vietnamese unless absolutely necessary.

During the first night there, I followed a cousin up a steep wooden ladder to a loft bed draped in pink tulle that made it look like a giant ballerina's tutu. Two girl cousins climbed in and motioned for Wendy and me to enter into the princess sanctuary. I asked why the bed was covered in fabric.

"Con muỗi," Minh Tâm said. *Mosquitoes*. It was a word forever seared into my brain because the next morning I woke up with over a hundred bites all over my body and streaks of dried blood up and down my arms and legs. My lean cousins and sister went unscathed. My host Aunt #6 looked at me, horrified, and then explained why I was the chosen victim.

"Tại máu con ngọt," she said. *Because your blood is sweet.* Meaning, my chubbiness made me the target. I was given an anti-itch cream. When I squeezed the tube, long brown plant fibers came out with the white paste. Má yelled whenever I scratched, but I couldn't stop. It wasn't until we went to the coastal town of Nha

Trang with its salty, muddy waters that I got better. An afternoon of jumping in the waves with my throng of cousins quickly patched up the wounds.

The next day, after a sweltering ten-hour car ride, we arrived at my parents' home village, Mỹ Xuyên. The locals called it Bải Xào, a Cambodian-derived word meaning *not fully cooked rice*. Once we pulled into our family home, I rushed into the outdoor shower stall to bathe myself from a giant clay drum. When the rainwater splashed on my skin, it was so refreshing. But when I was done, I realized I didn't have a towel. I peeked out of the stall and kept asking for a towel from anyone who walked by. "Towel? Towel. Towel!" Water was dripping from my hair, and my naked body was now a platter ready for mosquitoes. My cousin Minh Tâm poked her head out from the house and cheerily waved. She came back with a circular plastic bin used for washing clothes and vegetables. I shook my head.

"Towel!" I insisted. What else would a person need after a shower? She looked confused and then brought me back another plastic bin in a different color. I kept shaking my head with frustration as I began to slap at my body, fending off the mosquitoes closing in on me. I forgot the Vietnamese word for "towel," khăn. Minh Tâm found Wendy, who finally brought back a thin, two-foot-long kitchen towel. The English word "towel" sounded like the Vietnamese word for "container." So of course, all I got were containers.

At dinner, all the adults had a big laugh about the towel fiasco. I excused myself from the table to lie down in my net-draped bed. I hated where Má and Ba came from. I didn't belong here, and I would never be Vietnamese enough. I promised myself I would never come back ever again.

Now a fresh college grad, I knew this trip back to Việt Nam would be different. I wasn't a nine-year-old anymore; I was now a grown woman and responsible for my reality. I was in control of my life and could problem-solve my way out of anything.

How quickly I would be proven wrong. I soon learned that Việt Nam operated under a different, more mystical set of rules.

While my aunts didn't let me borrow money for Dahn, my desperate phone call reconnected us, and I arranged to go back with Dì Ngân just in time to celebrate Tết, *Lunar New Year*, a two-week holiday where the entire country shuts down to return to their respective home villages and eat with family. After we made our rounds from Bà Ngoại's grave to the homes of our bà con, we stopped by the Bat Temple.

As I asked the gods to help me with law school, my eyes stung from all the incense smoke. The incense holder was overstuffed with the hundreds of prayers that had already been made before mine. I jammed my incense stick in a small opening and then ran out of the temple as fast as I could. At the entrance, I sifted through knee-high piles of slippers and heels to find my shoes.

Outside the temple, Dì Ngân wore a blazer with oversize sleeves, a new handbag, and a little too much jewelry. This was in stark contrast to her home uniform, which consisted of faded Christmas pajama sets and a matching golden phoenix necklace Má used to have. But in Việt Nam, Dì Ngân looked rich. It was a thing so many Việt Kiều of their generation did when they came back. They signaled to others that they "made it," even if they still worked twelve-hour days, six days a week, in the nail salon.

I showed Dì Ngân my new Canon camera that I'd splurged on for the trip. As I scrolled through pictures of our family grave, Dì Ngân clucked at me.

"Không nên con," she said. *You shouldn't.* I shrugged her belief off. I walked around the temple grounds and found a small room with an altar of more than a hundred faces of the deceased. Many of the small black-and-white framed photos were caked with dust, pushed tightly against one another to make room for the color photos of the recently deceased. Sunlight blazed through the window onto all the photos. I zoomed in on the forgotten faces a few seconds each to awaken them.

I felt pity for them; if their families remembered them, then their photos would have been clean.

Back at our family home, I wanted to show my older boy cousin Thắng the photos from the day. But when I turned the camera on, all the photos on my memory card were wiped clean. Every moment I had captured in the last week was gone. The dishes Aunt #4 made me in Sài Gòn, the video where I was screaming in the wet market as the vendor killed the frogs, the inscription on Bà Ngoại's grave, the faces of my new dead friends. It was as if I'd turned on the camera for the first time. My cousin knew I had taken pictures of the dead, so he snickered and repeated Dì Ngân's premonition, "Không nên." When I plugged my camera back into my laptop, I was able to recover all my trip's photos except for the ones I had taken that day. It felt eerie, like I was being warned by the dead.

I spent the next week at our family home pestering my uncle, aunts, and cousins with questions about Má. I carried a digital tape recorder with me because I knew how fickle memory was, and if someone was finally going to give me answers, I wanted to never forget them. I asked Uncle Bình any memories he had of Má. He replied by pushing over a plate of crispy bánh tét, a glutinous rice cake with a mung bean and pork filling, wrapped and steamed in banana leaves. It was sliced, panfried, wrapped in lettuce and herbs, and then dipped in a zesty nước mắm, our *fish sauce vinaigrette*. The dish was a staple for Tết. Since the banana leaves preserved the meat longer, people could spend less time cooking and more time visiting with family. When I had a moment alone with Dì Ngọc, I asked her about Má's refugee escape, but she just swatted at the recorder, saying it was all too long ago. When I asked my cousin Sinh for any memories, he offered me a vodka shot and karaoke microphone.

All my insistence got me was an address for Má's first suitor in the next village over. With my recorder hidden in my shirt pocket, I watched the grown man cry, chain-smoke, and blubber about Má.

He had heard she died from a "stomach surgery." The only details he could share was that she was beautiful, smart, and a good person. Details so vague, the whole meeting was just a waste of time.

On the ride home, I started to doubt my grand plan. Here I was in a rural village in the middle of nowhere, searching for answers, when Ba, Má's partner of twenty-one years, was a gold mine of information. The answers I wanted weren't with the suitor but with the person who'd actually built a life with her. After two weeks with Má's family not budging, I gave up asking and indulged in eating instead.

There is an ancient custom of reburial in Việt Nam. Three years after death, bones are dug up, cleaned, rewrapped, and then stored in a new stone casket. It is only then that the deceased are freed from their spiritual limbo. With Má, we never dug up her bones. Her grave was in America. Sometimes I wonder what I would have found if we did have a reburial. If things stayed preserved, would there be a letter of regrets from Ba? A list of promises Dì Phương made to her? Confessions from Wendy? I bet I would find more clues in her casket because it was impossible to be vulnerable with the living.

With my search at a dead end, I focused on my career as a human rights lawyer. As I packed my bags for my big move from Sài Gòn to Hà Nội, where my internship was based, my relatives tried to convince me not to go. None of them had ever gone to Hà Nội. Their biggest worry?

"But what will you *eat* there?" Dì Ngọc asked. She was visibly stressed.

"Whatever they eat?" I replied.

A week into my internship, I found out my European manager was slimy and corrupt, a fitting introduction to human rights law, so I quit. I hung around the USAID office until they agreed to giving me an internship focused on sustainable cacao development. It felt serendipitous, since my sister and I had started a chocolate company when we were teenagers, selling handmade truffles in front of Ba's nail salon during the summer farmers market. Like our parents, we were hustlers.

This new opportunity allowed me to move back to Sài Gòn, where

I would live with Dì Ngọc and my cousin Minh Tâm, the kind cousin who had brought me a plastic tub when I needed a towel. Their front door was the width of a one-car garage, which opened up to an alleyway of crowing roosters, vendors pushing food carts, and grandmothers yelling at just about everyone. I spent my first morning following Minh Tâm as she dropped off kilos of rainbow-colored plastic bags to different vendors in the market. After our afternoon nap to beat the heat, she took me shopping for new clothes. Inside the first store, the shopkeeper looked me up and down and gave me a look of disgust.

"Cô không có XXL!" she yelled. *I don't have XXL!* Just existing in my body, I offended her. She pushed us out of the store like I had done something egregious. I officially felt like a whale. The next two shops did the same exact thing. It was as clear as day: I failed at being Vietnamese.

Strangers didn't know how to classify me. Vietnamese locals guessed I was Korean or Filipino. They were shocked that I understood Vietnamese and made fun of my clumsy attempts to speak. My internship had me traveling all over Việt Nam, and each time I checked into a hotel, the receptionist would squint at my passport and cock her head.

"Chị Liễu? Chị Liễu?" she would ask, confusing my last name for my first name. Even though a cacao farmer christened me with a name that most sounded like Susan, Xuân An, meaning *peaceful spring*, I continued to feel like a foreigner. I felt so stuck as a Vietnamese American. White colleagues got so much praise when they poorly pronounced greetings, not having any idea how much effort the local Vietnamese put into accommodating them. Even though I could understand more than I could say, I still spoke like a six-year-old, where none of my complex ideas could be communicated. Because of that, it felt like they treated me like a child.

My colleagues assumed I knew everything about Vietnamese culture, but there was so much subtext I was missing. I didn't even know what my last name meant. Finally, I asked my coworker Ngọc Anh.

"You don't know? It means *willow tree*. When the wind comes, the swaying branches sound like someone weeping," she explained. Willow trees were seen as sad trees because they moved downward; if they were happier, they would grow upward. It felt odd to come from a lineage of sorrow. Last names could be a nod to wealth like the meaning of gold in the name Huỳnh or the regal lineage of Nguyễn. I came from sadness.

After I had spent seven months in Việt Nam, Wendy made me a proposition on Skype. She had just returned to the States after visiting me for two weeks. I showed her the country I came to love: the coffee and cacao farms in Đắk Lắk; the legendary nem nướng restaurant run by our grandmother's younger sister; a street food stall singularly focused on one dish to satisfy a craving. She wanted me to move back to help her grow our chocolate business idea. It had always been a hobby, and she wanted to give it a real shot.

I thought about how much I had changed in the last year. I finally knew all my relatives' names and shared so many laugh-out-loud moments with them. My Vietnamese agricultural vocabulary had expanded, but I wasn't any closer to knowing my mother. And then here was my sister, who everyone said looked most like Má, asking me to help her with her dream. Ever since we were little, it was always Wendy looking out for me. She was the one who got me new pants when I got holes in the crotch. She would let me crash at her place in between my adventures and take me out to nice dinners. I never had much money to give back, but now there was something I could do for her.

I accepted that maybe this was all I could know about Má and booked my ticket home. I wasn't satisfied, but I didn't have any other leads. I hadn't found Má in Việt Nam, but I had found her family, our family. And as little as I knew about her, I was sure Má would have wanted me to put family first.

PART III

MÀ

But

The Hunt

For the next three years, Wendy and I were like Lucy and Ethel in a chocolate factory. After Wendy worked her corporate job during the day, we would meet to make chocolates out of our sister-in-law's doughnut shop, working well past midnight to finish production. Then during the day, I sampled our product to different Whole Foods Market buyers, trying to figure out how to improve our packaging and nail down our pricing so we would be featured on their shelves. Friends and family spent hours with us during production, selling at festivals, all in the hopes of realizing Wendy's dream. And when we had something that felt more like a business and less of a hobby, Wendy stopped moonlighting to grow Sôcôla Chocolatier full-time. I still felt a calling to be in the social impact space, and quite honestly, running a business with her started to break us. I awkwardly handed the baton to her and went to get an MBA across the country.

Up until that point, during every call I got from Ba, he expressed his disappointment that I still didn't have a master's degree. After getting jaded about law school from my nonexistent human rights law internship in Việt Nam, I applied to a slew of business schools because it seemed like the only type of graduate school I could get into. On the first day of school, my career counselor, Deepa, asked me what kind of job I wanted when I graduated.

"Corporate social responsibility or design thinking," I said confidently. She explained my salary would plateau and business school wouldn't be worth the hefty tuition price tag. To have a good return on investment, most of the students went hard to get the coveted investment banking, consulting, or tech jobs.

"What's your backup plan?" she asked, a bit concerned.

"Talk-show host?" I thought aloud. She gave a nervous laugh, and then we both realized the big mistake I had made. My desire to please my father trumped financial logic. But I had signed the loan documents and already enrolled. I had to deal with the consequences. At least Ba's nagging about getting a master's degree would stop.

Now at twenty-eight years old, I was in my second year at business school and, quite frankly, hadn't actually thought about Má for the six years since my trip to Việt Nam. I thought about her only once a year on her death anniversary, the only time our family got together to clean and present offerings to her grave. If I was in town, Wendy and I would stop by the Lucky grocery store at El Cerrito Plaza to buy twelve stems of Má's favorite yellow roses. Kang would bring incense, carefully chosen fruit, white spongy bánh bò (cool to the touch, this rice flour, inch-thick dessert was flavored with coconut milk and topped with salted sesame seeds), crispy thịt heo quay (*savory roasted pork belly*), bottles of freshly pressed rau má (forest-green pennywort juice oversweetened with sugar but known to cool the qi), and tart da ua, or sữa chua (the Vietnamese take on yogurt influenced by French colonial rule with a touch of condensed milk), all of which was made in-house at Cẩm Hương Deli, the place we've been going to since it opened in 1985. The owners were Vietnamese boat people too. Hang would bring a clear tarp, drinks, and Costco-size paper goods. When all of us siblings arrived at Sunset Lawn, everyone dropped into their task without much discussion. It was better to be busy than to emote.

Throw out deer-eaten, decomposing flower remnants on the grave from the last visitor (likely the aunts). Dump the mossy old water and refill it from the spigot twenty feet away that always sprayed water on your shoes. Arrange the flowers and food. Windex both sides of the marble tombstone. Build a pyramid with the fruit. I would squat down and try to block the flame from the wind, lighting incense until I saw red embers glow. Three sticks of incense handed to adults, just one stick for each of my nephews.

Then we would raise our joss sticks, and each of us would have our annual private conversation with her. My requests were usually pretty selfish, often related to good grades or money because I was so broke. Then I would ask for her to watch over all of us.

After all the prayers were cast, we would snack, totally not acknowledging we were at her grave. We found many other things to talk about, anything but her. We sat with our backs to her headstone as if she were sitting alongside us, enjoying the view of the Bay Bridge. After we threw away our trash, we got back in our cars and went to Hang's house, the closest to the cemetery, to watch a sports game and eat some more.

Má's death anniversary was the only time of year we acknowledged she was gone. I was so curious about their prayers. What did they tell her? What did they need? I always found it strange to not truly know the people who have known me my entire life.

Now at business school, I was trying to figure out how to use capitalism for good. I didn't exactly land on a solution, but I found other people who were asking the same question. As I was trying to figure out my next career move, my spiritual seeking did not stop. I had just come back from a meditation retreat from the Esalen Institute in Big Sur. There, soaking in their hot springs on a majestic cliff overlooking the infinite Pacific Ocean, my problems felt small and I felt a part of something bigger than myself. The trip was especially blessed because I convinced my school to pay for my trip in the name of "leadership development training."

Returning from the retreat with my rose-tinted glasses and open heart, I felt hopeful that Ba and I could finally develop an authentic relationship before he eventually died. He wasn't sick, but death was just so unpredictable. I wished that he could finally see me as I wanted to be seen. I daydreamed we could sidestep our egos and acknowledge how we had hurt each other in the past. Reaffirm our love for each other. Reframe the narrative to turn our pain into power! Above all, I wanted his validation.

We did well when he had a project to work on, and to engineer this father-daughter bond, I found the biggest project of all—seeking revenge on Má's plastic surgeon. I hadn't ever thought about tracking him down until I went to business school. My professors trained us to live in the world of possibility. Plus, I was about to get my second Ivy League degree. If anyone could track him down and make him pay, it was this version of me.

There were stories of women he had disfigured, women whose bodies were permanently damaged, twenty-four lawsuits altogether. What this doctor did to my mother wasn't just a fluke accident. He had a history of it, and he was still practicing in the Bay Area. I checked his license on the Medical Board of California website. Two decades after my mother's death, he was still on probation. My blood started to boil. What was the point of probation if there was no accountability? My strategy to take him down was simple: creep him out with targeted Facebook ads just to him; buy out a billboard by his clinic to publicly shame him; then pitch a local journalist to do an exposé on him. With all this negative coverage, he would crack. Then I would sue him under a group action lawsuit with all his victims together.

I gathered my courage and called Ba. When he picked up, I could hear the soft voice of Phil Collins in the background. We used to play his tapes on our standing stereo console when Má was alive. My throat did the tightening thing it always does when I see Ba's face on our video calls.

"Hel-lo! Anything new with you à?" asked Ba in his singsong voice.

"Hey, Ba, I want to talk about—"

"Ăn cơm chưa?" Ba asked. *Have you eaten yet?*

"Dạ, I already ate," I replied, affirming in my most dutiful daughter voice.

"Remember, too much rice not nice," warned Ba. He was always reminding me to be careful about how much I ate, as if I weren't aware of my pear-shaped body. But I was done with the pleasantries. Eager to transform our relationship, I ripped off the Band-Aid and just asked him point-blank what I wanted to know.

"Hey, Ba, I wanted to talk to you about Mom's plastic surgeon," I said, a bit detached, as if I were commenting on the weather.

"Chuyện đó qua rồi, đừng nhắc đi nhắc lại hoài," he said. *All of that's passed now, don't keep bringing it back up.*

"Come on, Ba. I just want—"

"Đừng đi sâu nữa," he ordered. *Don't go any deeper.* I knew Ba wanted me to stop, but I didn't want to live with any more regret. If I could get Ba the justice he was due, I had to let him know.

"Yeah, but here's the thing. We might have a case against him, Ba. We could sue him and get *money*." I was pretty proud of my clever plan, and I couldn't wait for Ba to praise me for it. But he just tsked like an angry squirrel.

"Đằng nào thì Má mày cũng mất rồi. Ngừng đi, đừng hiểu thêm. Làm gì được bây giờ? Có ích lợi gì đâu." *You know she passed, so that's it. So stop, don't keep trying to understand more. What is it going to do now? Nothing much is going to come of it.* "Bỏ qua đi," he stressed. *Let it go.* The same thing he'd said twenty years ago when I'd asked about Má. Didn't he want a payout for the pain we all went through? The money would never bring her back, but at least it would be something. Thanks to the California insurance-lobbying industry, a life lost during a medical malpractice incident was valued at $250,000. It was a number that was instilled by the California governor in 1975 and never adjusted to inflation, *ever*. Twenty-one years later, that was how the value of my mother's life was determined. After legal fees, Ba divided up the money five ways. I was to be given a $30,000 check when I turned twenty-one. That amount was supposed to replace my mother. But never once did we get an apology from the doctor.

"Just tell me the name of the law firm we worked with," I pleaded.

After a long pause, he spoke. "I don't know," he said quietly.

"You must have some papers somewhere."

Ba kept everything. Any important document he had was in a plastic bin with hanging folders on the floor of his closet. He didn't answer, so I continued to press to jog his memory.

"What about the doctor's name?"

But Ba abruptly ended the call, not even with a fake excuse. I felt terrible. Like a fool, I had called Ba thinking things could be different. Clearly, they were not.

Business school was wrapping up with a flurry of exams and job interviews, so I dropped my revenge plans. I was also preparing for a cross-country move. My relationship with my classmate Marvin was serious enough that he wanted me to move to Seattle, where he had gotten a job offer. I didn't know a soul there and had always intended to return to the Bay Area. But love happened and the man could cook, so my plans changed.

I actually met him over a five-pound piece of fat. It was orientation, and we were in the Yale Peabody Museum, where the exhibit was on the evolution of human food consumption. He was yards away from everyone else, completely removed from the crowds of overeager business school students rambling off their prior work experience. I found his ability to not succumb to social pressure intriguing. There he was in front of a plexiglass case of silicone fat. The sign asked, "How would your body feel if it was five pounds lighter?"—a hope I had tried to unsuccessfully actualize for years. Instead of shaking his hand, I asked him if he wanted to shake the fat with me. We stuck our hands in the two holes of the clear box and moved the fat up and down. I was charmed to find another weirdo.

Marvin and I arrived in Seattle and began our postgraduate lives together. Marvin became a product manager, and I got a gig as a digital marketing consultant. Once I felt settled, I opened up my investigation into the doctor again, this time roping in my college friend Kathy, a Harvard Law School grad and now a lawyer. When I wrote to her about what I was trying to do with the doctor, she started digging. Maybe she could figure out how I could sue this plastic surgeon in some form of group action lawsuit. The doctor had preyed on Vietnamese refugees—there had to be something there.

But when I got on the phone with her, she delivered unexpected news. The plastic surgeon had just died the month before from Parkinson's.

"Wait, what?" I must have heard her wrong. I started to feel agitated. My entire plan hinged on him being alive.

"Well, can we sue dead people?!" I asked out of desperation. Apparently, you can't. I had waited too long. I should have done something before I graduated. I had the chance, and now I had nothing to give to Ba. Kathy left me with the name of the law firm my family worked with during the arbitration against the doctor. I sent the law firm a note and left a voice mail. One week later when I was commuting home from work, I got a call from a San Francisco number and picked it up.

"Susan? Hi. It's Doris, a partner at the firm. I was involved with your family's litigation. How can I help?" I was shocked she still worked there. She was with my family when it all happened eighteen years ago.

"Do—do you remember our case?" I asked, wondering if she could recall anything. I could barely remember what I'd eaten for dinner the previous week.

"Of course I do. Out of thirty years of practice, this and one other civil rights case, well, have been my cornerstone cases."

"What do you mean?" I asked. What made our case so unique?

"The doctor not having malpractice insurance. That's rare. And the nurse he worked with—actually having malpractice insurance—that's rare too. The confluence of them both happening, well, the odds were one in a million." Doris spent the next thirty minutes on the phone nicely explaining legal clauses and recounting the past.

I had arrived at my apartment and sat there in the dimly lit underground garage with the car running, not wanting to lose this chance to talk to her. I begged her to send me anything about our case so I could review it. That week, she sent over the settlement agreement Ba had signed after the arbitration proceedings. The doctor was supposed to give him a portion of his income if he ever made more than $80,000 a year for the next twenty years. Nobody ever sent us a check.

What was I going to do now? I had a list of a few names of other women who'd tried to sue the doctor, but I didn't want to call them. There would be no group action lawsuit. I didn't have any more emotional energy to give. Following up with them wasn't going to give Ba or me resolve. I knew I needed to pivot, but how? I needed a big hairy distraction to take my mind off things. So I did what people do when they don't want to face the real problems in their life—I got married.

The Wedding Crasher

E verything about my wedding felt a little supernatural. Ten days before the big day, I got a call from Ignacio, the leader of our hired thirteen-piece mariachi band.

"Susana, it's on fire!" he exclaimed into the phone. The entire town of Twisp was being evacuated from the wildfires in eastern Washington, which included our venue, Sun Mountain Lodge. We looked at their webcam and saw clouds of black smoke on the property. Marvin and I had to plan another wedding at warp speed in Seattle proper, forcing us to shift the nuptials by a day. We cobbled together a new schedule of events and hoped for the best.

On our wedding day before all the fanfare began, Marvin and I were reviewing last-minute details with the event coordinator when I heard someone playfully shout, "Sú Sàn!" I turned to see Dì Phương and Dì Ngân beckon to me. Marvin and I bent down to hug both of them as they pretended to chastise us for putting our traditional Vietnamese hats on crooked. As they were readjusting our Vietnamese garb, my mother's absence loomed large. This was *the* day for mothers and daughters to be together. But her sisters were here in her stead, trying to fulfill her duty. My eyes glistened, and I hugged them both one more time before they lightly pinched, sniff-kissed, and smacked my cheek. They didn't want to ruin my makeup. Dì Phương whispered that I should try to have a baby soon. I laughed and sniff-kissed her right back. With our hats on straight, Marvin and I were now ready for our big day.

The wedding began with an outdoor Vietnamese tea ceremony against the rolling waves of the Puget Sound, stand-up paddleboarders and screaming seagulls rounding out our picturesque backdrop. Marvin and I sat across from Ba and my stepmother, Dì Nhung, while our seventy guests watched. There were the older generation of people born in Asia properly seated in the row of chairs and the younger generation of my idealistic friends next to Marvin's architecture and tech friends, all leaning against the patio railing. The tea table was set with two wooden ducks, a Korean symbol for lifelong partnership, a pot of vodka (Ba insisted it would help calm everyone's nerves), and two teacups. I poured a small amount for each of my elders.

Ba began with advice. "Listen to your mother-in-law. Don't get on her bad side. I learned this from the Korean dramas." Then Ba presented us with gold chains with the letters *M* and *S* welded together.

As Marvin and I received the gifts, we heard a clap of angry thunder. I stopped fake sipping my vodka tea. People always say it's good luck if it rains on your wedding day. I didn't know if that applied if you were already outside. I wasn't sure what kind of omen this was, but all I knew was I had to run.

Huge raindrops started to plop on my wedding áo dài made of red silk and golden threads. I covered my face with both of my hands so my makeup wouldn't get destroyed and rushed into the building as quickly as my hidden pink Mary Jane Crocs would allow. Groomsmen picked up the tea table. Guests moved with their folding chairs, and we all gathered inside watching the rain come down with haste like a monsoon in July. It was sunny without a cloud in the sky during our morning drive over to the venue. Could it be that the inclement weather was some form of divine intervention? Maybe it was Má storming in to take her place. Maybe she didn't like that her seat was occupied by another woman.

After we finished with my side of the family, Marvin and I rushed back to the bridal room to change into our Korean outfits. Mrs. Kim, my mother-in-law, designed the hanboks and had them shipped all the way from Korea. Marvin had just a simple pink silk long-sleeve top tied with a knot at his side and a pair of royal-blue pants. My outfit required a pit crew of three bridesmaids. They began by stripping off the Vietnamese red áo dài with snaps and hooks that ran from my throat across my chest and down to my armpit. My red khăn đóng hat, yellow silk pants, golden necklace, and golden earrings were quickly removed. In just my undergarments, I squatted on the floor as my two bridesmaids carefully placed a petticoat over my head without disturbing my hair. I stood up, holding the three pounds of pink fabric that extended from my bustline to my feet. A short pink jacket slipped on. On went the white sock liners and pink silk shoes that were reminiscent of the concubine era. One bridesmaid worked on a five-step Korean half bow while the other placed a blue hat with pearl strands on my head, fastened a brooch, and adorned me with even more pearls on my neck, finger, and wrist, all a gift from my mother-in-law, Mrs. Kim. A matching pink purse with zero contents glided onto my wrist past my french gel tips. This all used to take us five minutes. But after two hours of practice, we did it in thirty-four seconds flat. My bridesmaids and I high-fived. We were crushing time-intensive beauty standards.

I emerged from the bridal room with my hanbok, a traditional Korean outfit that made me look like the love child of a sumo wrestler and a baby doll. We continued the tea ceremony with all the Korean relatives by rank, starting with Marvin's parents. Some of my in-laws spoke only Korean, so there was a bit of earnest nodding, bowing, and the receiving of silver gifts, a Coach purse, and cash.

Now in front of scrutinizing Koreans, Marvin hoisted me up on his back, and my legs locked around his bony hips to begin what I called the "Fateful Piggyback Ride." Marvin started trotting around the guests in his flip-flops to show he could "carry me through life's obstacles." I began to slowly slip down his back, our frictionless silk hanboks sliding off each other. The only firm grip I had was around his Adam's apple. Once we made a full lap, everyone cheered.

Next was the "Determination of Offspring Quantity" game, a Korean wedding rite. Originally, Mrs. Kim didn't want us to do this part. She insisted that professionals were hired in Los Angeles and Korea to facilitate this with proper decorations and precise rites. It would be too complicated for us. I insisted and tasked my bridesmaid Brittany, who was white, to scour the internet for guidance. Mr. and Mrs. Kim threw chestnuts and goji berries at us. I knew it was just a game, but I became primal like a gorilla and caught thirteen in my hanbok (we were standing a tad too close). Once we announced that I would be pregnant for the next two decades, everyone whooped again! I knew we weren't doing it perfectly, but we were trying to honor our dual heritage by doing it in our way. Marvin and I returned triumphantly to the bridal room, and my bridesmaids undressed the ten-piece getup and helped me get into the American outfit—a glorious white wedding gown with tulle and feathers adorning the train, a gift from Wendy, my matron of honor, and her husband.

I was the last to come out of the bridal room and saw Ba waiting there for me. He gave me a small smile and then placed his hand on his hip. I held on to his elbow, and we started to walk down the aisle. I found it so odd to be touching my father that I almost forgot to look up at all my guests' eyeballs focused on me. The most important people in my life were there for my big day—and then, an empty chair right in the front row.

My mother should have been there. She would have complained when I was being too cheap and when I was paying too much. She would have said I looked nice, which would have meant she'd noticed I'd lost ten pounds. She would have effortlessly taken care of all the crises. She would have brought me my favorite snacks. I could feel tears welling up. I would make this wedding more disastrous with ugly crying. *Think happy thoughts, doofus.* We started to approach Marvin at the altar. *There are going to be panko chicken lollipops and mushroom tartlets soon!*

Ba stopped walking and then handed me off to Marvin. I faced my life partner and placed my hands in his. In full view of our Korean and Vietnamese elders, this felt racy. Couples were never supposed to touch in public. My sorrow quickly dissolved to smugness because I never thought I would make it to this moment. All my life, my aunts used to tell me to lose weight, warning me no one would ever love me if I wasn't a size zero, max size two. And there I was, an unfathomable size eight, and I married up—because he was *Korean*—the gold standard for Asian hotness. Koreans were superior. They have a gene where they don't have body odor, can eat all the cheese they want, and they created Hyundai with their one-hundred-thousand-mile guarantee. Ba reminded me that even white people bought Korean products, feeling dismay at Việt Nam's lack of exports outside of food and textiles. So if Marvin chose me, that meant I was desirable too, right?

After we exchanged our vows, we went outside to take pictures with our bridal party, my family of origin, and my new Korean family, since the rain had stopped. With the simple exchange of rings, the Lieu clan had grown again, adding another ethnic group to my rainbow of extended family. Kang had married a half-black, half-German woman, Hang an Iu Mien woman (a Chinese ethnic minority that made its way through Thailand via Laos), and Wendy a Kashmiri man (with a wedding led by an imam, no less).

And now, the Koreans had joined the flock. Squeezing together for our group photo, there was a pack of Lieus on the left with a wide range of heights and nose shapes, and a homogeneous group of tight-lipped Koreans on the right. This was the modern immigrant American family.

After a more playful photo shoot with my bridal party, I felt someone tug my wrist. It was my bridesmaid Jenny. She was the mastermind behind the flowers and feathers in my hair. She walked me away from the crowd to the water's edge.

"Look up," she whispered. I followed the direction of her finger and saw a yellow beam of light coming through the gray-blue rain clouds. It looked like a portal of some sort.

"She's here," she said delicately, holding my hand tightly.

"You think so?" I asked the clear sky. My shoulders dropped, a tension I didn't even know I was holding, and then I felt an ease in my body. I could feel my every heartbeat.

"I know so."

We looked straight ahead, breathing in the mystery of the other side. A bird glided by as the waves gently lapped against the shore. I could hear someone faintly call my name. It was time for dinner.

Wendy clinked her butter knife against her champagne glass and stood up.

"Marvin, you are a courageous man to marry my sister—she's a lot. But here's the three things I learned over the years to keep her happy."

My eyebrows shot up. I was expecting a canned matron-of-honor speech. Wendy hated public speaking. She could have just gone with a template from the internet.

"The key to Susan's heart is food. If she gets hungry, she gets hangry. Chips work every time."

The crowd chuckled.

"Second, everyone must be at the table when the food is ready. If the food gets cold, she will be upset. And finally, if you make her cà ri gà—with the vermicelli noodles, not the baguette—she'll always be by your side. To the newlyweds!" Wendy raised her glass, and we locked eyes. I nodded with approval. "Cheers!" No one knew me better than she did.

Now that the speeches were over, I could finally relax.

"I can't believe we pulled this off," I whispered to Marvin.

"I wasn't worried," he said nonchalantly, totally focused on his steak.

Maybe it was because of his middle-class upbringing, but he was never in a constant heightened state of anxiety like I was. After four months of dating, I met his parents in Hong Kong, where they took us to a fancy Korean barbecue restaurant. Picking up the spareribs with my fingers, my teeth cleaned the meat and cartilage off the bone with the same joy I had when I was a little girl eating chicken wings with Má in the car. I sucked the sweet marrow, licking up the charred crumbs around my lips. The table seemed a little too quiet. I looked up and realized my potential mother-in-law, Mrs. Kim, was staring at me with concern. Her meat scissors were frozen in midair.

"The bones are for the dogs," said Mrs. Kim, her first words of the evening. I looked at her plate. Her bones were still covered in meat and a few faint bite marks. I suddenly became very aware of our class difference. I kept trying to eat like she did, but all the uneaten meat started to bother me. So when Mrs. Kim wasn't looking, I moved my torso the other way and cleaned off my spareribs, hiding the bones on my napkin. Even though I wanted to win her approval, my conditioning to not waste food trumped the moment. I was a jungle Asian through and through.

My thoughts were interrupted by a hand on mine. It was Jenny again.

"There's something going on with your aunt . . . Your family needs you."

I looked over and saw my siblings hovered over Dì Phương, who was rocking back and forth—the same way Ba used to when he spirit channeled dead ghosts. I wasn't scared. I was just wondering why it took Má so long to make an appearance. When I got to my aunt, Wendy was crying into Dì Phương's hand. Hang and Kang seemed unusually tender.

"Dì ơi! Sàn ơi!" Dì Phương cried out, referring to the second syllable of our English names. My siblings folded me into the circle. I reached for my aunt and looked into her eyes to see if it was really Má. Dì Phương's body started to convulse as she wailed at me.

"Thấy ghét quá trời!" *Oh heavens, you look so hateable.* I gave her a big hug. Vietnamese people show our love through insults. Sometimes we say the opposite of what we really mean. I knew exactly what she meant. As I held her tightly, all I wanted was for her to come back and stay. I had so much I needed to tell her. I still had so much to ask.

"Con xin lỗi, Má!" I whispered. *I'm sorry, Mom.* I was still so ashamed of our last day.

"Come on. Let's go to the other room," said Hang, pulling up Dì Phương.

"Are you sure?" I asked.

Dì Phương was crying out a mess of Vietnamese gibberish. I wanted to go with them, but it didn't feel right to leave my own wedding reception. Kang and Hang hoisted her up, walking her limp, possessed body away. I wanted to run after them and ask if she ever forgave me, but I was worried about what she would say back—what if it ruined my night? I convinced myself that if she had more things to say, she would make herself known again.

I looked at Ba two tables away. His jaw was wide open as Wendy walked over to him. Everyone at my wedding was looking to me for a reaction. The entire room was quieter than a library. I shrugged, smiled, and then walked back to my scalloped potatoes. People saw what they saw, and I didn't need to explain it. As I took a sip of wine, I smiled to myself. The woman really knew how to make an entrance. I snuck a glance at my new Korean family. My mother-in-law and her relatives looked like they'd just seen a ghost.

Spirit Channeling

So, here's what I should tell you about spirit channeling. What happened to Dì Phương at my wedding was kind of like Whoopi Goldberg in the movie *Ghost*. My aunt was the Vietnamese Oda Mae Brown! Even though this was the first time I ever saw Dì Phương do it, spirit channeling was a completely normal part of my childhood. Communicating with the dead through mediums was as real as believing the Virgin Mary could have a baby without having sex. Same same, but different, right? I didn't see spirit channeling as folkloric or "mystical." It was a part of my culture and a way for people to get answers from the other side. I knew this because Ba was a spirit channeler.

When I was a kid, every few years Ba would have a spirit jump in his body, and my entire family and I would sit around him, asking him questions. I could still remember the first time I saw him do it. It was Tết, and I was ten.

It was a Sunday morning, and Wendy's top bunk and the aunts' room were empty. My mother's voice ricocheted around the house. She had an ability to be everywhere all at once. I jogged down the stairs to see my brothers cleaning out the fish tank with Ông Ngoại. A hose came through the backyard window to the tank. Five-gallon powder soap buckets were repurposed to house the swimming fish. Fish tank–cleaning day meant we were going to have a big house party.

When we moved up to Santa Rosa, Má upgraded our fish collection with angel fish, neon fish, and bottom feeders that were like mini catfish. Ông Ngoại took a big suck out of a long, clear plastic tube, and the cloudy, poopy algae water started to flow to the backyard.

I heard Ba's voice singing on his karaoke machine, echoing from the family room.

"Mười năm không gặp tưởng tình đã cũũũũũũ," he sang. The song was about being separated from a lover for ten years. Ba's eyes were closed, yet he was hitting every word as it lit up on the screen. Sundays were one of the few times I ever heard his gentle voice. With a microphone in hand, he was uncannily expressive and confident.

Bà Ngoại ordered me to light incense to our ancestors. After fanning out the flame, I closed my eyes and made a wish.

It would be really great if Chad Dawson would stop calling me "flat nose" and "four eyes." Please help me get all As this year. Please make Today's Nails #2 as busy as #1. And next time we go to the store, please let me get the white shark fruit snacks.

I placed my incense stick in front of my unknown ancestors. Each photo was surrounded by electric red candles permanently lit up and a pyramid stack of delicious Asian pears, small bowls of hot soup, slices of poached chicken, and a small dish of noodles. We were not allowed to eat the food until the dead spirits had a chance to eat it first. I bowed three times on the ground and then returned to the kitchen, where I had a front-row seat to Ba's ballads.

Moments later, the aunts and Cô Thảo came through with aluminum trays of egg rolls, lotus root salad, cases of Bud Light, and a big calendar with 365 tissue-thin sheets for each Western day and its corresponding lunar day. It helped us keep track of when we were supposed to eat vegetarian and light incense based on the lunar calendar. Whenever Bà Ngoại woke up at the crack of dawn, she would carefully tear the past day down and then use the paper to hold bones when we ate to reduce mess. At the top of the red calendar was a big 1995 and a picture of a pig. In two years would be my sign, the year of the ox. Some people say when it was your zodiac year, it would be unlucky. But if I had to wait twelve whole years for this, I secretly thought it should be my best year yet.

"Chúc mừng năm mới, người đẹp ơi!" hollered Cô Thảo. *Happy new year, beautiful people!* She seemed like she was in a particularly good mood. It was probably because of Tết. Bad luck could come back to you tenfold if you were negative during this propitious time.

"Bắt tay! Bắt tay!" said Dì Phương, making me cross my arms. I looked up and saw her waving red envelopes. Lì xì! I climbed down my stool and crossed my arms to receive my *lucky money*. Tết was like a Vietnamese Christmas, birthday, and Halloween rolled in one. "Chúc con dồi dào sức khỏe, học hành tấn tới, thành công trong mọi mặt!" Dì Phương looked so joyful saying all of this, but none of it registered. I held the red envelope in both of my hands as she held the other side of the envelope with both of hers. Proverbs. The only words I understood were something related to my health and that I should study well. I nodded and said the only phrase I knew back.

"Chúc mừng năm mới!" I said proudly. *Happy new year!* She squeezed my cheek hard and then sniff-kissed both sides. I got an envelope full of money, and then the doorbell rang.

"Khách tới, bà con ơi!" boomed Bà Ngoại like a cannon. *Family, the guests have arrived!* The aunts ushered Wendy and me upstairs to change our clothes. As we raced up the stairs, I heard the front door open. Wendy and I were pushing hangers to the left and right to find something nice to wear, and then I heard Má's voice playfully welcoming our guests.

After twelve hours of nonstop honoring of ancestors, grazing, drinking, singing, and Bầu Cua gambling, the house became quiet again. Everyone did their part to take out the trash, wipe the counters, and package the leftovers for tomorrow's lunch. Once we were all done, Wendy and I put the *Aladdin* LaserDisc into the karaoke machine so we could sing "A Whole New World." My sister turned up the volume with the remote control and we settled onto the couch. Wendy usually sang the girl's lyrics, and I did the boy ones.

Halfway through the song, I heard a high-pitched crying that didn't sound human. Wendy and I stopped singing. The background music kept playing, but the only audible voice was this thing coming from the living room. We ran over and saw all the adults sitting on their heels in a tight circle, focused on Ba, who was sitting cross-legged. His torso moved back and forth like a rocking chair. Má was by his side with her hand supporting him on his lower back and shoulder, preventing him from tipping over. Wendy and I took a seat on the sofa behind the aunts sitting on the floor.

"Ai đó?" asked Bà Ngoại with her eyes locked on Ba. *Who's there?* Ba's eyes were closed, his jaw and hands were clenched. He didn't answer.

"Thằng đó!" the thing inside Ba finally screamed out. *That man!*

"Thằng nào?" asked Má patiently. *Which man?* But whatever was going on with Ba had its own plan. Ba started to weep and laugh so intensely, the hairs on my arm stood up. I wasn't sure what he was talking about. I tried to breathe as quietly as possible so I didn't attract the thing's attention. Wendy crushed my hand tightly.

I looked over at Má. She was kneeling by Ba, slowly asking what the spirit wanted. Ba let out another shrill cry and kept laughing. Louder, higher, louder. Everyone just patiently waited. I looked over at Bà Ngoại. How come she wasn't fixing this? She was always doing black magic on me whenever I got sick, spitting black cobra juice all over my back, forcing me to eat weird organs like brains and intestines to become smart or else. How come she didn't know what to do? Ba started sobbing and then collapsed sideways into Má's arms. I thought for a moment he was dead. Bà Ngoại had Wendy fetch Ba some water.

"Kêu Ba lại đi con!" ordered Bà Ngoại. *Call your father back, child!* I knelt right by Ba and grabbed at his arm.

"Ba ơi! Ba ơi! Đừng làm vậy nữa!" I bawled out. *Father! Father! Don't do this anymore!*

Má cradled Ba's chin and slowly dribbled water into his mouth. I looked over to the cordless phone charging above our storage tower of rice. If Má said we should call 9-1-1, I was ready. Wendy tapped Ba's body, begging him to return.

Suddenly, Ba took a big gulp of air like he'd just come up from underwater, pushing away Bà Ngoại and Má. His eyes fluttered open.

"Có gì không?" he muttered. *Is there something wrong?*

We all took a collective breath. Dì Phương handed Má a foldable fan to cool down Ba.

"Mô Phật! A di Đà Phật!" cried out Bà Ngoại, clutching her chest. *Buddha! Oh, dear Buddha!* She always called Buddha when she was happy, sad, or scared. When Ba came to, he explained he was lighting incense to ancestors before he got possessed. Bà Ngoại insisted he rest. Má helped Ba carefully stand up, and he hobbled every step up to their room like he'd just had a bad fall. I went back to the living room, where the TV screen flashed a list of Disney songs to choose from. I turned off the TV and wrapped the microphone cords.

Tết was one of the most auspicious and suspicious days of the year. What did that mean for Ba? Was this a good or bad sign? Who was trying to channel him, and what message were they trying to send? Even worse, what if they came back again?

As I climbed the stairs, I looked down at the family altar and saw the last of the incense smoke curl up. The red bulbs of the artificial candles glowed around the portraits of Ba's parents. The worn carpet spot where Ba had his spiritual encounter. Did our ancestors *actually* hear our prayers on the other side? And how powerful were they really? Up until this point, I lit incense only because I had to. I didn't actually believe ancestors had any purpose except for a frame I had to dust once in a while. Their faces looked so serious, and I didn't even know their names. How could they help me if they were dead?

After that day, whenever I said a prayer in front of our family altar, I started to believe that there was something more than the eye could see. If I really needed help, maybe the supernatural was there after all. Maybe when people die, they were never, ever gone—they just existed in a different form.

This was the first of many times I saw Ba spirit channel the paranormal. Whenever the ghosts jumped into his body, our family would surround him, waiting to receive a message from our ancestors. Each time, it was equally tense. It was a power Ba had that he didn't want to cultivate. He had given it up in his early twenties after he got married and had kids. But the spirits kept coming. Ba was extremely introverted and never wanted the attention on him. So never for a moment did I ever think he was faking it. Most of the time, he just spoke in jumbled words. It wasn't coherent like when we would go to other mediums who did it for a living. Even still, I wondered if the spirits were trying to warn us of something big that was going to happen.

A week after my wedding, I was at our orange dining table, accounting for all the cash gifts in a spreadsheet. I kept thinking back to Dì Phương spirit channeling Má. Did that really happen? It felt normal at the time, but the more distance I had from it, the more it seemed like a dream. It never happened at my siblings' weddings, and it was the first time Dì Phương ever channeled.

The last time we had contact with Má was when she was in a coma, days before she died. She sent a message through Ba undeniably saying she was "too late." And that was the last time he ever channeled her. Why was she coming back now? Was there something she wanted me to know? It had been a year since I tried to hunt down the doctor and the trail went cold. Did she want me to keep going? The fire, the storm, the sunlight, and the spirit channeling on my wedding day. It felt like in a million ways she was reaching out to me. She wanted me to find her, but I had no idea how.

The Calling

Soon after I got married, the urgency to reconnect with my mother subsided because my work life was falling apart. To be fair, I was working a marketing consulting job I didn't want. On the long commutes to Microsoft, I would listen to NPR and hear about the world's travesties and feel disgusted with myself. Ever since I was a kid, I thought I would be a humanitarian do-gooder, not measuring click-through rates for a huge technology company. But it was the most I had ever been paid, so now I could finally give Ba a monthly allowance. I was a "good" daughter but a miserable wife. Two months after my wedding, I switched jobs for a hip young food delivery start-up, where I didn't feel like such a cog. Five months later, I got fired. All my life, I was an overachiever. Now I was unemployed.

My friend Julie tried to console me by encouraging me to explore my hushed desire to become a performer. I had tried stand-up comedy four years prior and was on a roll until I got heckled. I was so terrified of getting attacked again, I avoided the microphone for three years. I kept telling myself it was all a silly pipe dream. After all, I had grad school loans to pay. But as I searched for jobs, I noticed how I always kept a tab open on this auditioning class I heard about. I signed up on a whim.

My participation there got me an audition for a Prius commercial, which I was ecstatic about. But when I walked in, I found the seats filled with dozens of Asian women and white men, which sickened me. I wasn't special, I was just being typecast as an aspirational Pacific Northwest couple. When my fake husband and I sat down in our pretend Prius, they told us to act like a married couple. I went for it.

"David, why don't we travel anymore? We always talked about Spain. What happened to us?" I asked with my hands rotating the pretend steering wheel.

"*Well*, it's because we've been going on road trips in our Prius, which gets great gas mileage."

"And when are we going to start trying to have kids? All you've given me are nonanswers."

"Come *on*, let's take it one day at a time—in our Prius." I didn't get the gig, but I had a hell of a time getting into character. I continued my entertainer escapades with headshots so airbrushed, my husband didn't recognize me. I was an extra in a music video for free and waited around for my talent agent to get me gigs, but she never called. This whole performance thing was going nowhere. Meanwhile, I was getting nonstop calls from Ba and Dì Phương.

"You need to stop jumping from thing to thing! And when are you going to have a baby? When you get too old, it gets harder!" nagged Dì Phương.

"Are you allergic to work? Get a job! Why are you so hardheaded?" accused Ba.

There was no space to talk about my passion or purpose. My elders were just disgusted that I was such an overeducated failure. Then after nine months of interviewing for jobs, I became a consultant (yet again) and my client was Microsoft. It was corporate samsara. I detested it, but it paid well, so I gave myself a reward. I registered for a solo performance class.

I had cut a deal with Marvin. He was ready to start a family. But any mention of motherhood made me feel icky. I couldn't imagine raising a kid, telling them to "follow their bliss" when I was a complete coward in my own life. Marvin and I agreed to table the decision for two years. He would scratch his mountaineering adventure itch, and I would do the same with performance. Go all out before we had to become responsible parents, hence the acting class.

On the first day of class, I was just as surprised as the instructor when I began my five-minute story. "I wanted to avenge my mother's death—so I went to look for her killer," I confessed. I never thought my yearning would ever become public. But here I was, sharing the saddest secret of my life because my family wouldn't listen. I felt delicate that night but then dismissed the story again for the rest of the semester. I never had any intention of surfacing that ever again. My capstone performance was an Andy Kaufman–esque mime where I fed the audience raisins and then sat there meditating in a rainbow poncho, hovering my hand over a hammer for ten minutes. No one got it, but I thought it was hilarious.

A month after the class was over, I signed up for a twenty-five-minute slot for a solo festival happening at a community theater in Greenwood. Whether they booed me off or not, I would have faced my fear and then could finally take out my IUD. I would extend the absurdist piece in front of a real, breathing audience, and then I could be done. That was the plan anyway. But two weeks before showtime, everything I had been so sure of took a turn.

There I was, attending a workshop to refine my show for the festival. The orange-haired instructor, Ashlen, a woman who performed as a clown at kids' birthday parties, divided us into pairs to discuss our work. I was the odd one out, so she became my partner. We sat in the greenroom, where the walls were plastered with hundreds of messily collaged show flyers and name tags. We sat on a stained, sinking couch as I spread out all my notes on the scuffed coffee table, trying to figure out a splashy ending. But Ashlen kept gently asking me about my mother's story. I told her about it briefly when she asked how I got into theater. Then she suggested that Má should become the basis for my show. I laughed but dismissed the idea.

"The avenging stuff? Nobody wants to hear about that. It's not interesting. I could become the next Asian Kaufman. They wouldn't expect me to tap-dance. Maybe that could be my finale?"

"Her story seems really important to you, and I find that really interesting," she said softly. I looked up from my colored sticky notes, which mapped out the scenes of the show. This lady was actually serious.

"Who really wants to hear about my dead mom? Plus"—my voice lowered to a whisper—"it's my family's dirty laundry. They would be so pissed if they knew I was talking about her." I kept rearranging my sticky notes but thought about her point. Should I do what's easy or what's hard? Nothing was at stake with the performance art. Even if I put on that show, would I have fully confronted my fear, or would I have just checked the box? I let out a big sigh. Who was I kidding? I couldn't outsmart myself.

"Family is really complicated," she said. "Your mom sounds like a really big influence in your life." Ashlen listened so well, I could finally listen to myself.

"It is. She was. She is."

Ashlen offered me a hug, and then I cried into the workshop facilitator's chest. Everything I had been holding on to came rushing out in big sobs. I knew the show I created had to be about something that actually mattered to me. Otherwise I would still be a coward. When the tears finally stopped, I felt emboldened to take the high road. I would write a show about Má and memorize it in two weeks. I brainstormed thirty scenes, rearranging all the sticky notes as I talked it out loud with my coach. It was go time.

An hour before my performance, I placed a show program on each of the fifty seats. The cover was a photo of Má in heels standing on a boulder. Inside was the *San Francisco Examiner* exposé detailing what happened between the plastic surgeon and Má. I wanted everyone to know none of this was made up. Inside the greenroom, my heart was pounding. All the other artists were schmoozing with one another. I kept flipping through my script, repeating the lines over and over again as if cramming ever helped anyone. When my name was called, I pushed through the velvet curtain and took my starting mark. The lights went up, and then I saw eyeball upon eyeball in the dark, their faces expressionless. *Go, damn it!* I blanked on my line and started to sweat, waiting for them to shun me.

"So . . . ," I uttered, trying to buy myself time. But then the words came, just like on the first day of solo class. I paced the stage and told them about my last day with Má, the coma, my rage for the plastic surgeon, and the two decades of family silence. I played each of my family members, shifting my body and voice to match theirs. I pleaded, I joked, I fought. Finally, I gave myself permission to shine a spotlight on all the sorrow I held inside. I bared it all so I just wouldn't feel imprisoned by the shame anymore. I wanted so badly to be free.

When the lights went to blackout, I could feel the beads of sweat on my forehead, the snot dripping off my nose. People started to stand, but instead of getting their stuff to leave, they began to clap and cheer. I was stunned. No one made fun of me like the comedy club heckler years ago. I bowed and rushed backstage, uncontrollably laughing and crying at the same time. I pulled a long roll of toilet paper from the bathroom and wiped my messy face. I could see myself in the mirror, but I also felt outside my body, partly levitating. I was still shaking when I met Marvin in the lobby. I had him hand out copies of the plastic surgeon's obituary as patrons exited the theater.

"How'd it go?" I said in his ear. He never sugarcoated anything. I could count on him to tell me the truth.

"You cried like ninety percent of the time, babe."

I laughed and squeezed him tightly, jumping up and down. I'd faced my fear and now I felt *alive*. I turned to my friends and thanked them for coming out. My tech friend Ben tapped me on the shoulder.

"Susan, wow, that was the most raw theater I've seen in a long time, but . . ."

I wasn't sure if that was a good or bad thing and, boy, was I scared of what was going to come after next.

"But I just kept wondering the whole time—who was your mom? What was she like?" His words hit me like a ton of bricks. The only time Má was in the show, I was sitting by her bedside, talking to her while she lay in a coma. He was right. I had a whole show dedicated to her but didn't actually share anything about her.

"Yeah." I choked up. "I wish I knew too."

After the show, I kept mulling over Ben's comment. Maybe I would finally be ready to become a mother once I knew my own. All my other attempts to find out about her led me to a dead end, but somehow, this felt different. The adrenaline rush I felt onstage made me realize how much I had numbed my desire to know. I didn't realize how dead I had been. Now I felt a new kind of hunger, one that wanted to see where this would take me. I wanted to put on another show to answer what she was really like. I just had to find out first.

Resistance

The next month, I spent Christmas with my siblings at our annual five-day sleepover called "Extreme Indulgence." I screened a recording of my show, and the only sibling who showed up was Kang. "Emotional roller coaster" was all he said before he joined the rest of the party. Hang wasn't interested in watching, and Wendy requested I send it to her so she could watch in private. The following evening, I tried to start a conversation about our favorite memories of Má.

"Why'd you have to kill my buzz?" said Wendy bitterly.

"You're exploiting our family story," accused Hang. "Your emotions don't matter. Just get over them." I began to feel attacked, always the black sheep in the family. I looked down at the Tahoe cabin rug as if it were newly recovered Titanic jewelry, trying not to take his harsh words personally. But I felt totally crushed.

"Come on, sis. We're trying to relax," chimed in Kang a tad more diplomatically.

I sat there dumbfounded. I had hoped for fond reminiscing. Instead, I got stonewalled. There was never a good time to talk about her. I felt like a nuisance, just the annoying little sister I had always been. I poured myself another drink and then walked away to play with my nephews. They didn't really want to hang out with me, but at least they weren't cruel to my face.

After spending Christmas with my siblings, I drove to Dì Phương's house to eat dinner. I pulled up to her two-story house with large white gravel rocks in the front yard and two plastic life-size deer statues. I rang the doorbell and heard the quick slapping of slippers coming. She swung open the door and sniff-kissed both of my cheeks and gave me a firm slap on my face. We briskly headed toward her kitchen and addressed the most critical topic. Should I eat noodles or rice first?

"Bún nước lèo," I requested, going with the pungent fermented fish noodle soup, a specialty from Sóc Trăng province. The soup literally means *plain water soup*, and it's anything but plain. Dì Phương filled my bowl with a springy pile of vermicelli noodles and then artfully arranged three shrimp, a few pieces of roast pork, small pieces of white fish, blanched bean sprouts, and Chinese chives. She ladled in a simmering clear broth and handed me the piping-hot bowl. On the condiments plate, there were small half-moons of limes, curly strings of banana blossom flower, split water spinach stalks, Thai basil, and mint for a second layer of aromatics. A small saucer of green Thai chilies for those who liked spicy. A jar of gray fermented fish paste for those who liked to eat extra salty. Dì Phương's house was one of the few places in America where I could get this soup.

My family was not just Vietnamese; we were ethnically Chinese, and it showed with our facial features and the particular spelling of my last name. Liu was more common for Chinese nationals and Liễu evolved for the Chinese who made their way to Vietnam. My mother's side were Quảng Đông people and my father's side were Triều Châu. Both sides fled Guangdong Province because of oppressive Communist rule, migrating down to the Mekong Delta with other Chinese people like them.

When we arrived, we fell in love with this soup. But it wasn't native to Việt Nam; it was from Cambodia, the country that bordered the province. When the Vietnamese Kinh people had invaded Cambodia and declared our current provincial land as Việt Nam, bún nước lèo became a communal dish for multiple ethnic groups. The soup was flavored with fermented fish, rather than bones, which explains why it's called lèo. When my parents, grandparents, and aunts continued the lineage of seeking asylum, they brought this soup to their American kitchen. With just one sip of broth, I could taste my family's story of displacement. I came from a long line of people who never felt settled because it was never safe to do so. This soup was born from that collective struggle.

I shuttled my hot bowl to the table covered in newsprint—namely, the Walmart ads, and returned to the stove to get her bowl.

"Ăn rồi con." *I already ate.* Somehow she always ate before I came so she had hands free to keep feeding me. Perhaps it was her way of making up for all the years when the family was torn apart. She gave me her full attention now because she couldn't give it to me then.

"So, I want to know why my mom wanted plastic surgery," I nonchalantly requested as I tore up the aromatics.

"Trời đất ơi! How come you want to talk about sad things? What about happy things?" she complained. She tsked at me and then started rummaging through her pantry, showing me different dried things we could eat next. Long strips of banana slices cut horizontally across the fruit, Việt Nam's version of a fruit snack. Dried squid she could toast; its sweetness would come through with a few sips of Heineken.

"I'm just trying to find the truth," I explained.

"The truth? You only focus on how she died. What about how hard she worked for the family? Six, seven days a week, all those weekends. She sacrificed everything for you."

These were all things I already knew. This narrative was so one-dimensional. There had to be more. I sighed and just tried to enjoy my noodle soup. Dì Phương headed back to the stove, her place of safety.

"Hỏi để làm cái gì hả?" she asked with slight annoyance now. *You're asking to do what?*

I froze. Then quietly, I said, "Con chỉ muốn biết thôi." *I just want to know.*

American children asked the question "But why?" all the time. It was seen as charming curiosity, a sign of intelligence, the instinct for negotiation, and an annoying question parents have to tolerate for a few years. But Vietnamese elders didn't see that question as cute. It was seen as defiant and disrespectful. "But" was a word that divides, rather than deepens. The more I used it, the more I pushed my family away, and I was doing exactly that with my aunt.

Dì Phương fussed over getting me more food and then changed topics, asking if I was still employed. Then she invited me to Việt Nam to celebrate Tết and Ông Ngoại's ninety-ninth birthday. Kang would be coming with his family too. I could ask all the questions I wanted then, she promised. It had been seven years since my last visit. I wanted to introduce my husband to the clan, and who knew if the old man would make it to a hundred? Plus, I would get undivided time with my aunts.

I agreed, and then Dì Phương seemed to act like her old self again. She instructed me to get some used take-out containers from the oven to portion out leftovers for Wendy. Her generation, always so practical, used the oven and dishwasher as storage because they didn't have any other use for them. When everything was all packed, Dì Phương gave me two grocery bags of food for Wendy.

"Make sure you put it in the fridge when you get to her house so it don't spoil because sometime you so stupid, okay?" She gave me a sniff kiss and a slap on the cheek, waving at me from the door until she was fully out of sight from my rearview mirror.

....

Every year, one of my three America-based aunts (who all worked at the same shop) rotated out to go to Việt Nam for a month to celebrate Lunar New Year and their father's birthday. This year was Dì Ngân's turn. Just three months after my first solo show, I would be on a plane halfway across the world to get some answers. Maybe she would open up to me, her thirty-two-year-old niece, on the long car ride from Sài Gòn to our home village.

I spent time planning for the trip in my apartment den, the same one that still had taped clues about the plastic surgeon hung on the walls. I put my laptop on a small desk, wedged next to a rolling cart of messy files, comparing airline prices. After I crossed tickets off my list, I called Ba to get some intel. I wanted him to introduce me to his spirit-channeling master. I wanted to have a number of ways to get information about Má, and all the better to be able to communicate with her directly.

"Con tưởng cái này là trò chơi à?" he asked. *You think this is all a game?* At one point, he had said the youngest in the family had the gift. He was the youngest of his siblings and, depending on how you sliced it, I was the youngest of my siblings or my half sister was the youngest. Then he claimed he never had the gift in the first place!

"What? You used to do it when I was a kid, remember?" Was this an early onset of Alzheimer's, or was I bringing up a topic I wasn't supposed to talk about? Elders were so indirect, I could never be too sure.

"Thôi, bỏ qua đi, Sú Sàn, bỏ qua đi!" he said hastily, telling me to just *let it go*, just as he had done for twenty-two years. And instead of trying to find a spirit channeler, he urged me to finally grow up and start a family. Focus on the future, not the past, he said. Then he ended the call, claiming he had to pick up my stepmother from the nail salon. I guess I just had to find some other way.

My trip back to Má's home village with Marvin was full of dead

ends. Without a spirit-channeling contact from Ba, I followed the
Vietnamese method of crowdsourcing—just ask the next person you
see. A neighbor phoned a friend, who gave us an address, which led
Dì Ngân and me to a spirit channeler who spoke and swayed like a
Vietnamese Elvis. She was clearly a fake playing to my emotions,
never coming up with any specific information. I paid her one hundred thousand đồng anyway; the try was worth six bucks.

The day before Ông Ngoại's big party, I found him in the backyard
chopping wood with a small hand axe. He was almost deaf, so I had
to really raise my voice when I talked to him.

"Do you ever miss my mother?" I asked, practically screaming.

He let out a hissing sigh and rubbed his naked belly with his gnarled
old hands. "Chuyện cũ, con ơi!" *Old news, kid!*

Up until this point, I had never once ever asked him about Má. But
he was her father—he had to have some insight about her. I lobbed
him a softball to get some kind of reaction.

"What do you think about the doctor?" The small slits below his
eyelids dropped a bit. I had never seen the whites of his eyes before,
so it was always hard to read his expression. He got up to leave, returning with a pack of Oreos. He pushed the cookies at me. I really
didn't like sweets, but I ate the fake chocolatey bits to tease out more
information. He went on to tell me the doctor was an evil man. The
doctor, like all humans, would have his karma served to him one day.
In his Buddhist way, he was trying to give me some kind of assurance
that there was a prevailing order of right and wrong in this chaotic
world. That would be nice.

We stared at his lush garden. The papaya tree had three fruit growing on it, the yellow footballs wrapped in plastic bags so the bugs
wouldn't get to them. He fished for another cookie from the plastic
sleeve. He had been through so much war and poverty, he knew how
to savor a treat with small nibbles. We sat and felt the breeze together.
Neither of us needed to say anything more.

At his birthday party, the old man took cognac shots and happily ate dish upon dish of poached chicken cabbage salad, duck bamboo soup, and lotus-shaped white buns. When he was supposedly asleep, I did a double take. There he was on his veranda, swinging a fifteen-pound kettlebell back and forth at eye level. I elbowed Marvin to check out my genes in action.

After dinner, we all congregated on the tile floor for the evening's main event: eating a durian. I held Marvin's hand excitedly. He knew how much I loved fruit. This wasn't the frozen kind we got in America; this was the potent stuff straight from the source. Dì Ngân was squatting on the floor with a butcher knife. She cracked open the spiky porcupine fruit on a wooden chopping block over carefully laid-out newspaper. With one whack, she split open the husk, revealing three plump, canary-colored pieces in just one of the many compartments. She handed me a piece. I closed my eyes and inhaled its big perfume. I tore at the custard flesh like an animal, sucking the meat off the large chestnut-brown seed, leaving a thin film on my lips and threads of fiber in between my teeth. I licked my lips; I was ready for a second piece. Then Dì Ngân popped my joyful bubble.

"Mày mập quá, đừng ăn nữa!" she teased. *You're so fat, don't eat anymore!* All the people who understood Vietnamese cracked up—except for me. I bit my lower lip and looked away, pretending I didn't hear her. She didn't make fun of anyone else. After she cut through the whole fruit, three durian pieces were unaccounted for. I really wanted another, but I walked up the brown-gray marble stairs without saying good night. Marvin followed me upstairs. The group was dead silent, and then I could hear Dì Ngân's voice fading out, recounting every dish at Ông Ngoại's birthday meal. Inside our room, I shut the door quick to block out the mosquitoes. I crawled underneath the top sheet and turned on the AC with a remote control, hot tears dripping down the sides of my face, landing cold into my ears. I was not surprised by her words, but they still stung. Marvin didn't egg me on to fight back—he knew they would never change. It's more strategic to do nothing, he said.

"I just wished my body belonged to me" was all I could whisper.

Hours later, I woke up to an eerie blue twilight coming through the small window. I sensed someone calling me from the altar room. I waited to see if something spooky was going to happen. A twist of the doorknob, a sliding of the closet door, nothing. But the pull kept getting stronger, calling me out of my room. I gave Marvin a small shove, but he didn't move—his snores just got louder. I swung my feet out of the bed and ventured out alone.

The family altar loomed six feet by ten feet at the balcony by the top of the stairs. Each shelf had a different ancestor's photo with the electric red candles bookending each of the portraits and an incense holder inviting the prayers of the living. I crouched by Má's photo. It was the one from Kang's high school graduation. I didn't like that one, because both Hang's and Kang's arms were wrapped around her, which felt weird because they were still alive. It was as if she pulled them partly into the afterlife with her. Or maybe they were holding on to her.

I made my way to the stone bench while keeping my eye on Má's face, ready to receive what she had to say. The blue twilight beamed through the windows, forming a spotlight around her and me. I wondered if a spirit was going to take over my body. What if it got stuck and no one came to help? Ten minutes passed and then the pull seemed to melt away. I was too late.

The next morning, I told Dì Ngân what happened, and she scolded me for not getting her. I was still mad over the durian incident, but maybe she would have known what to do to get Má to communicate with us.

The day before I had to leave Má's home village, I pestered Dì Ngân again for answers. She motioned over to who I thought was the housekeeper, Cô Bảy. *Lady #7* wasn't hired help but Má's childhood best friend, on call to take care of Ông Ngoại while another relative was in Sài Gòn.

I spent that afternoon in the outdoor kitchen, hovering over her while she made thịt kho trứng, *caramelized clay pot pork belly with egg*, for dinner. Her hair was in a tight bun, and somehow she had not gotten a stain on her nice white blouse as she cooked. I guess this was what Má would look like, more or less, since they were the same age. Her pot had thick pieces of squishy pork belly stewing in molasses and coconut soda. The eggs were a light brown, dyed by the simmering sauce. A small jar of pickled bean sprouts and chives to cut the fattiness. These were the flavors of home, the sacred code of where I came from.

Cô Bảy emanated kindness. The older woman let me taste the sauce, and then we started to talk as she julienned ginger. Her cuts were so thin, it looked like the work of a mandoline. I bet my ginger slices would make her panic. They were too thick, uneven, and sometimes still had the skin on them. I had never cooked for my aunts, because I didn't think I would be able to handle their criticism.

As Cô Bảy continued to prep for dinner, I asked her about Má's first suitor. She laughed. Má never knew the guy since she spent all her free time playing in the banana groves after school with her and my father, chaperoned by my older uncle. I waited for more, but all I heard were the crisp cuts of green onions. I offered to help, which made her laugh even harder. We both knew she was the master chef.

"What was she like?" I asked. Cô Bảy kept moving about the outdoor kitchen, dolling out details periodically like she was tasting a dish, checking to see if it needed more seasoning. My mother had integrity and was mischievous, always initiating the next outing. Of course, everyone thought she was beautiful, but she was also kind, someone you could trust. Cô Bảy's eyes welled up, likely not from the alliums. There was no one like her, she said. Her spirit of adventure was infectious; it was too bad she died so young. Cô Bảy gave a quick wipe of her eyes and then encouraged me to go into the house "to take a nap" before dinner. She pushed at my back with surprising strength to go away. I obliged. The woman was able to open up, but maybe she'd hit her limit.

Back in my room, I told Marvin about Cô Bảy. She was the first person who didn't shame me for asking about Má. She didn't shut me down. She let me in as much as she could—but she also wasn't a relative. She dealt with the grief differently. Perhaps my family kept their guard up because they were too afraid of what they would admit if they let their guard down. Who knows what would come out and if they could ever recover.

The next day, Marvin and I traveled to Sài Gòn, where I dropped him off at the airport so he could visit his parents in Hong Kong. Then I headed to Dì Ngọc's house. I had one evening with her before I headed back to America. I had made attempts to interview her over the years, but she had been too shy to talk. My white-and-green Mai Linh taxi pulled up to a familiar intersection by an animal feed kiosk. And there Minh Tâm was in all her pajama daywear glory. She sniff-kissed me and then gave me a tight hug as scooters and old women selling banana desserts with coconut milk weaved around us. We pulled my luggage through the tight alleyway and then entered into their big open living room. The world that walked by could see everything in their home, and we could see everyone pass by.

When I arrived, Dì Ngọc motioned me into her dark kitchen. She turned off the flame of her faded green propane burner and placed a hot soup in the middle of the kitchen floor for us to eat. I saw two cockroaches scurry around the floor sink in between the large sacks of plastic bags. They made me feel a little queasy, but Dì Ngọc brought my attention back to the dishes she'd placed on the chipped tile floor. My cousin, aunt, and I sat cross-legged on the floor.

"Ăn đi con!" Dì Ngọc said, inviting me to eat. With just one bite of her food, I forgot how this kitchen looked different from mine and began to indulge in each of my favorite dishes, which I'd requested days in advance. Dì Ngọc didn't have her dentures in, which made her mouth look super tiny. She was Dì Ngân's size, about four feet tall. Like all my other maternal figures, she said she'd eaten earlier, and sat there monitoring the food levels, ready to refill anything that went too low.

Since this side of the family didn't attend Ông Ngoại's birthday party, I regaled them with stories about the fake spirit channeler and Ông Ngoại's kettlebell swings. The calling of the altar and the banana groves. They hung on every word, repeating lines and laughing with me. After dinner was over, Minh Tâm squeezed their metal gate shut and then snapped on four separate locks secured by a rusty chain. Dì Ngọc sat scrunched up against the tile wall at the foot of her stairs. Above her head, right by the corded phone, was Dì Phương's U.S. home and nail salon phone numbers written with permanent marker on the tile wall. Her two daughters' cell phone numbers were scrawled there too.

It was my last night in Việt Nam, so I took a chance and went for it. I told them I was still searching for stories about Má. I wanted to include it in my next show. People kept asking who Má was, and I felt stupid because I truly didn't know. I had come to a point where the need for answers overcame the need to belong. Asking "But why?" had led Má and me into a room of funhouse mirrors. I saw her image in mine, sometimes hideous and sometimes hilarious. I saw her life cut short in America, and I saw my own life that never could be in Việt Nam. But what I saw was still distorted. I kept asking for their help.

I looked back and forth between her and Minh Tâm. Here they were, a perfect pair, a mother and daughter still intact. Dì Ngọc sucked her pursed lips back and forth like a pacifier and then whacked me on the back of my head.

"Thôi, chơi luôn!" she said as if she were psyching herself up to gamble. *Fine, I'll play!* "Have you heard the story of your mother's feet? There was blood everywhere!" For the first time on my trip, I felt hopeful that I was finally getting something substantial about Má. I pulled out my tape recorder and put it in her hand. I wasn't hiding anymore, and neither was she.

"Con chưa nghe," I said with a big grin. *I haven't heard it yet.* Dì Ngọc got up and came back with three purple mangosteens and a small paring knife. She made an incision along the fruit's circumference. After a big twist, she offered me the tart ivory-white segments. Once the fruit was in my mouth, she began to tell me a story Má had told her years ago. This was the missing piece in my family's origin story. Merging stories I'd gathered from Ba and Dì Phương in half conversations over the years, I finally could see their refugee journey in its entirety.

PART IV

MÁ

Mother

Bloody Feet

To better understand Má, I had to comb through her lineage. Both sets of great-grandparents on my mother's side escaped from Guangdong, China, as refugees fleeing Communist rule. They settled in the Mekong Delta province of Sóc Trăng, in a tiny village called Mỹ Xuyên. Ông Ngoại's father, my great-grandfather, was a savvy linguist and leveraged his French to become a French-Vietnamese translator for dignitaries during French colonial rule. In 1920, Ông Ngoại was born and eventually sent to school to hone his French too. Bà Ngoại was never sent to school, typical for girls during those times, who had to take care of their family at an early age. She remained illiterate her whole life.

As a young man, Ông Ngoại had a close circle of friends. Since he was so remarkably short, his friends would toss the grown man in the air for fun, like how they kicked a white feathered shuttlecock around in a circle. In his village, he made a living as the "Chè Man," spending most of his waking hours making desserts.

Ever since Má was a little girl, she watched Ông Ngoại make seven types of chè, *Vietnamese pudding*. There was the chè đậu trắng, a sticky rice pudding with black-eyed peas, coconut cream, and pandan leaf essence. Made with the subtle sweetness of rock sugar and a few pinches of salt, a crowd favorite. Most of the desserts at room temperature were made with beans: green mung beans, red beans, a mix of yellow and green mung beans. Then there was chè mè đen, the one that looked like a small bowl of black ink. Served hot, this *black sesame seed pudding* was less sweet and had the health promise of improved digestion and shiny hair. Chè sâm bổ lượng, a refreshing Chinese medicinal one with seaweed, lotus seeds, jujubes, longans, and pearl barley. Each one had their own topping: crushed salted peanuts, toasted salted white sesame seeds, a drizzle of cooked coconut milk.

Ông Ngoại cooked the chè varieties all day at home while Bà Ngoại, who he met through an arranged marriage, sat at the market lending out books for a fee and selling small amounts of gasoline. When it turned dark, Má and her siblings would carry the many containers of chè one kilometer to the market so Bà Ngoại could sling the desserts to the local villagers. It was at night when people craved something sweet—and for good reason. Surviving poverty each day was reason enough for a small reward. For many, comfort came in a small plastic bag of chè.

But for the Hà clan, pudding barely made ends meet. There were long stretches when no one had money to buy dessert. To feed their eleven children, Bà Ngoại gave them small shards of rock sugar, a few fermented black beans, and rice porridge. It wasn't nutritious or appetizing, but it gave everyone the illusion of feeling full to make it through the night. Back then, meat was so rare, acquiring it was a black market transaction. Women traveled by bus from town to town with meat taped against their calves hidden underneath their pants to make a little money. Any leftover fat scraps were used to feed their families.

On April 30, 1975, the day Má turned seventeen, everything changed. It was the Fall of Sài Gòn. As the lucky southern Vietnamese with government ties ascended away by helicopter, an invisible prison enclosed around the ordinary citizens who were left behind.

People weren't allowed to run their own businesses. The currency value fluctuated wildly. Every action was monitored by Communist officials, and any resistance could result in labor camps, prison, or worse, disappearance. Word spread that the Chinese Vietnamese entrepreneurs in Chợ Lớn District in Sài Gòn were targeted by the Communists. Even though the war was over, the southern Vietnamese didn't experience freedom.

That year, Má dropped out of high school and got married to twenty-one-year-old Ba, a local village boy who was friends with her older brother Bình. There were other suitors, but she felt safe with him on their chaperoned walks in the banana groves. Following traditional custom, Má moved into Ba's house just a kilometer down the dirt road right by the market entrance. But since he was orphaned at an early age, they spent much of their time with Má's extended family. Ba earned a living fixing Honda scooters as a mechanic in front of their home. One year later, Kang was born. Two years later, Hang followed.

One outcome of the absolutist Communist rule was a newly instituted state-run lottery system, which piqued Má's interest. With more mouths to feed, she became an entrepreneur by running an underground gambling game called Số Đầu Đuôi Xổ Số. Every day at 4:00 p.m., the government announced a string of winning lottery numbers that were two-digits, three-digits, four-digits, five-digits, and six-digits long. But the real winning numbers for Má's covert game were the first two numbers, the đầu, or *head*, and the last two numbers of the six-digit string, the đuôi, or *tail*. If anyone bet the correct head or tail number from Má, they made their money back seventyfold. If they guessed wrong, Má was the house and kept their bets.

Má had a cadre of seven people selling numbers for her. The system was simple: tear a piece of paper out of a notebook and start collecting bets with their name, their head and tail numbers, and hold on to their money. At age twelve, Dì Phương would sprint out of grade school to sell numbers as fast as she could, making sure she got her sheet of nearly fifty bets to Má before the 4:00 p.m. deadline. She was eager to help, because all the sellers got a 10 percent commission of the total bets placed, regardless of whether they sold the winning number. Even though the poor just pit themselves against one another, everyone was invested in this game. Playing kept hope alive for everyone.

Since this was an illegal game, selling numbers had to be done in secret. The Communists always had the villagers on surveillance, so Má had her eye on the Communists during her transactions, casting glances over her shoulders for approaching officers. The irony was that the Communists were a part of the charade too. They regularly collected bribe payments from Má instead of arresting her. If they wanted a bigger payout, they hung around her house, which prevented people from approaching her to place a bet. A payment to them would buy her a week before they would come back again for more. Corrupt officials were simply a part of the operating cost of doing business.

A key part of Má's work was paying attention to signs. Má took dreams seriously because they were a direct line of communication from the ever-prudent ancestors. They also folded into her sales pitch.

"Did you have any dreams last night?" she asked the woman who peddled vegetables.

"I saw a dog," the old woman said as she plucked wilted leaves from her produce.

"Your grandson is the year of the dog, isn't he? Eight years old now? That could be your lucky number!" With an officer in sight, Má quickly changed the topic. "And this morning glory looks so fresh. It would be so delicious with garlic or fermented tofu."

Má would capitalize on dream information by pawning it onto other bullish customers, stretching the truth a bit to sell more numbers.

"Cô Quỳnh had a dream about a dog—two, in fact—a small one and a big one. And there was a fire she was running away from." The person placing the bet could make meaning from the dream, creating two-digit numbers from stories to rationalize their gambles. The birth date of the two people with that zodiac sign. The year any fire happened or the age of the person who caused it.

If someone's dream was especially compelling, Má would place her own bets with another gambling operation, of which there were dozens in the village. It was a way for her to curb her losses if she had to issue a payout and also a way for her to win big if the ancestors were right. And sometimes, they were.

From 1976 to 1979, Má made a sufficient living from her daily collections but started amassing wealth with divine intervention. The first time she hit the jackpot, it was because of someone else's dream. The first thing she did with her winnings was go buy delicacies from the market, which included green-clawed shrimp, snakehead fish, pork belly, and a ripe durian bigger than her head. She surprised Bà Ngoại with the haul, and that night, everyone went to bed truly full after the rare feast. Her second jackpot numbers came from the animals in her own dream, and the third came from a dead ancestor through her favorite fortune-teller.

Now with two toddler sons, twenty-one-year-old Má was ready to gamble it all for the *possibility* of a better life. The village was starting to thin out. She wanted to join the exodus of risk-takers who were trying to escape Việt Nam by boat. If they reached Malaysia, they would get a chance of getting sponsored to live in another country. And for many, the holy grail was America. With more than four ounces of gold saved, they had enough money to flee. Once Má got an idea in her head, she was stubborn, relentless, and aggravating to everyone around her. But Ba wasn't exactly on board.

Even though the ancestors answered Má's prayers for money, that was only the first obstacle. Reaching the dock without getting caught by the Communists was the next one. Boarding the overcrowded boat and braving the 550-kilometer journey, they would now be at the mercy of the elements. The untamed ocean and storms could capsize them. They could lose their way. Their engine could break, leaving them starving, or worse, dehydrated at sea. Then there were the Thai pirates who were known to steal, rape, and kill. Stories had a way of coming back with the tide.

One 215-passenger boat hid their gold in the water jugs and engine. The pirates saw the gleam and dumped the boat's communal supply of water, taking the engine with them. At night, passengers would stick straws in people's personal jugs to stay alive. Because of that, one matriarch tied her jug to her body with rope and slept over it, covering the opening. She rationed out the water, giving children one coffee spoon of water four times a day and the adults half a coffee spoon. Every day, several people died and their bodies had to be thrown overboard, sinking down to the ocean floor without a proper burial. Now out of water and her family on the brink of death, this matriarch found a tiny lemon on board and had her parched family of eight suck on small wedges so they could survive one more day. By the time a friendly fisherman towed them to Malaysia, they had been robbed eighteen times and now were just 155 refugees. And this was just one story of thousands of escapes.

Based on whispered hearsay, everyone knew there was only a 50 percent chance of making it to land. And even then, they could be forced to repatriate back to Việt Nam. The odds were stacked against them, yet Má was still determined to flee.

Ba tried to convince Má they could have a nicer house with all her winnings. She reminded him of the neighbors who were always watching them, ready to snitch to gain favor with the Communists. Had he not forgotten that his fellow brethren were even swindling him? He was sold cheap gasoline only to find out it was water with a splash of gasoline floating at the top. The local jeweler had appraised a gold necklace and then gotten tricked into buying a fake replica. A life in Việt Nam would mean living with constant distrust. The game of survival had no morals; that's just how it had to be played. Má was adamant that escaping was the only way. She was tired of following someone else's rules. She wanted to be in control of her destiny, and that would never happen if they stayed in Việt Nam.

In 1980, Má began making preparations. She bought four one-way tickets for the family, despite Ba's pleas. She paid the boat fee deposit to a man she trusted to smuggle them out. Dì Phương would stay longer at Má's house after the 4:00 p.m. bet cutoff time, sewing gold into the inner lining of the family's escape outfits. And when Má's contact fanned his hat in the market, Má knew it was the signal. She would bring the boys over to Bà Ngoại's house and spend the evening there, possibly the last time she would ever see her parents and siblings. The boys were instructed to say, "Đi ngoại chơi," if anyone asked—*off to play at their grandparents on their mother's side.* If they made it all the way to the dock and had to turn back home, the four- and two-year-old had to stick to the lie.

On escape days, Má would tell Dì Phương that she had to leave town to run errands, which meant Dì Phương was on point to act as Má's double. From far away, they looked nearly identical with their petite bodies, facial structure, and haircut. Plus her youngest sister regularly spent time at her house, so her presence wouldn't appear suspicious. For the Communists, it was more suspect if the house was empty.

At first, Dì Phương was terrified about getting caught, but then got used to it because Má had so many failed escapes. The first time they reached the dock, someone started fake coughing, which meant their cover had been blown. Everyone else started fake coughing while sprinting to the jungle to avoid getting caught. Má and Ba didn't know which way to go, so they had to pay the local barber and fellow escapee to lead them back to the village. That cost them an ounce of gold and a watch. On the way home, Ba was so thirsty, he drank water from a stream, which made him bedridden with a fever for days. Another time, the boat had been discovered hours before departure time, so the escape was called off. Every time Má returned to her house, Dì Phương would leave her post. Within a month or two, a new boat would be arranged, and then Dì Phương was back at Má's house, sweeping the floors and hanging the laundry outside as her sister's imposter.

On the fourth attempt, all the conditions seemed right. Hat signal, dinner at Bà Ngoại's, midnight ride to the docks. Along the way, Má gave Hang and Kang sleeping medicine so they wouldn't cry during boarding. When they got to the shore, there was no sign of the Communists. Our family loaded onto a small boat as the driver sped away. Other refugees emerged from the corners of the night, climbing into their small boats to get transferred to a larger one. But as the boats pushed off, a man cried out.

"Công An! Công An!" *Police! Police!* Everyone immediately dispersed. Má and Ba got out of the boat, splashing their feet in the water. Women and children were shrieking as the authorities closed in on the escapees. Ba dropped Kang by Má's feet on the shore and sprinted toward the jungle alone. Men who got caught went straight to prison. Hoisting up a limp Kang in her arms, Má had a four-year-old and two-year-old on each side of her hips. She started to run, but her wet slippers were slowing her down on the sand. She kicked them off and then started to gain speed. Her accomplice driver was nowhere to be found. The only way back was through the unforgiving maze in the dark jungle. She ran through a thorny bramble, her feet getting stabbed over and over again. She had no time to stop and check her wounds. They were on her heels, and the boys were weighing her down.

When Ba finally reached the village, his armpits were drenched from the adrenaline sweat of fighting for his life. He found a startled Dì Phương in the market selling chè.

"She's in the jungle with the boys," he sputtered out.

"How could you leave her?" Dì Phương cried out in shock. Everyone knew the danger of the jungle. "Why didn't you help her?" she accused him. "Why didn't you help her?"

The two walked the market and then hired a man to find her.

Back in the jungle, night turned to day and then night again. Má and the boys were so dehydrated, they licked drops of dew off leaves so they could stay alive. They wandered from tree to tree, licking for their lives. When the boys got tired of walking, they began to cry. Má would saddle them back up on her hips and inch her way forward through the thick vegetation. She was barely alert, her energy totally depleted. But she persisted. She had beaten the odds so many times. This was not how she would die.

When she finally found a couple who lived in the jungle, she begged them for help. All the jungle folk knew anyone trying to escape had all their valuables on them. Má knew they could kill her and take everything, or she could offer up the gold in Hang's and Kang's clothing. She promised them riches if they could just take her back to Mỹ Xuyên. The strangers took pity on her and then navigated her back home, straight to Bà Ngoại's house.

When the door cracked open, in came a barely coherent Má and the two boys. Dì Phương leaped up from her feet and embraced her older sister, who collapsed in her arms. Dì Phương supported Má to the green hammock in the living room, tracking blood all through the house. As Bà Ngoại fed the survivors, Dì Phương gasped at Má's feet. The entire bottom was so full of thorns, her skin appeared completely black. Armed with a needle and a shot of vodka (for sterilization and calming purposes), Dì Phương began to pull out the thick spikes as Má howled, gripping the metal frame of the hammock. When Má regained her strength, she pulled her sister close.

"I quit. I'm done trying to escape. Em ơi, I thought we were all dead—because of me. But I kept going, to save the children."

But two weeks later, Dì Phương was back at Má's house as her double, lighting an incense stick at the altar for her sister's safe passage. The family returned again the next day, the failed fifth attempt.

In 1981, right before Tết, there was an opening. Tết was a time to return to your home village and be with family. So for a good week, no one worked, including the usual patrol of Communist officers. Dì Phương tried to persuade Má not to go.

"I'd rather die trying than stay," Má said without hesitation. Finally, with no one watching, the family fled. Usually they came back the next day. But this time, they didn't. Dì Phương continued doing chores at Má's house every day, hoping for a sign.

Má and Ba made it to the tiny two-meter long boat that stealthily took them to another bay, where they boarded a four-meter-long boat. They hid beneath stalks of sugarcane as that boat took them to a beach where the twenty-meter boat was waiting. One hundred tickets were sold for boat number 500PB548, but 150 determined souls crammed their way into the lower and upper levels, pressing their bodies tightly against one another like a haul of flipping fish in one net. One lone dockman was paid off, and then the boat finally set sail.

On the first night at sea, it was frigid cold when the boat began to violently rock back and forth, smushing bodies together. Passengers screamed as fierce waves smashed the small windows on all sides of the boat. That's when the vomiting began. Ba threw up so many times, his bile became green and his mouth turned bitter. Everyone knew to be afraid of the government, but now the new enemy was the godless ocean and a thirst that could not be satisfied. As the waves continued to beat the boat, the parched passengers began stealing water. Má and Ba were among the first victims.

On the second night, Ba was on the upper deck getting some fresh air when a light shone on the boat. Immediately, the captain began turning the boat, making a hard ninety-degree turn to lose the likely Thai pirates. Everyone on the boat tried to keep as quiet as possible so the boat wouldn't be detected. Ba went back down to make sure Hang didn't cry. Women clutched onto their children and small pieces of coal, ready to mark their faces dirty so they could be spared from getting raped. After six hours of total silence, their boat was able to derail the predator, chartering the boat through a dense fog and away from the intruders. Once that danger subsided, the passengers became distrusting of one another again.

On the third night, Ba lost Hang. They were sleeping together in the lower level. But when Ba woke, Hang was gone, which sent him into a state of panic. Fearing the worst, Ba hurriedly searched up and down the boat, finally finding Hang sitting with another small boy in the upper level. Ba clutched his son, grateful he was still alive. On the fourth day, the captain saw land, and everyone on the overcrowded boat started to cheer. No one had died. Má and Ba were overjoyed. They weren't in the clear just yet, but they had made it past another obstacle, and that was something to celebrate.

Two weekends after Má's final escape, whispers snaked their way back to Dì Phương. The boat survived the open waters and made it to Malaysia. That meant she could finally stop pretending. A month after their departure, a letter arrived. Dì Phương saw foreign stamps and raced into the house loudly hollering for everyone to hear.

"Bà con ơi, vô đi! Vô đi!" *Family, come on in! Come on in!* Dì Phương trembled as she opened the letter. Bà Ngoại leaned in close, eager to listen to the words she wasn't able to read. Turned out, Má had made it to a Malaysian refugee camp on the island of Pulau Bidong! Everyone was doing okay. Overjoyed, Bà Ngoại headed straight to the market to buy an entire chicken. The ancestors had to be thanked and encouraged to keep helping Má. As Bà Ngoại made preparations, Dì Phương felt mixed. She was happy for her sister because her life would be better. But she was deeply distressed because it was unclear if they would ever see each other again.

For the next two years, Má and Ba tried to build structure into their uncertain lives in the refugee camp. They busied their days with ESL classes in the morning and then ran a small shop in the afternoon, selling clothes and cigarettes. Ba bought the storefront from his sister, who arrived a month prior and was now on her way to America. The most profitable item was cognac, which was sold in secret to the lucky ones about to leave. Any money my parents earned would go to the refugee women who took care of their now three children during school hours. In 1982, a year and a half after they arrived, they welcomed their first baby girl, my sister Wendy.

Every week, my parents would line up for their rations, which included instant noodles and Spam. As the days wore on, ESL classmates received either terrible news or wonderful news. Ba's sister had sent him a telegram saying America was indeed wonderful. The government there was providing a better life than what they had in Việt Nam. But not all refugees were that lucky. Some were not granted asylum and were forced to return to Việt Nam. Suicide was a common response; the Communist Party would not be so welcoming to people who tried to defy them. In 1982, after holding their breath for one year, the Liễu clan was assigned the most coveted country of all: the United States of America. They had done the impossible.

With their few possessions, they headed for Indonesia, where they learned English for another eight months, before transferring to Singapore to make the twenty-plus-hour transpacific flight to San Francisco. Once they arrived in the Bay Area, they lived in Ba's sister's basement for a month before moving into government-subsidized housing. Ba spent his first year learning English at the adult school and spent his second year delivering newspapers. But waking up at 3:00 a.m. and throwing papers until 7:00 a.m. at the minimum wage of $3.50 an hour took a toll on him. He wasn't allowed a single sick day. Meanwhile, Má started helping Ba's sister with her sewing company, working through large cloth bags of piecemeal work, sewing on buttons for pennies while taking care of the kids. But newspapers and dresses weren't going to get them off welfare. Má could sponsor her sisters and parents only if they became naturalized citizens and if they weren't reliant on government assistance. It didn't help that

Má was now pregnant with me, so the two of them started making moves.

Ba had the idea to start a gardening service with his friend, who I called Chú Kim. The friends pooled their life savings of $5,000 for all the landscaping equipment and a beat-up truck from an auction. They watched Mexican workers take care of yards from afar and then would practice on their relatives' yards. When they thought their work looked presentable, they launched their business. Ba found a landscaping flyer and then put our home phone number on top of it along with the business name, Tom's Gardening Service. He had just watched *Top Gun*, where Tom Cruise portrays the hero, the maverick, the guy who beat all the odds. Ba decided his English name would be Tom too. They made fifteen thousand copies and put flyers in every mailbox they saw, undercutting competitor prices. That first year, they had twenty-five customers, and the next year, they doubled.

But after two years of manicuring lawns, Chú Kim quit to buy a nail salon. Má took notice. By then, she had graduated beauty school to cut hair, but realized the real money was in nails. Ba kept gardening, but as his clientele grew, so did his back pain. Má decided they were ready to make another big bet—it was time to build a nail salon empire.

In 1989, Má opened our family nail salon, Susan's Nails, in the East Bay. The business took off. A friend helped cosign a loan, and then our family bought our first house. Ba sold the gardening business and then started working at the shop. That was the year that Má returned to Việt Nam wearing Ray-Ban sunglasses and announced she could sponsor over her parents and any unmarried siblings, which included Dì Phương. The following year, the paperwork process started. After two years of an agonizing wait, Má sent another letter telling them to go to the embassy. It was time to choose their travel day. Once Dì Phương had the date, she went a few houses down to the woman who had a landline to call Má. Then on April 28, 1992, the five relatives set foot in America at a chilly San Francisco airport. When Bà Ngoại entered the two-story house, she opened up all the kitchen cabinets. It was time to make this home.

When I was a kid, my job was to go to the three-foot-tall rectangular tower to fetch jasmine rice. Bà Ngoại would shout out the number of cups, and I would do some simple math, pressing a combination of one, two, or three cups to meet her wish. I pulled out the small box of rice and then poured it into the metal rice cooker bowl. I would wash the rice a few times until the water turned clear, putting in just enough water to the fill line and then turning the rice cooker on for that night's dinner.

On my second trip back to Việt Nam right after I graduated college, I visited my cousin, one of Aunt #1's many sons, who had a rice paddy. My new red leather New Balance sneakers got a little muddy as I squatted down to pull a thin green blade of grass from the earth. At the bottom was a very tiny grain of rice. No wonder Bà Ngoại would lose her shit every time I didn't finish my bowl. It was literal backbreaking work to get it from the field to the dinner table.

Ten years later, I visited my cousin again. Instead of one rice paddy, he had a giant tractor-like machine that he used to till everyone else's paddies. With a rice mill that separated the plants from the grains, he now had his own empire. It all started with the remittances Má sent back years ago to his mother, Tài Dì, the eldest sibling. Once Má sponsored over the aunts, those sisters sent money back to their siblings. Through unwavering persistence, each family was able to reinvest their earnings to fundamentally change their financial plight. I always knew Má was my hero; I just didn't realize she was everyone else's too.

Digging

O
n the plane ride from Sài Gòn to Seattle, I kept thinking back to my parents' journey to America. Despite every hurdle of impossibility, they beat the odds. This left me feeling guilty because I could get preoccupied with my first-world problems of not yet achieving coveted status symbols: giving a TED Talk, driving a Tesla, and wearing the "official" blue badge on Twitter. But in the moments I could remember that it was a privilege to have self-actualization crises instead of self-preservation ones, I could ground myself again. It was a miracle my family had even made it to America.

When she still lived in a tiny one-road village, Má's big, hairy, audacious goal was to eat meat every day of the week. And in America, we did. I knew money was tight, but I never actually felt poor. When it came to food, Má always made sure we ate with dignity and abundance. The curious thing is, every memory about her revolved around food. Her code for living life was embedded in these moments. For me, food was not a means to live, it was the way my hard-pressed mother communicated with me. One of my most cherished food memories was the night she took us all clamming. I can still feel the salty ocean air damp against my cheeks, full of reverence for my mother. Once we returned home with full buckets, Bà Ngoại prepared a feast with our foraged goods. We stayed up all night eating like a royal court.

I was seven years old and in the upstairs bathroom with Wendy, brushing our teeth after dinner. I heard Dì Hiệp holler from downstairs, "Mình sắp đi! Mình sắp đi rồi!" *We're about to go! We're about to go!*

Wendy and I looked at each other with our foaming white beards and then took turns running water into our cupped palms, slurping it into our mouths for a final rinse. I looked down the stairs and saw Bà Ngoại tying on her headscarf and the aunts zipping up their jackets. Wendy and I slid hip to hip down the plastic-lined stairs on our butts. I saw the edge of Má's coat flutter out the door. I raced after her, following her closely in the pitch-blackness. There were two cars to choose from: Dì Hiệp's Kool-Aid cherry-red two-door Honda Civic or Má's long station wagon. Dì Hiệp finally passed the driving test after trying three times. The last time I rode with Dì Hiệp, she drove up on the sidewalk by accident. She was nice and everything, but I was sticking with Má for safety.

I didn't know where we were going, but I heard ocean waves when we arrived. Dì Phương pulled a stack of buckets out of the trunk. We bought powdered soap in five-gallon buckets from Costco to wash all the towels at the shop. Once they were empty, Ông Ngoại used them to collect rainwater to water the plants or to collect food scraps from the kitchen to make compost. Ba used them when he was weeding his customers' yards. These buckets were versatile, and just like any plastic containers, we held on to them, just in case.

Dim yellow lights led us to the edge of the parking lot. Once we hit the sand, we relied on the moon to find our way. As my flip-flops sank into the mushy sand, I caught a breeze of wild fennel that smelled of sarsaparilla. We all moved toward the waves, stopping when we got to Má. Ông Ngoại came over to Wendy and me, grunted, and then gave each of us a stick. He squatted down and started to dig, so

Wendy copied him. I drew a heart in the sand and then started writing my name when I heard the sound of victory against the crashing waves.

"Con nghêu!" yelled Má. "Con nghêu!" *Clams! Clams!* Clams? The sound of stick scratching intensified. More excited shouts. And then the sound of shells hitting the buckets. *Clunk. Clunk, clunk, clunk.* Ông Ngoại unearthed one with his stubby fingers and showed me. He tossed it into our bucket. My stick hit something hard. I dug around with my hands, cold sand coming up my nails. I pulled out something that felt like a rock. In the moonlight, I saw tiny grains sparkling on the curved mollusk. My first foraged clam. I dusted off the sand and gently placed it in its new home. *Hey, little guy.* We were hunched over like we were harvesting rice. Má's booming voice kept us motivated.

"Tối nay mình ăn cho đã nhé!" *Tonight, we're going to eat for pleasure!* Not just to get full, but to eat gluttonously.

Every so often, Bà Ngoại yelled out, "Xe tới! Xe tới rồi!" *A car has come! A car has come!* We all would freeze and wait to see what happened next. Dì Ngân said if we got caught, we could go to jail. After the headlights drove away, we would go back to striking the sand, moving to the rhythm of the waves. Soon the buckets filled up. When my hands got too cold, I walked around to see who was the best clam digger—it was Má by a long shot. Má started pointing to the clams she partially unearthed, and then I crouched down to dig out the ones she found as she moved on.

"Mình đi về nhà!" Má called out as she picked up her bucket and headed back to the parking lot. At the car, I sat with my feet dangling outside the open door, clapping the bottoms of my flip-flops together to shake off the sand. When we arrived home, Bà Ngoại began her preparations. The clattering of the metal steamer getting stacked three layers high. The whacking of her cleaver on a wooden stump cutting board. The kitchen was fully alive, and this was Bà Ngoại's happy place, rummaging through plastic bags and opened drawers.

The aunts took orders from Bà Ngoại. We were a family sonata. Waiting for food to cook, I opened up a thick book of multiplication problems to pass the time until I heard her voice like clockwork.

"Bà con ơi, đến giờ ăn rồi!" bellowed Bà Ngoại from the bottom of the stairs. *Family, it's time to eat!* Ba and my brothers came running down the stairs as we all crowded around the dining table. The dishes started to come. Dì Hiệp balanced a wobbling pyramid of lemongrass-steamed clams, placing the plate down with clam juice glistening out of the open shells. Small dishes of fish sauce and Thai chilies lined the table.

"Ngọt thiệt!" exclaimed Dì Phương. *Truly sweet!* The sweetness was better than any candy I had ever tasted. Má got up and came back with two cans of Bud Light and a few coffee mugs. My aunts shook their heads and waved their hands no, bashful about drinking alcohol, but Má insisted.

"Lâu lâu mới uống một lần mà!" *We only drink every once in a while!*

"Uống đi! Uống đi!" encouraged Bà Ngoại, giving her blessing. The aunts collectively blushed and pulled their quarter-filled mugs toward them.

"Một, hai, ba, dzô!" whooped Má. *One, two, three, cheers!* All the mugs clinked together, and I joined in on the shouting too. All the adults took a tiny sip and then continued to binge eat. Bà Ngoại's next dish was a platter of clams coated in a shiny fermented black bean sauce and wilted scallions.

"Ai ăn cơm? Ai ăn cơm?" called out Dì Hiệp like a line cook, asking if anyone wanted rice. Small half bowls spun onto the table like oncoming Frisbees until each person had one. I licked the sauce off the shells, tore off the clam with my mouth, and then scratched off the tough small circle of meat with my thumbnail. I smacked my lips as a small morsel of rice cut the saltiness of the fermented black bean. Má finally sat down at the head of the table to stack her pile of empty shells on the newspaper. I gave any clams that were too hard to open to Ông Ngoại. If he couldn't open them and re-steaming didn't work, then they would be tossed in an empty soap bucket to compost in his garden.

Meanwhile, Bà Ngoại encouraged us to eat but didn't sit down herself. She loomed over us like an ocean, a source of life and a source of fear. When there were no clams left, we all cleaned up and headed to bed. With the lights off, Dì Phương kept exclaiming how sore her arms were from the weight of the buckets. Dì Ngân kept saying how she was so frightened that the police would arrest her. I drifted off to sleep, a little too full, and it was fantastic.

In my twenties, I took my then boyfriend to this same site for us to relive my nostalgia. At the parking lot, I saw a large warning sign. *DO NOT EAT SHELLFISH. TOXIC. Foragers will be subject to a fine.* That gave me a good laugh. No wonder we were so afraid of cop cars coming that night. But Má knew exactly what she was doing. She was always calculating risk for the family. She wasn't a big gambler at the casinos, but she bet big on herself and the power of our bà con. Three decades later, this night of digging is still so vivid for me. I can still recall the yellowness of the dining room light bulbs, the sound of dining chairs scooching against the linoleum floor, sucking up the clam broth and licking the black bean sauce off the shell exterior, the crumpling of newspaper and smell of fresh Windex when we cleaned the table. That night, I wasn't terrified of my elders or diminished to feel small. When there was an abundance of food, I could feel a collective release of tension. When we picked up our chopsticks, we could quiet the constant fight-or-flight feeling in our bones, at least for a few minutes. Eating had a way of helping us feel a deep sense of safety and security like nothing else.

The Messenger

ake your mark," said my director, Paul. I sighed and walked to the taped *x* on the floor to rehearse my second solo show, *Dr. X: Episode II.* It would focus on what I'd learned about my mother and what I still wished I could know.

"What was she like?" I said half-heartedly.

"No, say it like you're in Việt Nam and you're shouting across the ocean to America," he instructed, moving his pen in an arc.

"What was she like?" I had raised my voice a few decibels, but I was still so unsure.

"Like you need people to hear. They *have* to know. This is your only chance for them to know." He put two fingers over his mouth and rested his chin in his palm. I took a couple of deep breaths, jumped up and down, got all the wiggles out, and planted my feet. I looked downstage at an audience that wasn't there. I found the eyes of that tiny Susan who had been wanting to know Má her entire life. I reached deep from inside my diaphragm. I fought against the pressure to stay quiet, the paralyzing fear of messing up.

"What was she like?" I demanded with exasperation. For two hours, I waded through the script, trying out every word, madly scribbling notes on the pages. When rehearsal was over, we turned off all the lights except for the ghost light and headed home.

Later that night, I couldn't fall asleep, which was strange. Usually, I could fall asleep anywhere, but now it was 2:00 a.m., and I had been tossing for hours. I readjusted my pillow and began counting down from one hundred. When I got to eighty-eight, my heart started beating crazy fast, like four times faster than usual.

My forehead and cheeks started to heat up. My heart was pounding out of control. I felt like prey getting chased by a snarling predator, but my body was completely still. Was this a heart attack? Was I about to die? I tried to get up, but a gravity-defying force was pressing against my body. I pushed back with all my might, but I couldn't move. I kept trying to open my eyes, but all I could see was darkness. Was this a nightmare? Had I gone blind? I tried to wake up Marvin, but I was mute. I couldn't lift my neck. I couldn't wiggle my fingers and toes. I had no control of my body anymore. My mind started to race, trying to figure out another way. But then, I heard a woman's voice.

"Don't cover up the story." The hairs stood up on my arm, and I suddenly felt very cold. Who was this creepy intruder? I tried to see who it was, but it was too dark. I couldn't see a face. The voice got closer.

"Don't cover up the story," she said much more slowly. Her voice was oddly familiar. I racked my brain. Who would be saying this to me now and at this hour? I tried to defend myself, tell her to go away—anything—but my mouth felt sewn shut. I tried to pry it open and closed, but I was inaudible as a fish.

"Thấy ghét quá trời!" she exclaimed. *Oh, heavens, your face looks just so hateable!* A wave of warmth came near me. No, wait, it couldn't be. Má? It was she—it had to be. I became a giddy girl again. She had come for me! My feeble attempts to sit up were getting me nowhere. I wanted to see her. I needed to see her. But it was like I was the one in the ground, and she was above it. I could hear her, but she couldn't hear me. Then she said what I had been waiting two decades for her to say.

"Má nhớ con. Đừng quên." *Mom remembers and misses you, my child. Don't forget.* Cool tears fell out the corners of my eyes and into my ears. I had so much to ask her. I had so much to tell her, but the only thing working in my body was my ability to cry. I wanted to breathe in her presence. I wanted to have her fill me up. I wanted to remember this feeling of her right here. I took a slow breath. Take it all in. *Enjoy this, Susan.* I tried to give her a smile. When my heart slowed down, the air became strikingly cold again. Now I could feel the sheets against my skin, but that unnameable feeling of her was gone. I was in my body again. I could see everything in the twilight of the room. I sat up and touched all my limbs to make sure they were all there. Marvin was still snoring. It was now 2:20 a.m. I needed to see if she was still there. *It's now or never—go, Susan!*

I moved slowly out of bed, tiptoeing like I was going to sneak up on a robber. I snuck a glance into the kitchen. No one was there. I looked toward the living room. Maybe she was lying on the couch. No one was there. I leaned into my den that held all her clues. Empty. I kicked the bathroom door open and pulled the shower curtain back in one dramatic pull. Nothing.

Her being there and then not—it all made me feel so mixed, both relieved and disappointed. I grabbed a notepad and a pen and then sat down at the orange dining room table, jotting down everything she'd said. This was real. This had happened. I knew in the morning I wouldn't believe it. I knew days later my certainty would fade. But right at that moment, I would have bet my life on it. I climbed back into bed. The next thing I knew, my alarm was blaring. I saw the notepad on my nightstand and her five-sentence message to me. *Don't cover up the story. Don't cover up the story. Thấy ghét quá trời. Má nhớ con. Đừng quên.*

I read her message over and over again. There had been so many times I stopped searching because of my own self-doubt or the stinging comments from family. But Má coming last night, her message—it couldn't be any clearer. She wanted everyone else to know her story, our story. She gave her blessing. This was the permission I had been seeking. And now that it had been granted, I had the green light to give it my all. With just a mere two weeks until showtime and wind in my sails, I invited every single person I knew in Seattle to come. I spent my commute time listening to recordings of myself rereading the script over and over again to memorize the words. It was time to answer Ben's question.

My second show began with me handing out raisins with a pair of chopsticks to every guest in the narrow fifty-seat venue at 18th & Union. I instructed them to put the raisin in their mouths but not to chew. Squeezing through every aisle, I touched everyone's knees with my own. I bantered with my friends and made small talk with strangers. When I was done handing out raisins, I jogged back down the stairs of the black-box theater and pressed Play on an old, bulky cassette player. The song "Mười Năm Tình Cũ," the song Ba used to sing on karaoke Sundays, began. I took my seat on a chair at center stage and stared back at the audience. After a long, awkward thirty seconds, I started talking about the nature of mind and memory. Thoughts could become obsessive, incessant, and all-encompassing, perhaps like what they were feeling, wondering why the hell they had a raisin in their mouths. I let them chew it and started sharing everything I had learned: the lotto tickets, her bloody feet, her dream to eat meat every day.

Then I let them into the most intimate thoughts I had about Má. I recited the hundred questions I would ask her if she were still alive.

I've always wondered what it would be like if I could talk to my mom again, and not like a child-to-parent kind of conversation but the kind where you can see your parent as an equal human being. If I had a chance to ask her, I would ask:

1. *What do you think about all day?*
2. *Where are you now?*

3. *Are you ever near me or helping me?*

4. *How would I know for sure?*

Or I would ask her:

5. *That day when we were driving home on the Bay Bridge, why did you get out of the car and walk home?*

6. *What were you guys fighting about that got you so mad you walked on the freeway?*

7. *How did you get home that day?*

8. *Are you mad that Ba remarried, or are you happy for him?*

Or:

9. *Why plastic surgery?*

10. *What was the defining moment when you decided to get breast implants?*

11. *What did they feel like?*

12. *What did the aunts and Grandma think?*

13. *Did you feel beautiful enough for Ba?*

14. *Before or after the implants?*

I have to ask:

15. *What did you love about me?*

16. *Do you think I'll make it as a performer?*

17. *Did I disappoint you?*

18. *What's your advice for living life?*

And I'd definitely ask:

19. *Did you watch me sleep with all those men who weren't important to me?*

20. *Does it make you feel sad when I hate my body too?*

21. *Have you performed any miracles for us?*

22. *If so, which ones?*

23. *How does a spirit develop powers in the afterlife?*

24. *Are there exercises you do on a daily basis like Patrick Swayze did with the penny in the movie* Ghost?

25. *What was it about Dr. X's ad in the Vietnamese weekly that drew you to him?*

26. *Can you have his family open up to me?*

27. *How was I as a fetus?*

28. *What was I like when I was a toddler?*

29. *How can I summon you?*

30. *Could you tell me all of our happy moments together that I was too young to remember?*

31. *When will I see you again?*

32. *What do you smell like now?*

33. *When you went into the coma, could you see us in the hospital watching you, or were you already too far gone?*

34. *When I was three, I had a fever for ten days and almost died. Did you make a deal with the devil to bring me back?*

35. *What did you want to reincarnate into?*

36. *What did you reincarnate into?*

37. *When the white ladies say they can feel you in the room, are they telling the truth?*

38. *If so, how come I can't feel you?*

39. *What do you think of my husband, Marvin?*

40. *How much money will I make in my life?*

41. *Do you think the left-hand method to predict the number of kids you're going to have is accurate?*

42. *In other words, will I have three kids?*

43. *Be honest, who is your favorite child?*

44. *What is your biggest regret in life?*

45. *It's the year of the dog, so it's your year. Do they do anything special for you wherever you are?*

46. *Before you were born, did you make a choice to die young so all of the kids could develop grit?*

47. *So dying the way you did, was that part of your destiny, or do you wish it turned out different?*

Okay, be real with me:

48. *Should I become a vegetarian?*

49. *Do you think marijuana is sinful or natural?*

50. *Are you judging me when I eat edibles?*

51. *What should I be when I grow up?*

52. *Should I run my own start-up?*

53. *Are we all interconnected, and if so, do I interact with you all the time?*

54. *So when I order a cup of hot chocolate or when I ignore the same people who ask for money in front of my apartment every day, is that you?*

55. *How can we achieve world peace?*

56. *What makes you laugh?*

57. *What makes you cry?*

58. *What makes you smile?*

59. *When can you hold me again?*

60. *What is time?*

61. *Is it linear or just conceptual?*

62. *Seriously, are we in a simulation?*

63. *Have you ever met the Buddha, and if so, does he have a sense of humor?*

64. *He does, right?*

65. *Sometimes I cry when I'm really sad or really happy. When that happens, are you there with me?*

Má the general in a stylish pink jumper, standing on a tall rock in white heels.

From 1981 to 1983, Má and Ba (*standing*) and Kang and Hang (*seated*) hustled goods at the Pulau Bidong refugee camp while they awaited their asylum status.

Má (*front and center*) proudly displaying her graduation certificate from beauty school as a hair stylist. Two years later, she'd call it quits because she realized the money was in nails.

Entrepreneurial Ba, at 36, with his weed trimmer, gardening truck, and our home phone number spray-painted on plywood. (Tom Lieu)

Má (*left*), my aunt Tùa Cô (*center*), and Ba (*right*) lighting incense before we feast. I'm in Ba's arms eyeing the roast pork, bánh hỏi, and persimmons while Wendy looks away.

Me and Má cutting cake at our nail salon grand opening. The table is filled with delicious Vietnamese food, including a vat of fish sauce bigger than my head.

The grand opening of my namesake salon, Susan's Nail Salon, in Albany, California, 1989.

Strong matriarchs Bà Ngoại (*left*) and Má wearing their finest clothing, honoring ancestors with a giant pig in a Buddhist temple in Sóc Trăng, Vietnam.

Dì Phương (*left*) was a stand-in for Má during every escape attempt. The sister duo strikes a pose during Má's first visit back to Vietnam since fleeing.

My Vietnamese immigrant family in the early '90s, when big perm was in. *From left:* Hang, Kang, Wendy, Lầu Ý (Ba's aunt), me, Má, and Ba.

A rare moment when Ba and Má were not working, sitting on a pedicure chair at our second salon, Today's Nails, in Santa Rosa, California, 1995.

My family celebrating Kang's nineteenth birthday and my parents' twentieth wedding anniversary. Within one year, Má would pass away from her botched plastic surgery.

Me (*left, at 16*) and Wendy (*center, 19*), launching Socola Chocolatier in front of our nail salon at the Santa Rosa farmer's market in 2001. Ba (*right*) ziptied my hand-painted sign to a metal frame for our big debut.

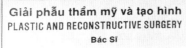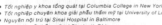

The plastic surgery advertisement Má saw in *Mõ Báo Magazine*, 1996. (The Southeast Asian Archive at UC Irvine)

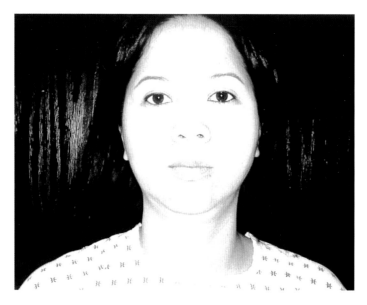

My mother's last photo, taken at her medical consult two days before her plastic surgery. I uncovered this photo and others while digging through old depositions.

My father and stepmother (*left*) giving Marvin and me (*right*) marriage advice during the tea ceremony at our very supernatural wedding. Moments later, thunder would clap and we'd all rush into the venue and away from the torrential downpour.

Me and Marvin at the summit of Mount Whitney, after a harrowing twenty-three-hour rock climb, 2019. I didn't know it then, but I was pregnant.

During my sequel *Over 140 LBS*, I slow dance, holding three generations close to my heart—ACT Theatre, Seattle, Washington, 2020. (Jenny Crooks)

Kang and Wendy having a good time at my sequel's postshow discussion, one of the few times we could talk about our late mother. (Jenny Crooks)

During Art's first Tết, I dressed him in an áo dài and introduced him to incense, lucky money, and his late Bà Ngoại.

66. *Are you trying to communicate with me ever?*

67. *How would I know for sure?*

68. *When you were a little girl, what did you want to be when you grew up?*

69. *And what attracted you to Ba?*

70. *When you were trying to escape Việt Nam, what were the first five attempts like?*

71. *And the sixth time, when you four made it to Malaysia?*

72. *What did you think you would become in the U.S.?*

73. *When I see yellow roses, I think of you. Do you think of me?*

74. *What is your favorite Vietnamese dish?*

75. *Knowing everything you know now, what are you most afraid of?*

76. *The last day I saw you, I yelled at you and told you I hated you. Will you forgive me?*

77. *How am I like you?*

78. *If I were to change one quality about myself, what should it be?*

79. *How should I take care of my skin?*

80. *Is Ba happy?*

81. *Is there anything more the kids can do for you to be happy?*

82. *For Ba to be happy?*

83. *If you could travel anywhere in the world, where would you go?*

84. *Can you fly?*

85. *Can you eat all the fries and chips you want without the calories?*

86. *What is your favorite American movie?*

87. *Are you a coffee person or a tea person?*

88. *When did your insecurity with your body begin?*

89. *Any advice on giving birth?*

90. *Who was your most difficult child?*

91. *Which grandson makes you smile the most?*

92. *Knowing everything you know now, would you do it all over again?*

93. *Did you ever want to divorce Ba?*

94. *Who else would you have wanted to be with?*

95. *Did you have any secret lovers?*

96. *What did you hate about Ba?*

97. *What did you love about Ba?*

98. *In past lives, what was your relationship to me?*

99. *Who should I stop trusting?*

100. *Do you believe in miracles?*

As the stage went dark, I felt a lightness come down from above my head, through my body, out my sacrum, and through to the audience. All the tension I had been carrying in my neck and shoulders dropped away. Since Má's visitation, I felt a new energy at rehearsal that transcended to that night's performance. I was now a believer in miracles because it happened at this show. She was in my room that night, and now she was onstage with me. I wasn't alone in my quest anymore. Má was now at my back, pushing me forward, coming along for the ride. Where it would take us, I wasn't sure. I was just grateful we got to spend some time together.

140 LBS

With all the stories I gathered in Việt Nam, I had a clearer picture of who Má was before I was born. Now I wanted to revisit who she was before we lost her. I became convinced that if I embodied her by following the same exact schedule on her last day, she would come through with another message. Detectives always went back to the scene of the crime. Why shouldn't I?

The plan was to fly from Seattle to San Francisco, and my even wilder idea was to reach out to the doctor's family. Maybe his family could give me the closure my family couldn't. When Má died, their lives changed too because the surgeon's license was suspended for a few years. Our world had been turned upside down. Hadn't theirs been too? If I got that confirmation, maybe it would help me forgive the man. Now that he had passed away, all I could do was reach out to his children.

Triangulating information from the doctor's obituary with the internet, I pieced together his family. He had five kids, and one of his sons, Ted, was a marriage and family therapist. Out of all of them, he probably would be the most interested in reconciliation. I made a spreadsheet of all the places where he worked and lived. Then I called his employers. Some had never heard of him. Some said he'd left years earlier. I narrowed my list down to three addresses, one of them just a mile away from Kang's house. My letter described the journey I had been on to search for my mother. I wanted to talk to him as part of my healing process and hoped to hear from him soon. I stuffed my correspondence in beautiful envelopes with dried flowers on them and addressed it in my best handwriting. Before I could rationalize my way out of this, I opened the apartment mailbox chute, slipped in the letters, and slammed the box shut.

All the letters were marked RETURNED TO SENDER except for one. Two weeks after I'd sealed the envelopes, I got a phone call. I was out celebrating my birthday with my siblings in Whistler for the weekend. Then I saw a name pop up on my phone: Tara Moglen. The doctor's daughter. Holy shit. HOLY SHIT. Ted must have given the letter to his baby sister. She ended up becoming a nurse just like her mother, who worked at her husband's plastic surgery clinic, but didn't operate on Má. I couldn't wait to talk to Tara, but a loud pub was totally the wrong place to take the call. I wanted our first conversation to be perfect. Plus, I hadn't even written down my list of questions yet. I let her call go to voice mail and then immediately listened.

Hey, Susan, it's Tara Moglen. I got your letter, and I'm really, really, really sorry about what happened to your family. And I think out of everyone in my family, you should talk to me the most. I'll explain when we talk. Okay, looking forward to talking to you soon. Bye.

I replayed her voice mail, trying to decipher every line. Why should I talk to her out of everyone in her family? What did she know or experience that was different from her siblings? She and I were both the youngest in our families and almost the same age when Má died. More than twenty years later, she remembered. My mom's life mattered.

I returned to my family to tell them the good news, but no one seemed interested.

"Can't you just deal with this in therapy?" commented my sister-in-law. I gave a light laugh and returned to eating poutine. Both of her parents were still alive. I couldn't expect her to understand. My siblings, though, left me disheartened. I was just the little sister who couldn't let things go, so I stopped talking about it with them and watched the game like a hollowed-out zombie.

On the drive home to Seattle, I texted Tara back some times I could chat. A few days passed. Nothing. I called and left a friendly voice mail.

"Hi. It's Susan, and it's such a relief to hear your voice. I can't wait to talk. Just give me a call back anytime." Nothing. Crap. Did she get scared? Did her brothers convince her not to talk to me? I called again.

"Hi, Tara. It's been a few days. My weekend is totally free. Just give me a ring." Still no answer. I waited a few more days and called again. I kept kicking myself for not picking up the phone when she'd had the courage to reach out. I gave it a few more days and tried not to sound desperate when I tried her again.

"Hi, Tara. I don't mean to bother you if you don't want to talk, but I'm going to be in San Francisco next week, and it would be so great to meet up for coffee. Just let me know." No answer. I decided that if she wouldn't communicate by phone, then I would try what worked in the past—snail mail. I hoped this could change her mind. Maybe her brothers talked her out of it. I sent off a letter but never heard back.

Then the trail went cold. I kept kicking myself; I should have picked up her call the first time. I was waiting for some kind of perfect moment, and now I'd lost my chance. What if Tara was the missing link? Worried, I called up the law firm who worked with my family and spoke with my old contact Doris. She told me I had to respect that family's privacy. But that just didn't feel fair. They had never respected our family, they never paid us a dime. I told Doris about the plays I was writing and that I was looking for more information.

After a long pause, she said she could give me access to all the depositions related to our case. California law firms were mandated to store documents for seven years, and then they could shred them. Somehow, twenty years later, all the depositions were still in their vaults. If I wanted, I could have all the transcribed accounts from the doctor, my family, and even myself. I still remember the day I was deposed in the San Francisco high-rise. The table had so many plastic water bottles on it and packaged chocolate chip cookies. I don't even remember what I said, but now I had a chance to open up the past with primary sources that hadn't been looked at for two decades.

When I received a link to the trove of documents in the cloud, I didn't open it. This all became too much for me. What if I learned something about Má that would taint her saintlike reputation? Whatever I read, I could not undo knowing. I could be satisfied with everything I'd learned up until this point, or I could keep on going. Ignorance could be bliss, or it could be devastating. There was only one way to find out, but I still felt apprehensive. All at once, I felt so isolated and alone, but also on the precipice of finally getting what I wanted.

Then one evening when Marvin was out, I got the courage. I opened my weed jar, made an intention, and then popped the gummy in my mouth. I went to the bathroom mirror and hyped myself up. *I deserve to know. This is what I wanted.* I paced around the apartment and then returned to the dining room table between the kitchen and the couch. I opened up my laptop. I had a yellow legal notepad, a bottle of IPA, and a few pens ready. When I opened the digital folder, I found more than a dozen depositions from my family, the doctor, and his staff that mostly took place in 1998, two years after Má's death. There were thousands of pages to comb through—who knew what I would find or how long it would take.

I opened the file for Tina, the nurse who'd assisted Dr. Moglen during Má's surgery. Tina was originally supposed to stay for extended observation of Má after the surgery. But when Má was rushed to Mount Zion hospital, Tina was left with Ba at the clinic. Dr. Moglen offered to put him up in a hotel, but Ba didn't want that. Dr. Moglen asked Tina to stay with him that night, making him as comfortable as possible. Tina offered Ba several options to sleep, and he eerily chose the bed in the recovery room, the same one Má would have stayed in if everything had gone fine. Dr. Moglen opted for the couch in his office. Tina never slept, roaming around the clinic looking for ways to help Ba. She encouraged him to lie down, trying to comfort him by giving him more blankets. When no one could sleep, the three of them made a late-night trip to the hospital to visit Má.

Tina thought Má would absolutely recover. She spoke with the emergency room nurses, who said Má was responding. She was doing okay, so they took her up to the critical care unit for observation. But when Má's tummy tuck incision was being closed up at the hospital, it was noted she was visibly tearing and grimacing.

For years, I had thought she had lost oxygen to her brain and then gone immediately into a coma before arriving at the hospital. But now I could see Má was completely conscious as her oxygen levels dropped during her tummy tuck. The fear she must have had getting wheeled past Ba in the plastic surgery clinic waiting room, riding in an ambulance and panicking because she knew something had gone terribly wrong. Crying to the nurses, in pain, fighting. When they stapled her stomach back at the three, six, and nine o'clock positions, she was awake. No one, not even the medical team at the hospital, thought she would die.

And if Ba stayed in the recovery room that night, that meant all of us siblings didn't visit Má on the day of her surgery like I used to think. We must have visited her the next day, which was a Friday, because I remember Hang expecting me to come home earlier from school. I read a medical board verdict, and it said she was in a coma for a total of five days before she was pronounced dead. I could have sworn it was two weeks. I checked all the dates and then calculated my age. I always thought I was twelve at the time of her death, but I was actually eleven. What else had I gotten wrong all these years? I wished my family could be uncovering all of this with me. I didn't want to do this alone, but if I didn't, no one ever would.

I opened Dr. Moglen's deposition and began to read. He completed general surgical training at UCSF Mount Zion. In 1971, he did a fellowship in hand surgery at Stanford and then spent part of the year as a volunteer through the American Medical Association in Việt Nam. In Buôn Ma Thuột, the capital of Đắk Lắk province, he served as the only civilian surgeon during the Tết Offensive, taking care of the civilian casualties caught in cross fire, for ten dollars a day. He was motivated to fine-tune his training since surgery was "born on the battlefield," he said. He was extremely proud of that experience, since he saved more lives during that period of time than he had in the rest of his medical practice.

When Dr. Moglen operated on my mom, he didn't have privileges at Mount Zion hospital, because he didn't carry liability insurance. He had been banned for the five years leading up to my mother's surgery. The last carrier to insure him was an offshore company that turned out to be a scam. He never attempted to secure liability insurance again, because the $80,000 cost was beyond his "financial means."

When he performed surgery on Má in 1996, over 30 percent of his patient population was Vietnamese. It all began in 1991, when he began advertising in the Vietnamese press. He placed an ad in the Vietnamese language edition of the San Francisco *Tenderloin Times*, offering to do free reconstructive surgery for any Vietnamese person who was injured during the Việt Nam War. The *San Francisco Chronicle* took notice and then wrote a feature on him, producing a certain amount of "goodwill," he called it. In his deposition, he admitted that he never performed a single free surgery, because nobody ever requested it. He also attributed his significant Vietnamese clientele to his advertisements in the Vietnamese magazines. Bingo. I knew exactly the publication. The logo had a suspension bridge that formed an *M* and a rising sun that made a big *O*. It was called *Báo Mõ* magazine, known as Northern Bay Area's largest Vietnamese weekly magazine, the same one Dì Phương used to read when she was on the toilet in our Jack-and-Jill bathroom. We used to pick up our copy from the nail salon supply store every Sunday.

Prior to Má's surgery, Dr. Moglen was a defendant in nineteen cases and had been placed on probation four years before operating on Má. He was not limited in any way in the types of procedures he could perform or the type of anesthesia he could administer, nor was he required to provide any particular information to prospective patients. Two years *after* Má's death, he was still on probation and still operating without consequence awaiting the medical board verdict from Má's case. What was the point of the medical board even putting a doctor on probation? Why were they so adamant to protect the doctor over the patient? Whenever I told people about what happened to Má, they would ask if her surgery was in Việt Nam. I would tell them San Francisco, 1996, and every time, their jaws dropped. The American health care system was worse than what they assumed of a country in the Global South.

I read on. Dr. Moglen remembered that Má was a very nervous, anxious patient. During the surgery consultation and on the day of surgery, she was very apprehensive. He found her nervousness unusual "to a degree," so he gave her ten milligrams of Valium to relax her. I jotted this detail down on my notepad. This was not the mother I knew. In my eleven short years, I would have never described her as nervous. So why was she on this day? Did she know something was up? Was her intuition telling her to get out? Or was she afraid that something might happen to her if she didn't go through with the surgery? For a woman who had been fearless her whole life, why was it the very surgery she signed up for that caused her trepidation? It's as if she already knew.

Then Dr. Moglen proceeded to claim the privilege against self-incrimination for every subsequent question: who monitored Má's vital signs, anything related to her procedure, when she was pronounced dead, the anesthesia he discussed with her prior to her surgery, any risks of the procedure, any concerns she expressed, the drugs she was given, the date he first met her, whether or not she spoke English well enough that he felt he could communicate directly with her in the absence of an interpreter, whether or not he made an incision on her, whether or not he asked anyone to call the paramedics, whether or not he called a code, whether or not he performed CPR on her before the paramedics arrived.

However, he did admit to a few things. He was the one who attempted to intubate Má. At one point, a Mount Zion physician had informed him that Má's condition was irreversible and terminal. And it was someone other than himself who communicated this to Ba. His deposition brought up more questions than answers. Why would someone continue to practice if he was uninsured and hurting people around him? Why would his staff work for him?

At the end of his deposition were a series of scanned forms that Má filled out during her consultation appointment on September 24, 1996. I touched her handwriting on my computer screen, my chest tightening. Under "How were you referred to this office?" she'd circled "Magazine."

With the question "What features do you want changed?" she'd circled "Abdomen" under "Lipo-Suction." And under previous operations performed, she'd written, "Implant Breast (2 yrs)." I had to look away. This meant Má wasn't new to plastic surgery at all. She had been chasing an ideal longer than I'd thought. I started to pace the apartment, shaking my head in disbelief. I couldn't unread it now. Why didn't anyone tell me? I lay on the couch, and then a strange memory from childhood came racing back. I put two and two together. It must have been the first time Má had gotten plastic surgery.

When I was seven, there was a weekend when all of us kids were home alone. Kang, the oldest at sixteen, was on point to make us "chunky pasta," a red sauce spaghetti with ground beef, zucchini, mushrooms, onions, and bell peppers. The secret ingredient was a teaspoon of sugar our Filipino neighbors swore by. We repurposed our phở noodle soup bowls to eat Italian that night, swapping our chopsticks for forks. My brothers forced my sister and me to watch Freddy Krueger in *A Nightmare on Elm Street*. I was on the couch, terrified, a red film around my lips.

An hour before midnight, when the movie was almost over, I heard the dead bolt click and saw the front door swing open. I for sure thought Freddy was there to kill us all. The silhouette of two large cloaked figures appeared, their hoods covering their faces, their jackets dripping wet. I clutched two decorative pillows against my body. A hallway light flickered on, and then I saw Ba taking off his jacket, shaking the rain off his hair. I ran up to them and reached for Má.

"Stop! Don't touch her," ordered Ba. He never raised his voice like that, so I knew something was off. Má was wearing dark sunglasses and just standing there, not responding, like a lifeless Frankenstein's monster. She didn't say a word—very not like her. It was like she didn't even see me. I again reached up to her face, but Ba swatted me away. Má's body creaked as she moved robotically up the stairs. I watched her clutch the handrail like an old woman, mechanically lifting each foot slowly. Ba followed behind and closed their bedroom door. In bed, I wrapped my leg around my floral body pillow and held on tightly. I was both afraid of my mother and for her. The next day, no one talked about it and then it was forgotten, like so many things we're not allowed to talk about.

I covered myself up with a blanket on the couch and kept replaying little Susan wanting to touch Má and her haunting walk upstairs as a new form. It didn't matter how much praise she got from others for being the family heroine. She was striving for an ideal that she'd thought only plastic surgery could fix. She couldn't get the look she wanted naturally, so she paid to have it done. I was heartbroken. If I met her on the street, I probably wouldn't want to be friends with her.

What she didn't realize was how her fixation on perfection would cut up her body, our family, and her future.

I continued reading the depositions. Then came a series of questions about her previous health conditions. "Do you have frequent head-aches, asthma, shortness of breath, joint or muscular trouble, chronic skin conditions?" At first, she circled "No" on the first five symptoms and then drew a line straight through the next twelve questions.

On the next page, she went back to circling "No." But then she circled "No" when she should have circled "Yes." "Do you under-stand that no surgeon can guarantee a good result in any operation that he performs?" No. "Do you understand that anyone undergoing any operation, no matter how minor, must assume certain risk?" No. Even though Dr. Moglen employed a Vietnamese translator, I won-dered how much support Má had when she filled out these forms—or if anyone reviewed them at all. The form was dated September 24, 1996, and signed by Jennifer Hà. At the salon, she insisted on all her customers calling her Jen-ni-fuh, even though I remembered her sig-nature as Phường Hà, because she had me forge them on school per-mission slips (she was too busy to do it herself). I traced this foreign signature on my computer screen. When did Má start identifying as this woman with an American name, so much so that she signed legal documents with it?

On the next page was an arbitration agreement that said in all uppercase letters:

BY SIGNING THIS CONTRACT, YOU ARE AGREEING TO HAVE ANY ISSUE OF MEDICAL MALPRACTICE DECIDED BY NEUTRAL ARBI-TRATION AND YOU ARE GIVING UP YOUR RIGHT TO A JURY OR COURT TRIAL.

I bet no one ever thought these liability release agreements would ever matter. In her case, it upended our lives. Without Má, Ba was tee-tering on the verge of financial and emotional bankruptcy for years.

A consult letter from Dr. Moglen describing her as a "well developed well nourished Asian female 5'1" and 110 pounds." His description of her made me want to vomit in my mouth. He recommended all the surgeries she requested: "an abdominoplasty with plication of the fascia of the rectus abdominus and liposuction of the flanks as well as submentum and conservative narrowing of the nostrils." When plastic surgery was written in scientific medical speak, it didn't appear dangerous at all. It must have been easy for Má to assume that if a doctor was in business in San Francisco, then everything should be fine. In 1996, Má did not have the awareness or capability to check his probation status. Why would she? He was a white, educated doctor who did his training at a big, reputable hospital. Legally, he didn't have to tell her anything about his problematic record. And his privilege as a white doctor allowed him to exploit unassuming Vietnamese refugees without any penalty for years.

I saw the receipt for her three procedures totaling $5,500. She had to do more than three hundred acrylic fills to get that kind of money. Based on our tax returns at the time, that was almost a fifth of our household income. Even after the botched surgery, the clinic never refunded us the money. Those bastards held on to it. Má thought she was going in for a routine operation. And instead of Má, all I had was an invoice.

Three years after Má died, Dr. Moglen's case was tried by the Medical Board of California. They took away his license for a few years. To make money, he tried selling medical equipment and even shoveled horse manure as a stable hand, but eventually, he started practicing again. He continued operating on unsuspecting women's bodies while on probation for another decade. The members on the medical board were mostly physicians who had strong ties to insurance lobbyists. And in the state of California, any case related to malpractice had a cap of $250,000, instituted since the 1970s. A life would never be worth more than that, no matter how high the damages, how gross the negligence. And because of that, lawyers weren't motivated to take on these cases. And because of that, the bad apple doctors never had to clean up their acts. The medical board didn't give a damn about patients like my mother.

I began to realize how racist and classist the system was, built to uphold the people in power. Low-income, less-educated people of color seemed more vulnerable to getting screwed. I just didn't think we would be the victims and that it would happen to us. But it did.

I read on. Buried deep in the medical board verdict was a very peculiar sentence describing Má. She was "140 pounds, though her reported weight in respondent's consultation notes was only 110 pounds." I reread the sentence three times just to be sure.

I never knew my body was also her body. I was also 140 pounds. Má was so insecure about her weight that she'd lied about it on her intake form. She wrote down the weight she wanted to be rather than the one she was. Má was going to become 110 pounds again, and by any means necessary.

A part of me wanted to dismiss her as shallow for wanting this. But I couldn't because I would be a hypocrite. Of course I sucked in my belly whenever someone took my picture. Of course I squeezed my excess belly fat and wished I could just trim it all off and start over again. I was repulsed by the reflection of my side profile in a shop window. I wished I could have someone else's body. But I had to have compassion for her. My pain was also her pain.

I continued to scroll through the rest of Dr. Moglen's deposition, and then my index finger stopped midair. Má was staring at me straight in the face. It was a huge photo of her wearing a medical gown, shot from her shoulders upward. The bright flash overexposed her face. The hairs on my arm turned prickly. I wasn't sure if she was going to pop out of my hallway closet next.

Her facial expression was neutral, her eyebrows nicely waxed, and her long hair tucked behind her ears. Her eyes were darkened with permanent eyeliner, an early '90s trend. The numbers in the bottom corner of the photo were "9 26 96." This photo was taken one day before her surgery. This was the last photo she ever took.

There were more pictures. Shots of her looking upward with the nostrils she wanted to narrow in center view. The left side of her face with a close-up of the double chin she wanted to reduce. The right side of her face looked like a spitting image of Wendy, which made me do a double take. The next photo was of her stomach area with the lower half of her breasts showing. The tummy she wanted to tuck. Faint stretch marks, permanent scars from giving birth, outlined the contours of her love handles. Honestly, she wasn't even fat.

The picture was cropped in a way where I could see her pubic hair at the top of her vulva. I moved in close, my nose an inch away from the computer screen. I never thought I would be gazing at my mom's pubes, but there they were, and they looked as black as mine with the same amount of curl.

I had been looking for Má everywhere, but I didn't expect to find her like this, literally face-to-face with me in Dr. Moglen's folder. Maybe this was a sign. All I felt were chills going up and down my spine. She was so "unusually nervous" that he gave her Valium to calm down. She knew something was wrong. The woman who was a queen in her nail salon didn't listen to her intuition. Because of that, she walked into his clinic and never walked out. Why was her self-worth so tied up with her body? But how could I blame her? Didn't I feel the same way about my own? Was anyone free from the self-hatred of our bodies?

I slammed my laptop shut feeling a nervousness rise in me. I'd had enough for one night. What if something weird and sci-fi happened, like her spirit in the picture switched places with my soul? What if I was mute and forever stuck in a JPEG, in a file, tucked in a folder? I was starting to freak out. As much as I wanted to call my family, I knew I couldn't. They wouldn't have sympathy. They would say I'd brought this all upon myself.

My first call was to Marvin, but he didn't pick up because he was in a mountaineering course. My director didn't pick up either. But my girlfriend Sinae answered, and she said she would come right over. When I hung up, the apartment was too quiet and the laptop was beckoning me. One moment it was a genie lamp giving me what I had always wanted, and now it was a mysterious way into another dimension.

I tried to distract myself by cooking the chunky pasta dish my siblings used to make when we were kids and home alone. As the garlic started to sizzle, I kept looking back at my laptop on the dining table. Was Má lonely in there? Come on, how could I be afraid of my own mother? I came out of her body. Plus, she seemed harmless enough. I had a change of heart. I brought the laptop to the kitchen counter and propped her face up by the stove, angling her toward me so she could watch me cook. There. Maybe it was time we got to know each other as adults.

Smoke Signals

The night I arrived in the Bay Area to begin retracing Má's last day, Kang gave me a dusty plastic-wrapped gold container while I unpacked my luggage in his guest room.

"It's Má's incense holder. From the old house," he said.

I carefully unwrapped the vessel, treating the incense ashes as if they had come from her body. I wiped the dust off the exterior with a wet paper towel, and then I saw a small piece of paper taped on the back. A date written in Vietnamese script. It wasn't her birthday or the day she died. It must have been the day she died on the lunar calendar. I polished the incense holder like it was her urn, my new companion for my adventure.

In the early morning, I woke up and drove to my childhood home in Rincon Valley, a neighborhood in Santa Rosa. When I pulled up to the tan two-story off Montecito Boulevard, I saw the rose trees were still there, neatly manicured just like Ba kept them. The yellow one was in bloom, Má's favorite. When the car clock blinked 6:00 a.m., Má's last day began. This was the same time eleven-year-old Susan was startled by Má in the kitchen. I got out of the car, lit an incense stick, and tried to have a more positive conversation with Má than our last argument that had regrettably played on loop my entire life.

Hey, Má, it's me. Look, I don't want to be chasing you forever. Could you just show me what I'm supposed to see? I want a sign, but make it obvious. It's too easy to read into things. I want to be sure that it's from you.

I put the stick on the edge of the lawn and bowed three times at the foot of my old driveway. I took a few deep inhales from some roses and hurried back into the car. I didn't want to creep out the current homeowners.

The next stop was the plastic surgery clinic an hour away in San Francisco. The clinic wasn't open yet, but it was located in a medical building, and the front door was unlocked. I took the elevator to the second floor and walked down a long, narrow hallway to suite 212. It was the last door on the left. I hovered my hand over the door handle. This is what Má touched on her last day. I wrapped my hand over it and held it tightly, as if I could transfer her touch back into me. The time was 7:37 a.m. At this point, Má would have been waiting to check in, and Ba would have just parked the car. She would have insisted he go back to work at the salon, but he would have gone into the café across the street to buy a doughnut and a coffee. Then Ba would have found a seat in the waiting room.

The hours on the door said the current tenant would open at 9:00 a.m. I called the office number and was rerouted to an answering service to see if I could come tour the office when they opened. The operator said she would relay the message. I camped out in front of the door and watched the hallway activity. A woman in scrubs walked into another office. I had an impulse to follow her, so I did. I found a receptionist and explained my situation. I wanted to know if she ever knew Dr. Moglen or if she remembered the day Má was wheeled out in a gurney. The receptionist hollered to another nurse, and after much chatter, she was sympathetic. It was years ago, and no one else worked in the building then. I thanked them and returned to my spot in front of the clinic door, prepared to wait another hour.

Then I got a phone call from Linh, whose name I recognized from the depositions. It was the Vietnamese translator who used to work at the plastic surgeon's office. She had signed forms that Má had signed, verifying that Má was given translation services. I had sent a physical letter in the mail and left two voice mails on numbers I'd found online. Here she was answering my cry for help.

I picked up the phone. Since she was about my mother's age, I addressed her as Cô Linh and told her about my quest and the shows I was putting on. We wept together. She said she wanted to help, so I started lobbing over questions. She divulged with great detail. She'd met Dr. Leslie Moglen when she was working as a translator in the local court system. He was there defending himself. She helped him create the ads in the Vietnamese weekly magazine and served as a translator with all his Vietnamese clients.

She said the number one customers for plastic surgery were middle-aged nail salon workers who were afraid their husbands would cheat on them with someone younger and sexier than they were, which I found fascinating and demoralizing. They wanted to feel desirable and confident, so they turned to plastic surgery. When they returned to their nail salon, they would get praised by their coworkers, causing more manicurists to flock to the clinic. It would start with tightening some loose skin around an eye, and then she would come back for a high-bridged nose and liposuction. It became an addiction because there was always another thing to fix.

I found her account utterly disturbing. These women were the heroines who beat the odds by boat, juggled homelife, and took care of their family at home and abroad, working themselves to the bone. And yet they found it necessary to save money for these procedures even when finances were already tight. These women were playing a game they would never win. Cô Linh thought most of them were pretty and didn't need any work done at all.

And after my mother died, Cô Linh was beside herself. She eventually quit. Now when Vietnamese people ask her if they should do plastic surgery or not, she tells them the cautionary tale of what happened to Má. Cô Linh was sympathetic and wanted to help any way she could, sending a warm sensation up and down my throat. Through my tears, I asked her to look through her archives for the ad Má probably saw. I wanted to see it. She agreed she would look and that she would come to my show one day. She reassured me that more people needed to know my family's story.

When we ended the call, I burst into tears. She was about Má's age, and talking to her helped me imagine what it would be like if I could interact with present-day Má. I wept because I was still grieving Má's death. I wept because women were still getting plastic surgery. But most importantly, I wept because I got approval from a living elder to keep going. I didn't realize how much I'd needed it until I'd received it.

Má was not forgotten, and Cô Linh, in her own way, was trying to make things right after all these years. To receive this call, on this day, was a good omen. Quite possibly a sign from Má that I was headed in the right direction.

I still had another thirty minutes to wait for the clinic staff to arrive, so I thought I would properly bless this moment by lighting incense and bowing three times. As my forehead touched the thin blue-gray carpet, I heard a high-pitched siren go off. I looked down at the smoking incense and up to the not-very-high popcorn ceiling. *Oh, shit. I set off the fire alarm!*

I grabbed Má's incense holder and sprinted to the elevator. The doors were so old they took a very long ten seconds to close. There was a brief jolt, and then it started to move down at a snail's pace. Incense smoke quickly filled the elevator, clouding my view of the buttons. Another thirty seconds passed just to go down one floor before the doors eked open. I booked it to my car across the street to drive away from the scene of the crime. I stomped the incense ember out, threw the stick on my car floor mat, and then slipped into the driver's seat. I looked up and saw my exit was blocked by a line of oncoming fire trucks. Two fire trucks parked in front of the building, and four firefighters ran in as new sirens squealed around the corner.

I slumped down below the car window, hoping they wouldn't ask me questions. I needed to make a run for it. I punched the next stop into my phone and then realized the hospital where the EMT took my mom was just one block away from the clinic. UCSF Mount Zion was in plain view in front of me. Estimating the response time from when I'd first lit the incense in the hallway to when the firefighters arrived, it had to have been three minutes, tops.

Má was without oxygen for fourteen minutes before the plastic surgeon made the 9-1-1 call. The human brain can go without oxygen for up to four minutes before permanent brain damage occurs. And when the paramedics came that day, they were able to resuscitate her right away. If the doctor had called when she first went code blue, she could have survived. He knew exactly what he was doing. I bet he wanted her to be fully incapacitated so the decision would have been easier for us to pull the plug. Then he wouldn't have been responsible for paying for a lifetime of twenty-four-hour care. Chó đẻ! *Son of a bitch!*

I snuck a look out my car window and saw more lights flashing. I closed my eyes and started to pray to Má.

Please help me. Get me out of here. I don't want to go to jail. Just tell me what to do.

All of a sudden, I felt a buzz from my phone and saw a new email come through. It was from Cindy Clifford, a gifted spirit medium and psychic, and Dì Phương's nail salon customer of twenty years. My aunt suggested I reach out to her on my trip back, but her waiting list was three months long. I reread the email again. Cindy had just had a cancellation and could see me first thing the next morning. I was planning for my final stop to be Má's grave, but now it seemed like Má had other plans. She was ready to talk.

The Psychic

All the spirit channelers I knew were robed Vietnamese monks in temples or elders in cramped apartments that smelled like mothballs. Psychic Cindy's meeting place was her home, a white mansion overlooking acres of lush sunbaked grapes. When her white-and-gold front door opened, a white suburban mom was excitedly waving to me. She dressed like she was stuck in the '90s with pressed high-waisted slacks, nude pantyhose as socks, and thick, chunky heels. Her hair had volume, floating two inches above her head like an aura. She escorted me through the foyer past the porcelain Dalmatian statues and oversize Renaissance paintings of angels. We entered her office, and she took her spot behind a bulky wooden executive desk bordered by eight hip-height baby angel statues. This place felt like *Scarface* for the spiritual seeker.

Cindy explained she had been a medium her whole life and had been doing it professionally for the past ten years. A few years earlier, Dì Phương was doing her nails, and Cindy requested she come over for a reading. Up until that point, Dì Phương didn't know that Cindy had a gift. My aunt was frightened but also intrigued, so she dragged Kang along. Cindy surprised them both when she said she could see

Bà Ngoại making Kang's favorite soup of canh gừng, the one that had pork, egg, ginger, and brandy. He didn't love phở the way he cherished that particular soup. That specific detail made them believers. But as I sat down and she began recording our session, I felt a little skeptical. How did I know she wasn't just going to regurgitate all the information she'd probably learned from her manicurist over almost two decades?

She started by telling me Bà Ngoại died from lung cancer even though she wasn't a smoker, which was true. Then she said I was a spitting image of my mother. My heart closed, and then I began to doubt her. Everyone always said Wendy looked like Má and I looked like Ba. Maybe she was just playing to my emotions. She went on to say Má died from surgery complications in an operating room. The person responsible didn't do due diligence on her allergies. They were irresponsible, and her soul crossed before her body left. All of it was true, but I could see my aunt telling her this story. I needed proof to trust her. I asked her to confirm my age when Má died. She said seventeen. No, but that was Hang's age at the time. She asked who was born in July. That was Wendy. Then she asked who was born in an "ember" month. November, that was Kang. Cindy clarified that Má was taking the time to acknowledge each of her children.

"We're not going to have a conversation like you and I would have," Cindy explained. "I will receive her messages, and you will validate them. In readings, you get the answers before I get the questions. It's through the energy field."

I tried to wrap my mind around this process. We only had sixty minutes, and this session wasn't cheap.

"You look just like her. You really do. Look in the mirror. You will see her in your eyes, you will see her in your smile."

I winced again. I had never considered I was like my mom. My rational mind told me she was manipulating me.

"Is there estrangement with your father?" she asked.

Now that was something my aunt wouldn't have disclosed. I rarely spoke to my aunt about Ba. Plus, that would be too shameful a topic to bring up to a customer.

"She said there's distance. She tries to heal and give you love and light around that because she doesn't want you to be sad because of her passing."

My dysfunctional relationship with Ba had always been a tender spot for me. But didn't everyone have daddy issues?

"Even though it was human error, it was her choice to have surgery. That was the cause for her transition."

For years, I had cursed the surgeon. But Má explaining it in this way showed how much agency she'd had in the whole ordeal. She was a victim, but she also wasn't a victim. And she'd used the word "transition," not "death," meaning she wasn't really gone. She was still here, just in a different form.

"She wants you to share your story with others. What you're doing now is important to her. It's important to her."

Her words helped me breathe a little easier. Hang's claim that I was exploiting our family story had been eating at me. I walked around with a tremendous amount of guilt and shame while trying to pursue this undeniable calling to perform. But now Má was giving me her explicit permission. Maybe I wasn't burdening everyone after all. I blew my nose. I didn't expect to come here for reassurance.

"It's part of your truth. You have to teach your lessons even though the outcome didn't come in your best favor, because you were denied your relationship with your mother. She lives in your heart, and she guides you always. She will always be that voice, that direction. She actually guided you to me. 'No, Susan will come to this reading,' she said. 'She will be here for this reading because I need to talk to her. I need to be a part of this.'" Cindy seamlessly transitioned between talking as herself and then taking on the direct words of Má.

I loved how Má was still giving orders from the other side. When she talked, people responded. Receiving the email from Cindy, the appointment being at a time I could make it, everything fell into place so Má could help me move forward. She was still a force to be reckoned with. Má went on to acknowledge her grandchildren and her siblings. For her, it was always family first.

But I still had a little doubt in my heart. I needed to ask one more question so I could know this woman was the real deal. "When my siblings were cleaning her tombstone for her birthday, did something unusual happen?" Cindy squinted as if she could see the cemetery.

"Was there a particle, something that I could hold in my hand?" she asked. "When they were cleaning the tombstone, was there a chip? Did something fall? I can pick something up."

Wendy had lit incense, and the stick broke off, burning her hand. I have probably lit hundreds of incense sticks and not once has that ever happened. Everything Cindy had said up until this point had been transformative for me. What else did I need her to say to help me believe? I didn't want to spend any more energy doubting. I wanted to use my time to be really present with Má.

Now Má was showing Cindy a roomful of gifts that had been left behind at her grave over the years.

"Pictures and energies from the grandchildren, things brothers have left as well." My ears perked up. I wondered what objects my brothers had left behind to her. I wished I could tune in to their private conversations with her.

"She says she communicates to you through birds, but not just every bird in the sky. One that would act out of the ordinary. That would hang longer. That would get closer to you, do you know what I mean? Hummingbirds, dragonflies, small birds, those things."

I always secretly believed flies were my mother. They would appear out of nowhere and hover over me, but maybe that's just what flies did. Cindy reassured me Má was at peace and with Bà Ngoại. Má came to all the birthdays and was at all my productions, but she had some advice for me.

"She says all the information is not there. Does that make sense to you? What would the audience need to understand because of the different perspectives?" This all made sense. I had planned on doing a third and fourth iteration. Retracing Má's last day was for the third show. Unpacking my relationship with my living family would be the fourth.

"She wants me to come back to the first and second installment. Why does she keep showing me the second one?" she asked. Cindy was puzzled.

"Because the second one was all about her and my relationship to her," I said.

"Ooooh! She loves that one!" Cindy gushed, having a grand time with Má. "Ooooh, I love that one! The second installment. She has been guiding you. Because of your memory, you try really hard to remember, the conversations, and your experience, and she tries to help you with that, honey. She does. She does."

I grabbed more tissues. Why could I remember only the times when I'd yelled at her or she'd yelled at me? I wanted to remember that there were good times. But I needed my family to help me remember.

"You are her legacy. You are her daughter. You are the baby, and that's what she says. She will comfort you, nurture you; she will guide you on that. What she holds closest to her heart, and her connection to you, is that second installment—your relationship with her. Because, honey, as you move forward on your path, you will continue to create this legacy, and it's going to be your experience and your growth, but she gets to be a part of it. And whether she was the reason that all of this happened, she's so grateful. But don't ever forget this is your path."

A warmth started to move through my body. Má and I were still bound together as mother and daughter. Má was justifying the search for the doctor, the trips back to Việt Nam, the shows, all of it. I never felt truly supported by my family in my quest, but I knew in my gut I had to keep going. Here she was trying to reassure me that all of this was part of my path, a greater plan.

"Am I supposed to be a performer?" I asked meekly. I had been so insecure around not having formal training, that I was foolish to pursue the non-lucrative arts.

"Yes! You are! You've got a reason now. And through the performance, through the vibrations and sensory, this work expands over to other lifetimes. It's going to be her legacy and yours. But she says she assists you in making all this happen with her. It's healing. It's a mother's love. That's all it is, a mother's love."

And healing it had been, indeed.

Cindy explained that Má wasn't able to fulfill her maternal experience since she'd died young. She still had a soul contract to be a mother figure with each of her children and grandchildren. Family groups were connected through the soul contract, and it wouldn't break until I crossed over. During my life review, I would see all the challenges I experienced and my evolution of self. Cindy's guide told her to tell me that I would push my habits aside, and each day would be different as I continue to evolve through life experience.

"You know that you came here as such a powerful vibration, so your soul will survive the human sentiments, the human experiences of loss because there is no such thing as a soul death. There is only the physical death, the physical vessel that is here that returns to dust. But the connections to the soul live on. That is why I'm able to channel spirit on the other side, because they still exist and their relationship is still there."

Cindy's words comforted me. Intuitively, I believed her in my heart even though I knew my mind didn't. After we talked about business advice for my brothers and sister, I asked about the day I got married.

"Was she at my wedding, and what did she think of Dì Phương that day?" I had been curious for so long.

"She's got a sense of humor." Cindy giggled, covering her mouth. "What is Dì Phương?"

"Her younger sister, Kim, who does your nails," I clarified.

Cindy looked confused. "Your mother keeps shrugging her shoulders and lifting her eyebrows. Did something happen at the wedding?" she asked.

"Yes. Kim channeled my mom, but did she really channel my mom or did she not?"

Cindy gazed through me again. "I love Kim. But your mom keeps shrugging. Kim loves her sister very much, and she loves you very much. She is a mother figure to you. So did she channel through her heart chakra? Yes, she did! But did she channel like I am doing? I don't know. That's why your mother went like 'eh' like, 'I'm not going to answer yes or no.' So it's best not said. I'm tapping into Kim at the wedding. It seems like she was very emotional because she was missing your mother."

I could still recall my siblings' eyes that day. All of us felt so much joy. They missed her too. I know they believed Má really came. But as the years wore on, everyone stopped believing except for me. That was the thing with the supernatural. It could feel so real one moment and then like a total illusion the next. The mind had a way of believing anything it wanted to believe. I guess I believed Dì Phương a little too much.

"But she was there. She honored and she blessed it. And your mother was there at each of the births of the grandchildren as well."

"What does she think of my husband?"

"Let me look here. She doesn't know him. She—" Cindy burst out laughing. "She's cute. She says you are very happy in this relationship." She paused a bit. "He wishes he knew her. He's a very good man, but the part of your heart that is sad and grieving the loss of your mother, he cannot fulfill that part. He can be a good support, friendship, relationship, but she said always remember that you're going to have to be independent. That you're going to be empowered as a woman, as a mindful being, and as a spirit. You will have abundance in this life. Much abundance."

"Financial abundance?" I clarified. I wanted to make sure it included this one too.

"Yes, you will have financial abundance," underscored Cindy. "But you and I both know what the most important thing is, don't we?" she said sweetly.

I racked my brain but came up with nothing. It would be great to know.

"And that's love of self," continued Cindy. "I too lost my mom at a young age, and I too know how hard that is. I know you miss her every single day. But I also know I find a lot of comfort knowing she is with me. She's the wind at my back; she's the numbers when they line up on the clock. She will always be there to guide you as a mother figure. But you make her very, very proud."

I closed my eyes and touched my heart. I wanted to never forget Má's precious message. This multiyear journey to know her had wrecked me but also finally filled what seemed like a bottomless hole in my heart. The path to my own salvation had taken work, but the method was now crystal clear: *when we feel, we heal.*

"She loves her children so much and she is so sorry it was her time to go, but she says she comes around. All four of her children are very unique and artistic. She draws me arrows going in all different directions. She and your father have fulfilled their journey together on the earth plane. Although she brings him love, light, and healing, she says there is no unfinished business with her and him. So he's free to go to live his life, and she honors him by bowing to him with gratitude for her children. All right, we have time for one last question!"

I had been waiting the whole session to ask. I took a deep breath and asked her the question that had been weighing on me: "Why did she want to get plastic surgery?" After all these years, I just wanted to know.

"Because she thought it would look pretty. She was a beautiful woman, and she thought she would feel better."

An answer so honest, how could I deny it? It's not like I never tried the ten-day Master Cleanse liquid diet. The cayenne pepper from the lemon maple syrup drink sent me dashing to the bathroom throughout a conference call. Má wasn't a demigod; she was human, just like me.

A timer went off on Cindy's desk. She smiled at me and reached into her blouse, pulling a small pink heart-shaped stone from her bra. "This is a crystal that has absorbed your mother's energy today. Keep it with you to protect you." She put it in a burgundy velvet pouch and then handed me a recording of our session on an outdated CD. At least I now had evidence of Má's wishes.

That night, I played the recording for Wendy and hoped I could get her blessing too. The psychic began speaking in full force and then I heard a woman so soft-spoken, I barely recognized myself. I sounded so fragile and timid, my life direction hinging on the words of a gifted stranger. As Wendy listened solemnly, I tried to study her face. When Cindy said Má was at the births of all her grandchildren, Wendy wiped away a few tears. She took copious notes when Má gave her advice for her chocolate company, one that was growing with employees and would bring her future success. When the recording ended, I took a deep breath and then braced myself for any blowback. Wendy cleared her throat.

"So all the shows and everything—it's not about you?" she asked.

I shook my head. Somehow the psychic was able to get through to Wendy in a way I couldn't. That moment would have been the right time to ask my sister questions about how she'd coped with Má's death over the years. Her thoughts on motherhood without Má around. But my words were stuck. I had learned the hard way that my sister was an internal processor, and she hated being put on the spot. After Extreme Indulgence, I sent her my first show, but we never talked about it. I was sure she watched it, but she never brought it up. Now I waited for her to make the next move.

Wendy closed her notebook and then said she would come to my next show, which surprised me. We used to be so close when we'd shared bunk beds, but the last few years, we had grown apart. Every communication I had with her had to be scrutinized before it was sent. But now she was giving me an opening. For so long, I'd wanted my family to acknowledge my feelings. Her coming to my show would do that for me. Wendy wasn't much of a hugger with me, so I tried to contain my excitement. I didn't want her to renege on her promise.

"Cool" was all I said. I guess she wasn't the only one who had trouble talking about the past. Even though I was adamant, actually talking about death was uncomfortable, because we had never done it. At least now we were one step closer.

I shared the recording with my brother Hang since Má gave him business advice. Later that night, I got a text from him.

"Cindy's advice makes sense." It was quickly followed by another text. "For my business."

Then I got a call from Ba asking what Cindy charged per hour. Ba usually frequented a monk with paranormal powers, named Uncle #9, in Houston, but he was curious about people with the gift. I guessed Wendy must have shared the recording with the entire family. We didn't keep any secrets from one another except for our hidden emotions about Má.

A part of me felt hopeful because all of them listened. They wanted to know if Má had a message for them—we all did. But no one spoke to my sobbing on the recording. I found it disheartening that they could listen to all of that and not ask the simple question "Are you okay?" or admit their own grief. I didn't need the living to fix anything, I just wanted to be heard and do the same for them. I believed that once they validated my experience, I could finally free myself from the haunting journey of going through Má's death alone.

The next month, Wendy flew up to Seattle to watch my third installment. It started with a picture of my belly on a large projector screen.

"This is my friend Fat. I think about my friend more than my husband on a given day." I talked about Má's body and the anxiety I felt about Bà Ngoại, who monitored and controlled everyone's eating. The constant body-shaming. How my elders drilled it into my head: no one would ever love me if I wasn't slender. My failure to lose weight over the years and my ongoing struggle with perfectionism. My search for closure with Dr. Moglen. I read my letter to the plastic surgeon's son and then played the voice mail from his daughter. I let them in on exactly the crazy roller coaster I had been on for the last year.

After the show, I talked with some audience members and saw Wendy out of the corner of my eye. She had the hearing of a hawk. She heard a Chinese American woman's confession of her eating disorders. A mother who lost her child through a devastating medical procedure. A trans person who had been ousted by their family and yet was still trying to find compassion for their relatives. Wendy stood by and witnessed how my story, our family story, sparked reflection in others.

On the drive home, I finally had the courage to get vulnerable with her. "Hey, Wen, I'm really glad you're here." She didn't say much back. For some families, this wasn't going deep. But for us, the floodgates had just opened.

We spent the rest of the night drinking wine and eating snacks. She filled up my wineglass with a twinkle in her eye. We didn't talk about the show, but her being there meant the world to me. She was my witness tonight, and hopefully she could be the bridge so I could get through to everyone else in the family too.

Paris by Night

As I was preparing for my next show, I had this hunch that there was a clue in *Paris by Night*, a diasporic Vietnamese variety show with song, dance, and theater. Sunday mornings were the only time our entire family spent together, because the nail salon opened at 11:00 a.m. instead of 9:30 a.m. I would wake up to Ba's karaoke echoing from downstairs. In the kitchen, Bà Ngoại would be doling out Styrofoam bowls of her shredded chicken quail egg soup sprinkled with white pepper. All the women would huddle around the coffee table, kneeling, slurping soup with plastic spoons as Ba switched the input to the VHS player. He would drive an hour to San Jose to bring back the show on tapes we rented from the Vietnamese video store. Once the tape was pushed in, the two hours of glamour would begin.

The MCs hosted like it was the Oscars, weaving in witty banter and a sense of dignity that my parents could never communicate in English. My favorite singer was Lynda Trang Đài, our Vietnamese Madonna, who wore risqué outfits and sometimes sang in English. One time, she came out kicking open a saloon door with a chic Western outfit and an entourage of flirty backup dancers. Most of the time, though, the Vietnamese women wore traditional áo dài with flowing silk pants and long tunics with slits that cut above the hip to show a scandalous inch of skin. It was extremely formfitting around the bust, neck, and arms, all held together with small metal snaps from the waist to the throat. I hated wearing them because they only "fit" when they were suffocating me.

When a new act began, my mother and aunts would go at it, debating who wore the áo dài best or who'd gained weight since the last tape. The curvier ones, with the one exception of Hương Lan, would be dismissed by my family and eventually disappear from the show. Occasionally, there would be the rare wonder of a white person who spoke and sang perfect Vietnamese, which always drew praise from my family. Dì Phương joked they spoke better than I did, which was true, but her comment was cutting, making me feel even more self-conscious to keep practicing. It's not like I spoke our mother tongue with my siblings. They also chose assimilation, so eventually, the melody of their six tones dried up too, erased from their mouths.

Paris by Night was still being produced but was at its height in the late '80s and early '90s, with over a hundred episodes in its vault. It was the epitome of Vietnamese feminine beauty and Má's favorite show. I had to get my hands on the recordings from my mother's era. If I wanted to get in her mind, I needed to see what she put into it. In my mother's medical report, it was noted that she had excess fat typical of multiple-term pregnancies. But I think our constant fixation on perfection was what finally got to her.

I called up my girlfriend Thanh, who came to my first performance and who was also a self-professed *Paris by Night* mega-fan. She invited me to have a sleepover at her mother's house, who had the entire collection. We were grown women in our thirties going back to her childhood home to stay up all night soaking up nostalgia and munching on snacks her parents made. Of course I was in.

Sitting cross-legged in Thanh's bed with my pajamas on, I pushed the tape in like Ba used to so many years ago. We had a stack of the shows produced between 1990 and 1996 and were determined to get through as many as we could before we fell asleep. Each show had the same structure. Female solo, male solo, duets. Long-haired petite women plucking zithers, singing about a lover they lost in the war. Sketch comedy with a fat man dressed in drag as an overbearing grandmother.

At the midpoint of every show, there was a long advertisement by Bà Hạnh Phước, a past beauty pageant winner and owner of a plastic surgery clinic in Houston, Texas. The camera would pan her lying poolside. From her voluminous hair, down her black one-piece swimsuit, to her pantyhose oddly covering her legs and toes. Green lasers sparked from the supposed operating room, and the commercial narrator kept repeating their phone number, "1-800-ĐẸP-NHƯ-Ý," which meant "1-800-Pretty-As-You-Wish." After the commercial, the show would cut to Bà Hạnh Phước, who sat in the front row of the theater as one of the show's biggest sponsors. Episode after episode had the same commercial, and the impact was apparent. So many of the performers started with their real noses, and then, after a few tapes, the same type of fake nose started to trend on their once-beautiful faces. My family never commented on the ad, but I did notice that after I saw a face wash ad on the show, Má had a few bottles of it on her bathroom counter a month later.

After the *Paris by Night* marathon, I felt uneasy. This show illuminated the rich talent of our community and brought up immense pride, albeit for a few hours since my family was still working seven days a week. When we watched, we weren't othered, made to feel inferior or like a piece of charity. Instead, we were watching Vietnamese people, not white people, be the stars. But even within our own ethnic group, the women were still objects up for critique, still subject to the Vietnamese male gaze. Beauty was binary, and it felt unsettling to watch the older women in my life take part in perpetuating what "pretty enough" looked like. They privately beat themselves up when they couldn't meet these impossible beauty standards and then passed it on to their daughters.

Uncle #9

When I returned to my day job after the third show about body image, a bomb dropped. I was served a termination letter from my management consulting gig. I didn't particularly love the work, but the timing was terrible—Marvin and I had just bought our first home, and I was still paying steep grad school loans. With the shows gaining momentum with press and ticket sales, I was at a crossroads. Make this hobby-turned-life-calling into my full-time work or find the highest-paying job I could get? My gut told me to pursue the arts and see where it would take me. Marvin felt otherwise. For two weeks, it was tense in the house until I made my demands clear: "I'm not asking for your permission, I'm asking for your support!" These last few years of investigation and art making had been the most thrilling of my life. I wasn't giving up now. When I floated divorce, he agreed to a one-year experiment with financial targets. If I didn't hit them, I would go back to corporate America. We shook on it.

Hot off the heels of getting fired, I called Ba to see if I could visit him for some R&R given my suddenly open schedule. Our video call went how it typically went. Ba asked what time it was in Seattle and if I had eaten yet. Like usual, he messed up rotating his video camera, and then I spent the next five minutes instructing him how to flip the screen back as I talked to his bare feet. When he asked if there was anything new with me, he was hoping to hear just two things: if I was pregnant or if I gotten promoted. This time, I was unemployed, which made him sigh a little bit longer than usual. I mentioned I could visit him, and he responded with a simple "When?"

I had two motives for the trip. Yes, I was craving Vietnamese food, but I also had to break the news to him in person that I wasn't returning to the corporate world—I was all in with this art thing that we both avoided talking about.

As much as I complained that Ba didn't care about me, he immediately started making preparations after the call. With Wendy also coming, all he could talk about on every subsequent call were the menus. Once we arrived, the food discussions continued. I wanted canh khổ qua, a clear soup made with cored bitter melon stuffed with ground pork, wood ear mushrooms, and bean thread noodles. And tôm kho tàu too, large freshwater prawns caramelized in a bright orange tomalley sauce made from its head fat. By dinner, both dishes were hot on the table.

Ba's cooking was so much better than my own clumsy attempts. After he moved to Texas, leaving a nail salon behind him, his cooking expanded to more family-style dishes because he simply had more time to himself. He attempted to work at someone else's shop, but the transition to becoming an employee after being the boss all those years just didn't work for him. So he spent all his spare time in "semi-retirement," recovering from chronic health issues and perfecting dishes learned through YouTube.

"Hey, Ba, can we visit Cậu Chín tomorrow?" I captured a one-inch-thick round of the sliced gourd from the communal soup bowl. I dipped it into my nước mắm saucer dotted with a few slivers of red Thai chilies fresh from their garden. A little broth and fish sauce dripped into my rice bowl. I opened my mouth wide like I was at the dentist and took my first bite. The hotness scalded the roof of my mouth.

"Ừ, được chứ." *Yes, of course.* Visiting Cậu Chín, which literally translates to *Uncle #9*, was one of the few family events everyone got really pumped about. If we went to a restaurant, it was because one person was craving their món đặc biệt, *the house special.* But when we got to go to Cậu Chín, everyone had something they wanted him to answer. He was a Buddhist monk renowned for his fortune-telling and spirit-channeling abilities. Direct and sassy, he didn't charge for his services. Temple donations were optional. And he was not our actual uncle; he was everyone's uncle. My family had been going to him for years, and his hit rate for accuracy was about 80 to 85 percent. Wendy, Hang, and I were big Uncle #9 fans.

On the other hand, Kang wasn't as enthusiastic about the fourth dimension. It wasn't that he was a skeptic; he had seen it all firsthand. When he was ten, he'd gotten into an argument with Ba about religion. He was sitting on the couch with Hang in our small Emeryville apartment when we lived in subsidized housing. Our parents had enrolled Kang and Hang into Chinese Christian school even though we were Buddhist (who could turn down a private school that gave scholarships?). Kang argued with Ba about whether there was a God. Ba said there was much more than what we could see and that he would prove it.

Ba lit an incense stick, whispered a few sayings, and gave a high-pitched yell. He started to fly around the small living room, doing wide kicks and swift punches a hair away from the boys' faces. The telephone book flew off the table, and Ba leaped off the walls as a primal scream echoed through the rental complex. The boys scrambled on top of the couch with their backs pressed against the wall, trying to get as far away as they could. After that, Kang stopped being an atheist.

A few years later, Kang had to go with Má and Ba to see Bé Rơi, a spirit channeler whose possessed voice sounds like a baby girl's. Her apartment smelled like an odd cross between mothballs and urinal deodorizer. As Má got her monthly fortune read, Bé Rơi sensed Kang's doubt. She excused herself from the kitchen table and approached him on the living room sofa.

"I know you smoked a cigarette with that boy yesterday," she hissed into his ear. Kang was shocked that she knew his secret. He had checked to make sure no one was watching. How could she have possibly known?

As an adult, Kang didn't want to have anything to do with the spiritual realm. "What good would it do to know your fate in advance?" he explained to me. Maybe knowing too much would make life more miserable. But even though he resisted, whenever Kang visited Ba in Texas, he still made a point to visit Uncle #9 because the spirit medium was *that* good.

Ba agreed to take me to see Cậu Chín the next day. When we were done eating, Ba set out a plastic-wrapped plate of pandan green honeydew cubes and a small cylindrical container of toothpicks. I shook it a few times until a stick poked out. Wendy stacked all the rice bowls and raised her eyebrows at me. I quickly rose and took dishes out of Dì Nhung's always-moving hands. My stepmother's arthritis in her hands and wrists had gotten worse after all these years doing pedicures. She was an aging nail salon worker who was still making minimum wage and exposed to toxic chemicals. Clearing the table was the least I could do for her years of sacrifice to raise us.

The next morning, I rolled over to check the time and then bolted up. How was it already 9:00 a.m.? Whenever I stayed at Ba's house, I slept in late like I was a high schooler all over again. I jogged downstairs and saw Ba and Wendy drinking coffee and eating pirouette hazelnut cookies. Then I saw plastic bags by the garage door filled with Filipino champagne mangoes and plump Korean pears. Before I even woke up, Ba drove thirty minutes to the nearby Vietnamese supermarket to get our temple offering. When I finally got my act together, Ba, Dì Nhung, Wendy, and I made the forty-five-minute drive to Uncle #9.

At the temple steps, we tossed our shoes into the whirlpool of heels, sneakers, and sandals. Inside the temple hall, I got a powerful punch of incense up the nose. Twelve rows of hotel conference room chairs spanned the entire width of the hall separated by a middle aisle leading up to the giant golden Buddha shrine. Mini golden Buddhas in clear boxes lined the wall from floor to ceiling, maybe three hundred in total. There were about twenty-five other people milling about, some in chairs and others making offerings, many of them not Vietnamese. We joined hopeful Mexican, Black, and white believers who waited patiently to be in the wise presence of Uncle #9. Those who had already seen him were drinking from Kirkland Signature water bottles with small pieces of red yarn tied on them.

We took a lap of the temple, and then Ba and Dì Nhung put the fruit bags down, settling on an altar with fewer offerings than the other stations. Wendy and I removed the soft white Styrofoam sleeves protecting the pears. We all quietly worked on the sacred art of fruit arrangement. When Dì Nhung was satisfied with the symmetry, she said, "Coi được." *It looks right, presentable.* That was the phrase elders would use to praise Wendy's body when she wore an áo dài. No one ever said it to me. We lit our incense and then sat down in the front row. There was no ticket or waiting list. Fifteen minutes passed, and we still hadn't talked to anyone. I saw a woman emerge from a closed door near the altar. She was not in robes, but she looked more comfortable in the space than we visitors did. I approached her and learned she was a volunteer. She was Vietnamese and in her midtwenties, wearing oversize gold-rimmed glasses and a mesh Adidas shirt with a camisole underneath. It was hot in Texas, even in a temple. I wanted to make sure she knew where we were in this amorphous line.

"When can we see him?" I asked.

"Thầy? Oh." *Teacher, master.* I could see a few drops of sweat glistening on her forehead as she scanned the hall. "You know, I don't think he can see you today. Maybe you come back tomorrow." I was leaving tomorrow. Despite her advice, my family decided to stay and try our luck. Over the next hour, the woman escorted small groups to the doorway by the giant Buddha. Some people came out sobbing, others beaming. Some visits took five minutes while others were twenty minutes. On their way out, all the visitors passed by a padlocked dark red wooden box with a slot where they could show their gratitude.

As the crowd thinned, the woman came up to me. "I'm sorry, Thầy is tired. Tomorrow from ten to one, okay?"

I nodded, a bit dejected. I'd tried. We gathered our things and headed toward the exit.

"Come." I heard a high-pitched male voice behind me. I turned and saw it was Cậu Chín, an effeminate, lanky, bald Vietnamese man in his fifties. He was wearing a flowing set of dark brown Vietnamese pajamas adorned with tiny flowers. He looked like a younger version of Thích Nhất Hạnh with Bà Ngoại's fashion of pajama daywear. And he was giving *me* a look. Cậu Chín stretched his arm out and flapped his palm twice like Bruce Lee signaling the beginning of a fight. He turned around and disappeared into his doorway. We rushed behind him.

Once through the coveted doorway, I saw his bed lined with a purple Korean mink blanket with a few beautiful roses on the corners. The four of us sat cross-legged on the floor while he sat on his bed. Cậu Chín pointed at my legs with a disapproving look.

"Next time you come, don't be so disrespectful."

I was wearing a skort. I quickly sat up on my knees and darted Ba a glance. How come he didn't warn me this morning?

Now he looked at Wendy. "Don't worry. Your hands will make you famous. Keep doing what you're doing."

Then he looked to Ba, switching between English and Vietnamese for each generation. "Now what do you want to know?"

Ba cleared his throat. "When is a good time to start a new business?" he shyly asked.

Cậu Chín smiled brightly and closed his eyes. He started speaking in the methodical cadence. "You need to rest. You need to pray. You need to be in your garden. You will know when it is time. Your first wife wants you to pray for forty days. Do that first."

Then Cậu Chín looked back at me. I felt ashamed that I offended him. I was scared of what he would say. "Thirty-eight, forty, forty-one, forty-two, forty-four, you live your best life. Forty-two, forty-four, forty-five, don't sit in a red car. Forty-seven, forty-eight, fifty, good money. Fifty-two, fifty-four, fifty-six, fifty-seven, fifty-eight, fifty-nine, sixty, sixty-two, sixty-four, sixty-five, all good."

I scribbled all the numbers in my journal, trying to capture his predictions.

Then Ba interrupted. "Thầy ơi, my daughter has a problem. She doesn't know how to work."

I looked up from recording my lucky years. What was he talking about? I had become a bona fide workaholic since going into the performing arts.

"It's like she's sick in the head." This was all news to me. "She wants to do a new type of job, but she doesn't have any training in it. She didn't study it in school."

He was talking about my transition to becoming a full-time artist. I'd tried to explain it to Ba, but since my work involved what happened to Má, he didn't want to talk about it. We pretended my shows were not real like we had pretended Má never existed. "It's like she's allergic to work!" he exclaimed. His assessment was infuriating.

Cậu Chín returned to his singing cadence. "She will do better in this than anything she has ever done. She will make more money than ever before." Then Uncle #9 turned to me. "Your mind a rock, okay? People don't want eat rock soup, right?" I wasn't sure where this was going, but I continued to nod. "So stop being stubborn like rock! Nobody like rock soup! It don't taste good!" Was he talking about my and Ba's relationship? Or all the self-doubt I felt as an artist? He clapped his hands right in front of my face and stopped singing. He spoke slowly. "You are too stubborn. You think you have a lot of problems. But you only have one problem. You." Wow, my fortune was a lot harsher than everyone else's. I made a note to definitely wear pants next time. "You create all your problem, okay?"

He blinked slowly into my eyes to make sure I heard him. I knew he was right. Perfectionism and imposter syndrome had paralyzed me countless times. My mental episodes could shut me down for two or three days at a time. But was it really that simple? I just needed to "stop" being stubborn?

Cậu Chín broke his gaze and then looked back and forth between Wendy and me. "Your mother love you very much. She watch you all the time. She always there to protect you."

Tears streamed down my and Wendy's faces. No one had told him about Má being gone. He just knew. Dì Nhung pulled out a small tissue packet from her purse and gave it to Wendy without breaking gaze with Cậu Chín. We were all in a hypnotic trance.

"Anything else?" he asked us all sweetly. And then it happened. It always happened when we saw mediums. We forgot all the questions we had going in. It was like a brain full of doubts and fears were wiped clean when we were in the presence of people with the gift. He stood up, and we all bowed and thanked him. Ba slipped a red envelope in the donation box, and we shook our palms one last time in the direction of Buddha for the blessings we received.

On the car ride home, we were quiet for a few moments before we erupted into the post-session recap.

Wendy punched my arm. "Skirt. So dumb."

I punched her back.

"Ba, how come you didn't tell me! And it's a skort!"

Ba just laughed and laughed, reminding us to write down our questions on paper before we went in. We were all in good spirits on the drive home. It was a rare thing to talk about Má, so it was such a treat that Cậu Chín let us know she was still around, watching over us, helping us.

That night, Ba made Wendy's requested dish of bánh xèo, a savory turmeric crêpe with shrimp, pork belly, mung beans, and bean sprouts. Ba added a little beer to make the rice flour batter with coconut milk extra crispy. We tore off sections with our chopsticks, making lettuce wraps with mint leaves, Thai basil, and perilla leaves from Ba's garden. One dip into the vinegary nước mắm made the warm, crunchy bite divine. Ba kept making them on the skillet until we were stuffed. Even then, he made an extra one and put it on the table in case we changed our minds.

The next morning, Ba took me to the airport first because I had a much earlier flight than Wendy. He had green tea ready in a disposable plastic cup and a few wrapped bánh mì with chả lụa, just like the old days. Food on the airplane was too expensive, he insisted. Ba pulled up to Departures and turned off the car, getting out to say goodbye.

"Okay," he said awkwardly. "Think about have baby." We looked at each other a few feet apart, both of us not saying a word. For some reason, Ba's presence always provoked my throat to close and dry up, cutting off what I would feel comfortable saying to most any stranger.

As we stood there motionless on the curb, it dawned on me how much of a joke I was. This self-professed artist who touted the value of vulnerability could not say what needed to be said. All this time, I had invested so much energy in knowing a dead parent when I knew so little about the living one right in front of me. I was interacting with him as if he would always be around. But if I'd learned anything from Má's death, it was that when we die is known to no one. Rich or poor, it was out of our hands. As I turned to catch my flight, his arms clasped me quickly like a lemon squeezer. I waved him goodbye as he stood by the trunk of the car. He was confused by American love, but he was trying.

Back in Seattle, I opened up the depositions again. I was so obsessed with the doctor that I had glossed over Ba's testimonial. I revisited his deposition, trying to unearth what he may never be able to tell me directly.

April 21, 1999

Page 13

A. (cont'd) . . . I was a gardener.

Q. Now, what was your occupation in Vietnam?

A. I repair motorcycle.

Q. Is it fair to say that since you started working, you worked first as a mechanic and then as a deliveryman, next a gardener and currently a manicurist?

A. That's correct.

I saw Ba's limited command of English and his life summed up as a laborer in just one breath. I thought about how different his life experiences had been, the opportunities he never had access to that I took for granted all the time. I never saw my father as a blue-collar worker. His authority loomed so large over me that it never occurred to me how much he struggled with communicating in a second language, trying to make a life in America, thousands of miles from his homeland. Then the lawyer asked Ba about an interaction he had with the plastic surgeon.

Page 45

Q. What did he say?

A. He said: "We hope she wakes up."

Q. Did he tell you what happened?

A. No.

Q. Did anybody, including the paramedics or any doctor at Mount Zion, anybody whatsoever, ever give you an explanation as to what happened?

A. No.

Q. Did you ever learn what happened to your wife?

A. No. Until now, I do not know. I think that the doctor's

office, that the surgery at the doctor's office, he might
make some kind of mistake. That's why my wife died.

Q. Did anybody ever tell you that?

A. No.

He could never give me an explanation because even he didn't
know what happened. I got to the end of his deposition and felt re-
morse. Instead of the disapproving father who had been withholding
information and telling me no all my life, I saw a confused immigrant
painstakingly trying to pick up the pieces. He became a widower at
forty-two with four children—and the woman who used to manage
everything was gone. He had been traumatized as an orphan, a refugee, an immigrant, and now as a widower.

Over the years, I'd pushed Ba as far away as I could to protect
myself. I hated how phone calls with him would wreck me for days.
I hated how he never made an effort to understand me. If I lived the
life he prescribed for me, every day would be hell. But if I pursued
the life I wanted, which I did, then every talk became a fight. I began
to feel ashamed of how I had treated him. He clothed and fed me.
He never drank or beat me. By some Vietnamese standards, I had a
blessed childhood.

I began to long for the days when I was his little girl. I wanted
to feel safe with him again. I thought back to the last time we were
happy together. Could it be when I was six years old?

Ba came by Susan's Nails in his gardening truck, and I got to tag along
with him to this Chinese restaurant where we shared a heaping plate
of beef chow fun. This was unusual because I typically saw him at the
end of the day at home with a big bucket of KFC or a rotisserie chicken
and a baguette on the table for dinner. While we waited for everyone
to come to the dining table, he would call me over, and I would get
up on a step stool and massage his shoulders, karate chopping down

his back because of his back pain. That was the only time we ever had physical contact.

When we finished off the noodles, the plate was just a pool of gravy and thick-cut scallions. The waiter took the plate away and returned with caramelized fried bananas and two scoops of vanilla ice cream. This was a major upgrade from the free orange slices and fortune cookies I was used to. But it wasn't anyone's birthday. Ba did it just because. I took delight in making spoonfuls of banana and melting ice cream. Then Ba's beeper went off, ending our special afternoon. He paid the bill and came back with a toothpick sticking out of the corner of his mouth like a farmer. He slipped two dollars under his teacup and we were off.

Back at Susan's Nails, I tasked myself with organizing the wall of nail polish by number order. As I moved the glass bottles like an abacus, I remembered the lunch I'd just had with Ba and enjoyed it all over again. I got to have his full attention, not because I was in trouble but because he wanted me there.

Now as an adult, whenever I feel particularly homesick, I go to the nearest Chinese restaurant for beef chow fun. How could I channel this tenderness back to us?

If I were to interpret Ba's behavior through an objective clinical lens, his emotional distance made sense. If I could strip my personal hurt and expectations out of the equation, I could cultivate and extend compassion toward him. Uncle #9 was right. My own stubbornness was getting in the way of empathizing with Ba. I was so attached to taking everything he did and said so personally, I couldn't see the fragility of him or the situation.

Maybe Ba pushed back on answering my questions over the years because it felt safer to bury the memories of a period that crippled him. Could it be that the intimidating parent I remembered didn't actually know what to do? Would it be possible for me to accept him as imperfect as I was? On a fundamental level, isn't that what I wished he could do for me? His emotional distance and cutting comments over the years were and weren't about me—and in realizing that, I found my own liberation.

World Premiere

I had four months until the biggest show of my life, the show where
I would put everything I'd learned in one place. This play would
be my homage to Má and my moment to finally realize my own
life calling as a performer. I didn't want to live a life in spite of Má; I
wanted to live a life because of her.

During the day, I hustled to find nonprofit consulting clients, work
I could actually stomach, to pay the bills. At night, I went to rehearsal
with my director, Sara, where she would review my pages and then
give me new writing prompts. The one I kept getting stuck on was
about my family's perspective on my mother's death. My characters
were too "one-dimensional," she said.

"Write about how your mother's death changed them," she
guided me.

"But how can I if they don't let me in?"

"Become them. Imagine what they went through."

As I inhabited their words, their gestures, their voices, my percep-
tion of them began to change. They were just as flawed and messy
as I was, navigating their own demons, also alone. The anger and
frustration I held against them began to soften. Of course I knew Má's
death mattered to them, but this exercise unlocked something new in

my understanding of them. My energy toward them shifted, and so did their communication with me. Wendy texted me every time she had a dream about Má. Kang quickly sent me photos I'd requested for the show. Ba completed his forty days of prayer for Má. Hang was still his same old reclusive self.

By Christmastime, my life felt like it was finally coming together. I had two nonprofit consulting clients, and my script was really shaping up. And with two of my siblings' newfound engagement in my work, I couldn't wait to share my progress with them at the next weeklong Extreme Indulgence sleepover.

Wendy and her husband, Sameer, had just finished their entry in the food competition with an elaborate Spanish paella dinner. The trophy was gleaming on the dining room table. The winning couple with the best meal would get their names and their dish inscribed on our modern-day family heirloom. The kids had run upstairs to build a Star Wars LEGO set. After a big dinner cleanup, all of us siblings were drinking wine on the couch. This was the moment to fill them in on my recent discoveries.

"Guys, I've been reading the depositions we gave years ago. Did you know the doctor had twenty lawsuits against him and had tried to buy insurance from an offshore scam company but—"

"Susan, we're trying to relax, okay?" Hang cut me off.

"Yeah, but did you know Má had *breast implants* even before—"

"We all have our own businesses, and we're tired, all right? We all have a *real* job, unlike you." Hang looked down at his phone.

I kept on. "It's just interesting because—"

"Susan, it's *Christmas*. Don't be so rude!" said Wendy.

"I just thought that you guys would—"

"Well, we don't. Okay?" Wendy got up to go to the kitchen.

I looked over at Kang. He was watching everyone else, and I couldn't read his face. I felt so confused. One-on-one, Wendy and Kang were more open to talking. What was with the sudden change?

"Come on, Harvard. Didn't the Ivy Leagues teach you you're not the center of the universe?" sneered Hang.

I looked at all three of them in disbelief. They blinked right back at me, probably thinking the same thing. I didn't understand why I kept coming back year after year if we weren't actually going to be authentic with one another. I totally got that we'd all had rough childhoods, but that didn't justify them shutting me down like this. I thought this would be the year where we would connect on a heart level. I was wrong.

I picked up the hardcover green book called *Family Christmas*, which I'd bought from Goodwill. It had prompts for people to write their favorite memories.

"Fine. I'm done." I took the book and started walking to my bedroom. I turned back toward them to have the last word. "You know what, though? I bought this book, and no one writes in it but me!"

I tossed the book on an end table and stomped off to my room. I was tired of being the family historian. What was the point if nobody cared? I put on my headphones and worked on my script. Once I released this show out to the world, I would have proven to myself that I was not a coward. After the world premiere in six weeks, I would take out my IUD and start my own motherhood journey, creating a family where we actually listened to one another.

The next morning, I saw the green book on the long kitchen island where we ate breakfast. I opened it up and saw entries from my brothers' spouses, Oriana and Gaina, and one from Kang. My eldest brother, Kang, doled out a bowl of rice porridge made with leftovers from his cooking night. He served it to me with some freshly chopped cilantro, slivered ginger, and green onions.

"Hey, sis, I've been thinking about your questions."

"Really?" I said half-heartedly, grinding pepper for my soup.

"I don't know if this is helpful, but . . . I was the one who pulled the plug," said Kang.

I stopped twisting. "No, you didn't." I kept my eyes locked on him while I found a blank sheet of paper and a pen on the kitchen counter.

"Yeah, I did. And I'm not mad at the doctor. I forgave him the first day Má was in the hospital." He ladled himself a bowl and told me about the choice he'd had to make when he was just nineteen years old. The doctors showed him the data. Má was going to spend the rest of her life as a vegetable hooked up to a machine. The Má we knew would have never wanted a life like that. Ba had completely deferred to Kang to make the decision because he was the oldest son. My brother didn't appear regretful for what he had done. He really was at peace with it all. He agreed to let me put this detail in the show, and we hugged it out. I was so grateful he trusted me enough to tell me and trusted that I would disclose it honorably for the family.

After Extreme Indulgence, I returned home to Seattle and looked through the depositions again, this time to reexamine my other brother. Who was Má to him when she was still alive? I opened up Hang's file.

April 21, 1999

Page 9

Q. What did you do there as a rule when you were at home on those weekends?

A. Homework.

Q. Did you go out with the family, do anything social with your mother?

A. We had family dinners. We celebrated holidays. We would take family trips, planned trips. It was only a couple of months into the semester before she passed away.

Q. I see. That's right. It was in October. The semester started in September?

A. Yes.

Q. While you were in school during those few months, did
    your mother call you often?

A. Very often, yes.

Q. About how often?

A. Three times a week.

My heart broke. My sometimes threatening big brother was just a freshman at UC Berkeley when she died. A little baby whose mom checked on him all the time, calling from the nail salon when it wasn't busy. Most college kids worry about parties and hooking up. For Hang, he carried a much different burden as a motherless, first-generation college student.

I reread the part where Hang commented on our family trips. I could only recall three family vacations we ever went on: Việt Nam, Yosemite, and the time we went to Circus Circus. That was where Má introduced me to the casino and indoctrinated the rules of buffet eating with tough love. It was before all our relatives came to move in with us, so I had to have been seven years old.

"Where are we?" I asked Má as the elevator doors opened to a place buzzing with energy.

"Circus Circus," she said with gravitas. I shook my head, not understanding. "Sòng bài ở Re-no." Oh. *A casino in Reno.* The place had a strong whiff of cigarettes. In this grand room, red sirens were blaring and whirling in all directions on top of slot machines. Bells kept going off like it was the end of recess, and coins would come clinking out of machines into small plastic buckets in the laps of old people. Má left to go check in, and Ba whipped out his camera and JVC camcorder from a large black suitcase to document our family vacation.

"Nói cheese đi!" encouraged Ba.

"Cheeeeeeeeese!" Wendy and I sang.

Ba's camera flashed brightly, which made me see a few stars as I blinked.

When Má returned, she handed Kang a single gold key, forty dollars, and instructions on where to meet for dinner. I looked over to Wendy, wide-eyed—we were rich! On some Sundays, Má would drop us siblings off at the giant Chuck E. Cheese in San Jose with just one twenty-dollar bill. All of us had to make it last a few hours while our parents ran errands. Tonight, she gave us double, which meant we could live it up like kings.

After we put our luggage down and freshened up, the six of us piled into the elevator, and two different buttons were pressed. I glanced up at Má. She lightly hit Ba on the elbow and had a mischievous grin on her face. She was wearing a strong perfume that smelled almost like flowers. And she was wearing black net stockings and heels. It must be a special night.

"Bà ham chơi hoài!" Ba chuckled back. *You always want to play!* I rarely saw them like this. After school whenever I was with Má at the shop, she was always busy with customers, making me do homework or chores. At home, while Má made dinner, Ba would press Play on the answering machine, listening to customer messages and then calling them back. I hardly ever saw both of them not working at the same time.

The door dinged open, and my parents stepped off and waved bye to us, their two hands coming together to touch as the elevator doors closed. When the doors opened again, we were back in the chaos of lights and sound. Men on headsets calling us over to play at their booth. Balloons got filled up by squirting water into a clown's mouth. Wiffle balls bounced in and out of barrels. A plastic horse race that advanced by rolling weighted balls into holes. Plush neon raccoons dangled from the ceilings. Gleaming, beeping, ringing, and I heard just one volume—fun. Kang fed our money into the change machine, and tokens spilled out like we'd just won big.

We made our way through the ocean of games and prizes. Hang wanted us to do a full lap before we started spending money. After an hour of our brothers winning small dolls and trading up, I came out with a neon-pink bunny, and Wendy had a classic brown dog. I named mine Bertha.

When it was time, Kang got us back into the elevator, where we rode up another level, opening up to the biggest buffet I had ever seen in my life. The Japanese sushi place we went to once a year had four stations. This one had at least twelve. Má and Ba were at the front of the line and waved us over. Má told me to lie about my age so we could get the discount price. Then she handed me a warm brown tray and a ceramic white plate from a tall cart. We entered the brightly lit room. But instead of starting with the salad bar like everybody else, Má broke away. I ran after her to a station full of king crab legs, raw oysters, and cocktail shrimp on ice. She was focused, her tongs darting around to get the best pieces.

"Did you win any money?" I asked.

She laughed. "Hên xui, con ơi." *It's up to the gods, kiddo.* Then she placed two plump cocktail shrimp on my plate. I wandered off to watch the man slicing hot meat under the heat lamp and then made my way to the chicken tenders, onion rings, minestrone soup, and the ice cream bar with a rainbow of toppings. Potato salad, macaroni salad, pasta salad. Even a baked potato bar with all the fixings. It was all the American food I could ever want!

When I arrived at our family's table, everyone was using their hands, tearing through the meat. Ribs and those king crab legs. I dipped curly fries in ranch dressing like I saw my friends do at school. As I stretched out the springy potato morsel, Má began to lecture.

"Sao mày ngu quá vậy?" *Why are you so stupid?* I wasn't sure what I did wrong this time. She explained meat was more expensive than what I'd chosen. I looked down at my prized mac and cheese, chicken nuggets, and chocolate chip cookie. I didn't want to eat now. I blinked a few tears back.

"Sao con nhõng nhẽo quá vậy? Đi rửa mặt đi!!" ordered Má. *Why are you so emotional? Go wash your face!*

Má pushed Wendy out of the booth to help take care of me. My sister sighed loudly, as she always had to be the one to walk me to the bathroom. In a stall, I laid down two toilet seat covers like Má always said, and sat. Why was I the one always messing up? I dabbed my eyes with toilet paper and blew my nose. I wanted to stay there and be left all alone, but I knew that would make Má even madder. At the sink, I splashed off any remains of sadness and patted my face dry with a paper towel.

"What does Kang always say?" asked Wendy.

"Calm [hiccup], cool, composure [hiccup, hiccup]," I recited.

Má's cardinal rule was never to waste anything, be it money, time, and especially food. Because we were immigrants, the odds were already stacked against us. Even at an all-you-can-eat buffet, Má expected we only eat the high-value items. That's what Má respected. To survive, we Liễus had to be the cleverest ones in the classroom and the nail salon. I went to get another plate and walked past all the things I actually wanted, dragging my feet to the seafood cart like a good girl.

The center of my universe was governed by Má. As much as she was thrilling, she was terrorizing. She made up all the rules and everything would be fine as long as I never pissed her off. And so, gradually, this became my truth; my relationship to food was really about my relationship to family.

After reminiscing about Circus Circus, I turned to Kang's deposition.

April 21, 1999

Page 12

A. When I went home, I studied when my parents weren't home, had dinner with them when they were home. Once in a blue moon, I would try to cook a dish that I learned to make. Sometimes we would go out to eat at a restaurant or go on an outing.

Q. Did you go on the outings during the days?

A. After she gets off work on Sundays. Maybe just go down to
   Bodega Bay and have a little picnic or family outing.

Q. You may have heard your father testify that she usually got
   home around 5:00 on Sundays. Would you then go out in
   the evening after that?

A. Yes.

I smiled reading how Kang's fond family memories were so inter-
twined with food. It wasn't just me who couldn't separate the two,
it was something he cherished too. Reading his statement about my
mother's seven-day workweek made me see how devoted she was to
the family. On Sundays, she would close the shop a few hours early,
and even then, her little free time went to the family. Rarely did this
woman ever make time for herself. I could see how plastic surgery
became a rare gift she felt entitled to after giving so much of herself
to the family.

Seeing my parents' journey to America in its entirety with the buf-
fets, the clam digging, even the chives, I began to understand just
how precious and complicated my childhood had been with food. It
came with incredible joy and also an inherited trauma from refugees
who had fought to survive.

Just as our family happiness completely revolved around food, so
did my own emotional struggles. When any family member criticized
my body and then quickly followed it up with force-feeding me, I
couldn't enjoy the food. All I wanted was to leave. Whenever I felt
worried or unstable, I tried to soothe myself with food. This of course
led to more weight gain, which made me feel even more insecure. The
taste of Vietnamese food was both the nostalgia of when my mother
was alive and the unworthiness I felt around family. Needless to say,
I had a complicated relationship with food. Now as an adult, I could
change the narrative around food, love, and body standards. And all
these realizations would be baked into my one-woman show.

....

Inside the long orange hallway of Theatre Off Jackson, I wore two rolls of blue painter's tape on my wrists like they were jade bracelets. I tore off pieces and made small inside-out loops so Jenny, my stage manager and assistant director, could tape up about a hundred pictures of my family on the twenty-foot-wide orange wall. We were in the narrow interior hallway leading to the theater doors. Opening night was in one week, and this was how we spent our meal breaks during tech week—building the lobby installation of my multiyear family investigation.

I took a step back. Jenny and I had created a collage of my old family photos. My first visit to Việt Nam in 1994, pictures of the family at the Malaysian refugee camp where Wendy was born, Má's early '90s glamour shots, our last family vacation to Yosemite. All of this was woven around deposition pages with highlights, notations, and many exclamation points. The medical board decision. The driving directions to track Má's last day. The plastic surgeon's obituary. My letters to his children. My neurotic CSI investigation on full display. Jenny was assessing our handiwork, placing photos in empty holes, adjusting to make sure key information was at eye level.

"You know, your mom really liked standing on rocks with heels on," she said, laughing. I searched to see the pattern. There were at least five photos of her doing that.

"Yeah, she could do anything in heels," I murmured with admiration. On the left side of the hallway was the collage. On the right side were two long tables against the wall with an altar and portrait of Má. There were stacked *Paris by Night* tapes, a few Vietnamese records from the 1970s, lottery tickets from Việt Nam, even Buy One Get One Free Sizzler coupons Jenny found. We laid out binders of all the depositions. The green *Family Christmas* book. The plastic surgery ad Má saw (recovered by the UC Irvine Southeast Asian Archive), blown up on a vinyl poster. And the three-foot-long Hello Kitty that I'd beaten up years earlier. She sat propped up against the wall, watching over all the artifacts. The lobby music was set with Madonna's *Immaculate Collection*, the CD I used to listen to when Má was at the wheel. My yellow show poster was plastered all over Seattle, and the press was rolling in with hype about the show. I was at the theater fifteen hours a day, had become a vegan, and completely stopped drinking alcohol. It was almost showtime, and I had to be at peak performance.

My team of designers were working with a diligent and spirited hum against the deadline. Erin laid out all the audio tracks to create an ethereal container. The closing song ripped my heart open every time I heard it. Emily's lighting was so detailed and moody in all the right ways and at all the right moments. Derek made a preshow video overlaying Ba and Dì Phương's filmed interviews with landscapes of Việt Nam and San Francisco. And my director, Sara, and I were still making edits to the script. As I said the words out loud, some of them just didn't sound right. The following morning, I would bring in fresh scripts for the team.

This would be the world premiere of my family story, *140 LBS: How Beauty Killed My Mother*, and I was giving it everything I had. And even before opening night, the production had exceeded my expectations. Even if no one liked it, I didn't care. I was at peace now. This was my homage to Má, and I knew she would have loved it.

A few hours before opening, I rehearsed the entire show in the empty theater, said a prayer, and bowed three times, asking for Má's help. I went backstage, put on my makeup and costume, and visualized the entire show. I did my warm-up movement exercises until Jenny came backstage with a five-minute call time. I sniff-kissed both of her cheeks and gave her a playful slap on the face. She did it right back. One minute until showtime, I looked in the mirror and said, "I thank you, I love you, and I forgive you." I said it both to Má and me. Then what I did next surprised me. I channeled Junior from *Cool Runnings* who gets inspired from Yul to believe in himself. I said most of his lines, but put a spin on a few words to make them my own.

"I see pride, I see power, I see a bad-ass motherfucker who don't take shit from nobody!" I said it three times, spitting more fierceness into the mirror each time. Then I glided to the curtain. I got into character for Má and Susan's last day together. Susan practiced her volleyball serve while Má packed for her overnight stay at the plastic surgery clinic. Right when I heard the "zig-a-zig-ahhhh" from the Spice Girls track "Wannabe," I walked onstage.

The first fifteen minutes were disorienting, and I wondered if any of this was getting through to the audience. Then I delivered an obvious joke, and thankfully, they laughed. I had just given them permission to laugh even when things were tragic. I could feel the audience with me on my journey to find the truth. Even when I was frantically searching for a line, I could feel the audience encouraging me to keep going. Sometimes, they laughed at lines that weren't written as jokes, which was weird. Sometimes, they groaned. And sometimes, I could hear weeping. The show ended, and the theater went to blackout.

When the lights came up, the audience surprised me with a standing ovation. The applause was electric. I was floored. This was one of the most important nights of my life, and the audience was letting me know our family story mattered. We were all in it together. For years, the secret I'd kept about my mother made me feel like a part of me was dormant and dead. But tonight, after my own "coming out," I felt totally alive. I finally finished what I'd set out to do.

After my third bow, I ran backstage to get into the lobby through the back door. When I arrived at my merch table, I was taken aback. There was an actual line, and I couldn't see the end of it. There were people staring at my family photos. People were flipping through the deposition binders. My family story meant something to them.

The night felt like a cross between a wedding and a funeral. Each person had a different story to share, a different moment that touched them, a different reason why they had come. The last time I had hugged this many people in one hour was at a personal growth workshop. My audience arrived as strangers, and now they felt like family—well, at least the kind that shared their feelings. Night after night, the magic happened again and again, filling my previously broken heart. Even with a freak snow blizzard called "Snowpocalypse" that took over Seattle, the entire two-week run was sold out, shocking everyone, including me.

During the last weekend run, Wendy and Kang flew up to watch the show. They had agreed to be a part of the postshow talkback. For the first time ever, we would have a substantial conversation about Má, but in front of a live audience. Hang declined the invitation by text. I didn't even try with Ba. He had been clear from the beginning that he was not comfortable, and I completely understood his boundary.

At the top of the show, I heard my sound cue, and I stepped onstage, performing the first scene as I always had. As I transitioned to directly addressing the audience, I saw Wendy sitting dead center. She locked eyes with me, and then I forgot my line! I turned my head to look at someone else, anyone else, to recover. Now I knew exactly where they were sitting. After the incredibly emotional hospital scene where eleven-year-old Susan was holding Má's cold comatose hands begging for her to return, I snuck a peek at Wendy's face as the lights changed. Tears glistened on her face. She remembered that time too.

The show continued with my search to know the truth and then ended in a fantastical dim sum scene between Susan and Má, spirit channeled through Ba. Má showed Susan how each of her children dealt with her death, alone and in their own ways.

....

MÁ: Family has always been there for you.

SUSAN: But they're not you.

MÁ: They are me.

SUSAN: Nobody cares about what I need.

MÁ (irritated noise): Saying they don't care for you? Doesn't

Kang always give you free cleaning when you're unemployed? Remember in college how he want the job to save the trees. How you say? Environmentalist. In the end, he become dentist like I always want—for family! He always good boy. Make the hard decision for family.

SUSAN: What do you mean?

(Lights change, Kang with Ba and Doctor.)

KANG: Hey, Doc, you wanted to see us?

DOCTOR: Welcome. Please sit. Thank you for meeting with me today.

KANG: You can just give it to us straight, Doc.

DOCTOR: Of course. Anthony, Mr. Lieu. Your mother and wife has suffered from cerebral anoxia, a complete lack of oxygen to her brain, which has resulted in permanent brain damage. She is currently in a comatose state, and unfortunately, her brain and organs cannot function on their own anymore. She needs a ventilator machine, feeding tube, and twenty-four-hour care to live. I'm very sorry. Mr. Lieu, how would you like to proceed?

KANG: Doc, could you give us a few minutes?

DOCTOR: Of course. I'll be in the hallway; let me know when you're ready. (Doctor exits)

BA: Kang, what the doctor say?

KANG: She's not going to wake up.

BA: Kang, I have to tell you something.

KANG: Yeah, Ba?

BA: Your mom, she come to me yesterday. Nhập vô. She say she try to come back but too late.

KANG: Too late? What should we do, Ba?

BA: I cannot. . . . You decide. You the oldest son.

KANG: I'm only nineteen, Ba. (beat). . . . Mom wouldn't want a life like this. She wouldn't want to be a burden. She wouldn't be happy. Ba, I think we should pull the plug.

BA: Ừ, làm đi.

KANG (opens the door and brings doctor back in): Hey, Doc, my father would like to move forward with taking my mom off life support.

(Lights change back to Susan and Má.)

MÁ: You see? Kang care for the family, and he care for you.

SUSAN: But what about Hang—he's such an asshole now. AND WE USED TO BE SO COOL! Before you died, we had this Yoda-Jedi relationship and he taught me how to be street-smart. But now he's so mean. Whenever I ask about you, he doesn't text back.

MÁ (beat): He the most loyal one you know.

SUSAN: No!

MÁ: Yeah, he the only one who come to my grave every week, and I get to see my grandson too.

(Lights change, at Má's grave.)

HANG: Warren, hold the incense to your forehead and ask your grandma to help you.

WARREN: But I've never met her.

HANG: It don't matter. You wouldn't be here without your ancestors. Do it.

WARREN: Hey, Dad?

HANG: Yeah?

WARREN (while holding an incense stick to his forehead): Why do we bring roast pork and bánh hỏi every week? Don't you kinda get sick of it?

HANG: That was your grandma's favorite.

WARREN: Oh, okay. (beat) Hey, Dad?

HANG: Yeah?

WARREN: Do you miss her?

HANG: What kind of question is that? Of course. Every day.

(Lights change back to Má and Susan.)

SUSAN: I didn't know that.

MÁ: He care in his own way.

SUSAN: But Wendy—she's such a bitch! Like right when she picks up the phone, she's already mad at me, and she doesn't even know what I'm going to say! She's always blaming me that she had to be the mom to me, and I never asked her to do that—

MÁ: Hey, she only fourteen when I die, you know.

(Lights change, Wendy in the closet talking to Má.)

WENDY: Did you have to go right before Lupita's quinceañera? Everyone was asking me why I missed her party, and what was I supposed to say? And Brian Scott, he asked me to homecoming, and I know you said I couldn't have a boyfriend until I get my master's degree, but is it okay if—

SUSAN (from offstage): Wendy! Where are you?

WENDY: And what am I going to do about Susan? She's always asking me what's the purpose of life and why are we here? I miss you, Mom.

SUSAN: Wendy? Who are you talking to?

WENDY (startled): Nobody. Hey, Susan, come here. We need to put all of Mom's stuff into trash bags and take them to Goodwill before dinner.

SUSAN: Do we have to?

WENDY: It makes Dad sad every day he gets dressed. Do you want to make Dad sad?

SUSAN: No. (slowly begins to put clothes in bags, deep inhale of clothes) It still smells like she's alive.

WENDY: She always liked her jasmine perfume. Giống quê, right? Homeland. Now, hurry up. We got a lot to go through before Dad comes home.

SUSAN: But . . . it just feels wrong! It's too soon. Maybe a miracle will happen like in those soap operas, and Mom comes back and she'd be really mad if she had nothing to wear. We can't waste all her money. We gotta make sure there's something here for her if she comes back—Wendy, stop! Stop putting her clothes in trash bags!

WENDY (whipping around and pushing Susan down): Don't be stupid, Susan! She's not coming back. If you're not gonna help, then just get out of here!

(Susan, crying, starts to slowly put things in bags. Wendy looks at her.)

WENDY: Dad said we can keep one piece each.

SUSAN: Really?

WENDY: Yeah.

SUSAN: If we put all this stuff in Tupperware, do you think we could keep her smell forever?

WENDY (stuffing clothes into bags): Probably, but who has that size Tupperware? Hey, Mom's purple dress! (smells it) Maybe one day I can wear it to your wedding.

SUSAN: The peacock is nice.

WENDY: I'll keep it. Come on. After we do this, I'll get you a Strawberry Shortcake from the ice cream truck. But it comes in two hours!

SUSAN: OK. (wipes nose)

(*Back to dim sum scene.*)

SUSAN: I guess I forgot that.

MÁ: You try so hard to remember the dead, but you need to remember the living. Your father still alive, and you only call him to make him sad. Have you thought to ask about how your half sister is doing in college? Or your stepmom arthritis?

SUSAN (realizing she is caught): But—

MÁ: And cut the avenge-my-mother stuff. Not cute.

SUSAN: But he got away with murder.

MÁ (disapproving squirrel click): Bỏ qua đi. His kids got his destiny like you got mine. I see everything. Let that one go. Su ơi, I start to fade. You don't have to tip them here, already included. And stop smoking the marijuana and going on Facebook—your post not funny.

SUSAN: Wait—my wedding day—did Dì Phương really channel you?

MÁ (smiles, shaking her head no): Sometime, the heart is sad.

SUSAN: I knew it! We had bets, so it wasn't—

MÁ: BUT, remember the ray of light after the rain? In all the photo? Mommy. See you next—

SUSAN (in earnest): What's your advice for living life?

MÁ: One heart, one mind, two hand—remember? You just like everyone else. Do something with your life. Don't be lazy. And call your father every week. He miss you, he don't know how to say.

SUSAN: Wait—do you think I'll make a good mom?

MÁ: Everyone have their own destiny.

SUSAN: Wait—I still have one regret. That last day, the last

thing I said to you—I've been holding on to this for twenty
years—

MÁ: I just want you to focus on school because I never finish
ninth grade. I know what you mean. Trời đất ơi, you're my
daughter. (extends arm)

SUSAN: Wait! (grabs arm)

Could you tell me all of our happy moments together?

When I light incense and ask you for help, does it really work?

How would I know for sure?

*The spirit channeler says you come to me in the form of small
birds. Is that true, or is she just trying to make me feel better?*

Do you believe in destiny or free will?

Knowing everything you know now, what are you most afraid of?

Did I disappoint you?

Any advice on giving birth?

If I have a daughter, how can I make her love her body?

How can I summon you?

How am I like you?

MÁ: You know now. Má nhớ con. Đừng quên. [Mom remembers and misses you my child. Don't forget.]

....

When the show was over, my stage manager brought chairs onstage for my siblings; our moderator, Thanh; and me. This postshow Q&A would be the first time my family would process Má's death as a group. It just happened to be in front of 140 people.

"So, what has all of this been like? Being a part of Susan's artistic process and watching your family tragedy performed onstage?" asked Thanh.

"Well, first off, I'm the oldest brother, the cool one," Kang clarified. The audience laughed. "And second, I always took the position of my dad and aunts. After my mom passed away, I just had to move on with my life. But with Susan, there was an emptiness, especially after my dad remarried. Your mind just replaces your mom with someone new, but that probably created a bigger void. So for Susan to do this project, it actually made me open up a lot of emotions that were somehow repressed with time. In retrospect, I felt sad and empty just like her."

His words surprised me. He had always claimed he was so at peace with everything. I didn't realize my last year of probing made him go on his own emotional roller coaster. He continued.

"I became a little Americanized over the years. I always lit incense at my aunt's house, but I never practiced that in my house. But after this process, I actually put up an altar for my mom, and I offer her fruits and desserts during special moments with my family. It made me realize we have to connect with our ancestors, our past, so we can move on to the future with more confidence and more closure."

I was amazed at my eldest brother. He had been doing deep reflection on his own and made a point to keep Má's memory alive with his children. She lived on.

Wendy shifted in her seat and then finally spoke.

"When Susan first said she wanted to do this process, I was really against it. I was grieving in my own way—it was such a personal thing—but I also closed that whole chapter and didn't want to think about it again. But then I went to one of her shows and saw how her work was changing people. Then I realized it wasn't about Susan getting attention." The crowd roared. "It was more about helping other people to go through grief. I was happy for her and continue to support it. Now seeing the whole show end to end, it's really helped me process our mother's death more. And hearing the recording from Cindy the psychic took me over the top. I told her, 'You go do it, Susan!'"

My heart melted. Wendy had never verbalized any of this to me. I knew she was going out of her way to fly up to Seattle for my world premiere, but I had no idea how much she had been processing since the psychic visit eight months prior. I felt even more touched. My sister sitting on a chair with me onstage meant she had done a complete 180. She was completely out of her comfort zone, and she was doing it for me. The evidence was right in front of me. It was possible for family to change. Thanh shifted the conversation back to Kang.

"As the oldest, you had to carry everyone through this, but you were so young. Is there anything you wish you knew then that you know now?" she asked.

"After looking at the hypoxia data and talking to the doctors, it was pretty clear. I didn't hesitate when she flatlined. I knew it was going to give us some closure and take us out of the hospital. We were there so long—a week, two weeks," recalled Kang.

"No, I went through all the records. It was just five days," I corrected him. Trauma had a way of warping facts. I always thought it was two weeks too.

"It seemed like forever," he continued. "If you have a tragic loss, like a car accident, they die instantly. Here it was dragging out, people crying for a long time. I still think about that, and I would have done the same thing. She might still be alive on a respirator until today. My dad says life is a journey that's a process for you to get to where you need to go. That was her destiny." Even though Kang didn't regret his decision, he took on the emotional weight for all the grieving adults and children. The burden my nineteen-year-old brother had to carry, then, and his entire life. "I think we all swallowed the pill and moved on as best as we could. I'm sure Susan has gotten less closure—"

"I had to put on a whole show to get closure, dude!" I teased.

"And my brother, Kevin, he might have been affected the most by this. He's become a harder, stiffer, meaner guy with life. He built a world around him so no one can get to him anymore. That's the one regret I have; maybe he needed more emotional help. He's not in any turmoil, but he's not lovable like Susan or Wendy."

"Wendy, were you surprised by anything Susan found out in this journey about your mother—who she was as a person?" asked Thanh.

"No, not really. All the different scenes she goes through, it's nice to see it in chronological order. I only remember certain parts that happened. I didn't actually know that Anthony pulled the plug. After the show just now, I asked him, 'Did you really make that call?' I remember they went in the hallway and had a conversation, but I didn't know my dad put that decision on him."

"Since you are all going through this grieving process publicly, does this change the dynamics in your family?" asked Thanh.

"Nay," Kang immediately responded. "We're a pretty strong unit. We love each other to death. But for a while, I was like, 'Is Susan employed? Does she have a paying job?'" More laughter. "She graduated from Harvard and Yale, so . . . this is nice for me to see Susan do this."

He'd never brought those concerns up with me. I found it fascinating how much I was learning from my siblings in a room full of strangers than with all the wrangling I had done privately. What was it about being publicly witnessed that made them communicate more fluidly than ever before? Kang continued telling his perspective.

"The legal process took a lot of emotion out of us, but I didn't care what came out of it, because I forgave the doctor the day I left the hospital. But the thing that hurt us the most—next to losing my mom—was when my aunts and dad had a rift. It divided the family and totally affected Wendy and Susan. They didn't know how to approach my aunts, who to side with. I told them, 'Look, the decision has to be made in the presence of Mom. What would she think if you didn't say hello to the aunts or go over there for dinner? Use that as the basis of your emotional decision. Clear your head with that.'"

Him saying those words brought me right back to that confusing time. It took me almost a decade before I was ready to have a relationship with the aunts again. I know Má wouldn't have wanted that, but choosing between living relatives was more consequential and complicated than pleasing the dead.

"Wendy, your mother passed away from elective surgery, which is so tied up with how she viewed herself, beauty standards, you know. I'm just wondering how you processed that," probed Thanh.

"Gosh, I can only accept it. I can't say she died of something else. When people want to do surgery, I'm very much against it. I can only voice my experience, but it is tough thinking about it again," she admitted. "But what are you going to do?" she whispered.

"Well, I'm in the medical profession," chimed Kang. "I don't fully agree with avoiding medical procedures, even if it is for cosmetic procedures. There are good surgeons and bad surgeons, like in many professions. You just need to find the right person. In life, we make choices, and I don't think my mom made a mistake for choosing what was going to make her happy at that time. She did make a bad choice, and she didn't google this guy—"

I interrupted him right there. "She couldn't—it was '96, dude! The point here is to do your homework. People need to make smart decisions so they don't die a senseless death," I said adamantly.

We had time for just a few more questions, so we opened up the floor to the audience.

"How did Susan involve you in her creative process?" asked a middle-aged Asian man.

Kang went first. "She would ask these questions, but I couldn't remember. I didn't know my mother's intentions or what was said exactly. In life, you just go through it, and you remember what you selectively want to remember. And I dug through a lot of photos that were set aside in a bin in the garage. But I think everybody's journey is different from what they remember. For me, I tried my best, but she did a lot of investigation to get the little details. It's nice. Now I don't have to figure it out. She already [did]." The crowd burst out laughing. "I just watch the show and piece it together."

Right then and there, I realized the play had become an artifact for the entire family. This work would live on for our children and their children to remember where they came from.

"It was very natural," added Wendy. "It became half our phone call. 'Do you have this dress? This picture? This video?' 'No, I'll check when I get home.' It just became a part of daily life."

Both of their answers were so sweet. At some point, both of them decided to join me on my quest, because it was our collective journey. We were children who had tragically lost our mother. Two decades later, I could finally stop because we had found her, through one another.

PART V

MẠ

Newborn Rice
Seedling

The Bird

After the world premiere of *140 LBS*, I had to tend to my marriage. Marvin's love language was quality time, and his idea of a romantic getaway was a multiday alpine rock climb up Mount Whitney, the highest peak in the lower forty-eight states. Like a fool, I agreed. Marvin had dragged me on mountaineering trips like this before, up the terrain of Mount Rainier, the Bugaboos, and Mount Baker. Each time, I went reluctantly, eventually sitting down in the middle of the trail in mutiny, telling him just to move on without me (but to leave the Cheez-Its). But after this whirlwind of a year when he'd supported my wild dreams, I felt like I owed it to him.

After a grueling six-hour hike with a fifty-pound pack, we reached base camp. The next morning at 3:00 a.m. we put on our headlamps and gaiters, hiking through deep snow to reach the foot of our rock climb. Marvin would climb a full length of rope and I would follow him to complete one pitch. The East Face route was a thirteen-pitch climb, a total of one thousand vertical feet. But what we planned as an eight-hour rock climb turned into a twenty-three-hour horror story.

Everything was going great until halfway through. I had to climb up a tight chimney, two parallel faces of rock wide enough for a body to fit. I could move up only by wedging my arms and legs against the rock like a superhero. But the ice axes on my pack kept scraping against the rock, dragging me down. My muscles began to shudder from exhaustion. For the next few hours, Marvin had to haul up the pack and sometimes me. All of this wasted a lot of time. Then it got dark, which meant it got cold. When I reached him, I whined to turn back. But we couldn't rappel down because there weren't any obvious paths. We could end up without enough rope, lost on a ledge in the dark. The only way back to camp was up. I berated him. How could he put us in this situation? If I actually knew where we were and how to get back, I would have left him dead for the marmots. He didn't respond, he just continued to climb.

On one of the last pitches, Marvin couldn't figure out which route to take, so he left for an hour to explore. When he radioed me to climb, my numb fingertips couldn't find anything to grip. Every additional attempt made me slower, clumsier, and more frustrated. When I got to him, it was 11:00 p.m. With just one granola bar and a few splashes of water left, I slumped down next to him.

"Can't. Tired. Helicopter," I blubbered. But Marvin said no one would come because we weren't at risk of losing our lives or limbs. Besides, they wouldn't come until daylight anyway. I insisted he break my legs so that maybe a helicopter would be deployed. We were at over fourteen thousand feet, and the high altitude made every breath a task. Marvin switched gear with me and then moved on without talking. He started to climb, and I sat there letting the rope slide through my belay gloves. My life had been full. No regrets. I was okay to go. I radioed Marvin one last time.

"Love you. Over and out." I closed my eyes and let go of the rope. My body gave out. My mind gave out. All I wanted was sleep. Then, in my delirious state, I thought I heard a high-pitched chirp right by my side. A bird. I was trying to die from hypothermia, but this annoying sound was getting in the way. With all my remaining energy, my eyelids opened. A small robin with a gray head and peach chest quickly hopped around me, trying to get my attention. What was this bird doing here? I hadn't seen another living creature since lunchtime. Psychic Cindy's voice echoed in my mind. Má would appear in the form of a bird. It would act unusual, she said.

Then the bird started to sing. The melody was so familiar. I had heard it before.

Why have you come to earth? Do you remember?

It was the theme song from the personal growth retreats I used to do in my teens and twenties. They would play it when we lay down on the floor after screaming "No!" until all our rage dissolved. I was usually one of the last ones standing.

To loooooooove, serve, and remember.

My cracked lips sort of smiled. I started to whisper the song with the bird. And even though my mind and body had shut down, I felt a greater force pulling me back up. I needed to get up. I had to get up. That bird, that song. That was what helped me stand back up and begin to climb. When I finally got to Marvin, I nuzzled his face with my ice-cold nose, and we forged on.

By 1:00 a.m., Marvin and I finally summited the fucking mountain. We had done it, and Marvin said there was a shelter up top, which lifted my spirits. If only he had told me there was one earlier! I ran there, ready to rest. I imagined a guest host with a bowl of steaming instant ramen, chicken flavor. Playing Yahtzee and laughing about this with other climbers. A guestbook where I would regale our brush with death. I pushed the shelter door open, but it got stuck on snow. I squeezed into the room and found just a small, empty room with something that looked like a twin-size bed, but it was also just made of more snow. Marvin began to nest, instructing me to put all the sharp objects and any provisions we had left in a corner. Without any camping or sleeping gear, we used our climbing rope as a sleeping pad. Marvin squeezed into our one emergency blanket, the reflective thermal kind given to marathon runners.

"Get on top of me," he said in the most unromantic voice.

We lay there in our snow igloo, waiting for sunrise. I was grateful we didn't have to move anymore, but we were shivering.

In the morning, I heard male voices.

"Weird. This place looks like someone died in here. Wait. Holy shit!" shouted a loud male voice. I was so depleted and my mouth so chapped, I couldn't even muster a cry for help. The voices faded away. Oh well. Back to feeling empty and cold. Time passed, and then I heard voices again. It was a woman this time, asking if we needed help.

"Yes," I gasped through my cotton ball mouth. I peeled open my crusted-over eyes with my fingers, ripping a few eyelashes. "Need help," I muttered. I stuck my hand out of the foil burrito and flopped it around so she wouldn't leave. And then this incredible goddess of a woman gave me the most delicious thing I had ever put into my body. A s'mores Pop-Tart. I gave one half to Marvin, and then I sucked on the sugar coating. I used all my energy to sit up and savor this treat sent from the heavens. The glucose sent signals to my brain, and my system started to reboot.

She insisted on giving us water. I was a bit embarrassed to take it. But then she showed me her stash surplus. Between her and her partner, they had three full Nalgenes. These reasonable people came up the hikers' route fit and prepared. Their climb wasn't exactly easy, but it wasn't the hell we had gone up. Here we were at sunrise, and they were already at the summit flush with water.

"Angel?" I asked her. She showered us with even more gifts of peanut butter and jerky before waving goodbye. After ten minutes of eating in silence, Marvin and I started to speak in full sentences again. I also didn't want to kill him anymore. We soon emerged from the shelter to revel in the sunrise. By the grace of my ancestors, we had another day to live. Hikers started to crowd the summit. Usually, this would annoy us, but it was nice to be in civilization again.

As Marvin dabbed some sunscreen on his face, he let me know the way down wouldn't exactly be easy. Since we rock climbed up, we had to descend to our base camp using the mountaineers' route, requiring more technical skill and gear. In layman's terms, that meant it was going to be hard. When I got to the beginning of the trail, I looked down at the steep drop-off. The snow was so hard, it was almost ice. That's when I stopped talking to him.

To move downward, I had to hold on for dear life to my ice axe, facing the mountain, kicking my crampons into the icy snow, searching for a tiny toehold so I wouldn't go sliding fifteen miles per hour like an overturned turtle. My leg muscles were in total fatigue, trembling the whole way down. After hours of banging my right big toe against my mountaineering boots, we made it back to base camp. That was when Marvin informed me we had taken the wrong way down. There was a less steep route just twenty feet from the trailhead we'd taken. I continued fuming.

When we reached our car, we found out the only vacant lodging was a $230 overpriced Best Western. They were price gouging, but I was willing to pay anything for a hot shower. It pained me, but I handed over my credit card. The next morning at the buffet breakfast, I was eating a chalky, unripe banana when I read an article that left me pondering. Birds typically fly below five hundred feet. During migration, most species cruise at an altitude of two thousand to five thousand feet, while some could reach up to twenty thousand feet. But birds only migrate in a flock. When that bird came to me near the summit, it came solo, and we were at fourteen thousand feet. The circumstances for that bird to be up there at that time just seemed too unusual. Was it too much of a coincidence to think that bird was Má?

On the drive to the airport, Marvin finally broke the silence. "When you said you wanted to quit climbing, it's like saying you don't ever want to eat a meal with me ever again."

I finally made eye contact with him and raised my eyebrows. "You can't compare walking on a glacier to eating brunch! Two totally different things," I said with a light laugh. Then I saw his face and realized he was actually serious. It meant that much to him that I'd gone on a grueling suffer-fest with him, even though I'd hated every moment of it.

Nobody told me that marriage would be so complicated. Here we were, two people with divergent interests trying to make a life together and completely missing each other with our love languages. Marvin sucked at giving me words of affirmations. Instead of doting on me with validation, he wrote a program for the Alexa virtual assistant to give me compliments. How was I supposed to feel when her computer voice said my eyes looked like grapes? That my cheeks were his favorite body part? In relationships, I knew we were supposed to make compromises, but did I have to show how much I cared by mountaineering with him, a sport where we could literally die out in the wilderness? My robotic, unemotional husband with catlike tendencies was trying, in his own way, to be vulnerable.

Maybe I was being a little dramatic. What happened on Mount Whitney was nothing compared to the risk my parents took as boat people crossing a dangerous ocean. Má and Ba were the real adventure seekers. They ran through the jungles incognito, trying not to get caught by the Communists, squeezing onto an overcrowded boat knowing very well they could die. They beat those odds, and when they finally came to America, Má used to climb tall rocks in her heels with Ba right by her side photographing her. And now here I was with my life partner climbing our own tall rocks, braving a different type of uncertain world together.

Both couples, a generation apart, had to negotiate risk to manifest each other's dreams. Má set her sights on America and a nail salon empire. Marvin wanted to traverse crevasses and watch the sunrise on epic peaks. Ba was frightened of leaving Việt Nam, and I had no place being up here in the mountains. Má wanted to have her pre-kid body, and I wanted to become an artist. That night up on the summit, Marvin showed me he had more faith in me than I did in myself. It was the kind of faith Ba and Má had for each other to beat the odds, the kind that binds you when things go wrong. They had radically different personalities, but they were each other's safety nets, leaning on each other to go on. It was never just Má out there being the hero on her own; she was because he was.

I leaned my head out of the car window and let the wind blow into my face. Marvin and I had just gone to hell and back together. His choice of words were terrible, but his actions spoke volumes. He was going to be by my side, no matter what. It's funny how I had been pining for someone to give me unconditional love most of my life and the person I chose to be with for the next foreseeable forever was very similar to Ba, in all the best ways. I didn't see that coming at all.

Six weeks later, I was having an annual girls' weekend when I decided to take a pregnancy test on a whim. Something felt off. I did not enjoy eating sweets, but lately, I had been finishing doughnuts. Seconds later, I saw a thick and bold plus sign. That couldn't be right. I shook it again. I wasn't ready yet. I didn't feel like I had the nurturing qualities of a mother, one that intuitively always knew what to do. I still felt like a mess in my own life. I needed a second opinion.

I showed the stick to my girlfriend Diana, who had two kids. She shrieked. While all the other women joyfully clinked their wineglasses, I poured a LaCroix into my glass with a little less enthusiasm. I phoned Marvin, and his monotone voice went up a few octaves. Everyone was more excited than I was.

Moments later, I got a call from Dì Phương, and she didn't sound like herself. She told me Ông Ngoại had just fallen and he had been rushed to a hospital in Sài Gòn. She was flying back to Việt Nam the next day and was inviting me to pay my respects. I wasn't exactly ready to share my news so soon. Việt Nam had Zika cases, which meant going back could endanger my fetus. I let her know I was pregnant. She insisted that I not go.

"Con buồn để trong lòng là được rồi," she said. *When you are sad, keep it at the bottom of your heart, then that's enough already.* I knew she was right, but I still felt guilty. Before I hung up, I told her about my sugar cravings.

"Chết cha rồi! Mày có con trai rồi!" It was clear to her as day. That meant I was going to have a boy.

During my initial ultrasound, the first thing I blurted to the technician was "Don't tell me!" For now, Marvin and I decided we would just call it "Cletus the Fetus." The technician fed my love of surprises with another surprise. I was already ten weeks pregnant, further along than we thought. I calculated the conception date. That meant Cletus survived that night on the mountain too. We had a little mountaineer on our hands. Marvin was beaming.

I started to connect the dots. We had conceived the baby just two days before we climbed Mount Whitney. The bird that came out of fucking nowhere was my mom. Má came to me to remind me I still had things to do. She came to remind me that I don't live life just for myself but to honor the people that I came from and the people that come after me. Má wanted me to know I had something to live for.

My grandparents paved the way for Má, she did the same for me, and now it was my turn to continue the lineage of our culture, but hopefully not our trauma. So when this child arrives and decides to be whatever they want to be, I would get to learn from them and teach them. It would be my duty as a mother to protect them every day— from the things that messed up Má, that made it so hard for Ba to express his emotions, that prevented my siblings from articulating their grief. And parenting with this intention would be possible because of the strength and wisdom I got directly from my ancestors. Má, with my father, created my family, and no matter what my child decided to be in the world, it was my duty to create a space for them to make their own choices—and so on for the next generation.

That was what powered me to keep climbing that night. This was all a part of my số, my *destiny*. It was official. I was no longer just the daughter. My rite of passage had come. It was time for me to finally become the mother.

Slow Dancing

looked at my bump from the side in the greenroom mirror, my little nugget protruding. It was twenty minutes until showtime. I was in Chicago, the third stop in my national tour. But at five months pregnant, I couldn't do my forty-squat warm-up like I used to. I had convinced myself that putting on a ten-city national tour would be a great idea. Everyone said I would be at my physical best during my second trimester. I wanted to build as much momentum as I could for my arts career before the baby came. But here I was, exhausted and kicking myself.

Up until I found out I was pregnant, I was terrified to sign venue contracts because I was scared no one would show up. Not only that, if my tour was an utter failure, I would have to return to corporate life. But the pregnancy gave me a real deadline. I had to be real with myself. Once the baby came, I knew everything could change. I was at high-risk for postpartum anxiety and could spiral after I gave birth. Who knew if I would ever perform again? It was now or never to give my arts career everything I had. I couldn't drag my feet any longer.

The window for the tour dates became anchored to the development of my fetus. If I wanted to be onstage, it had to be when I was three to six months pregnant. I pulled the trigger and dropped thousands of dollars in venue deposits. I searched for people by city, messaging every non-awkward contact, begging them to come to my show. I locked in the tour dates, sent poster tubes to strangers on social media who offered to plaster their city, took calls with the press while I repaired my costume, and fundraised $6,000 to subsidize tickets for refugee and immigrant communities. I planned for almost everything.

What I didn't anticipate was the loneliness of being pregnant on the road. Most nights, I woke up in a panic with charley horse cramps in my calves, my muscles twisting with electric shocks up and down my legs. But instead of waking my husband to comfort me, I was alone on a friend's air mattress.

Standing in the greenroom, looking in the mirror, I felt like a hypocrite. Night after night, I was telling this beautiful mother-daughter story, but in truth, I was afraid to love my own baby. Some moms-to-be sing and read to their babies. I didn't do any of it. After everything I went through with Má, I just couldn't. I figured if I was less attached, then maybe I wouldn't suffer as much if I lost the fetus. But my distance with my baby started to show up in my performance.

The preshow butterflies I used to get were starting to fade. There were some shows where I had to force myself to get excited when really I just wanted it all to be over with. In one of the final lines of the play, I ask Má, "If I have a daughter, how do I make her love her body?" The energy I used to bring to that scene before I was pregnant just wasn't coming through. There were times when I felt like I was just regurgitating the script instead of connecting with the audience on my arduous journey with redemption. I got only one chance to make an impression on people who showed up, and I couldn't mess up my big debut. I knew I was cheating them and I needed to change, fast.

A part of me felt sour about becoming a mom. Ba had pressured me nonstop since I got married to start having kids. But when he saw my pregnant belly, the only thing he said was that he hoped my kid would yell at me as much as I yelled at him. "Karma," he said with a sneer. His words choked my vocal cords. I said nothing, waddling to my room to call Marvin for a sanity check. A simple congratulations would do. When I told my mother-in-law how far along I was, she shook her head and said at seven months I was "too big," which sent me into a sobbing fit in her guest room. She thought I was "sick" from drinking too much seltzer water, so she banned it from the house and forbade me from drinking it. All I wanted was to feel supported; all I felt was wrong.

I thought becoming a mother was going to be the perfect way to heal my relationships with the older generation. But even after I announced my pregnancy, they still found ways to judge me, which sent me into a perpetual self-hating cycle. My rational brain could explain their stinging one-liners with their experienced trauma or cultural conditioning, but I wasn't immune to feeling hurt. Perhaps if Má were alive, she would have found something to nitpick. But at least she could relate to the uncertainty and impending joy of growing a tiny human inside of her. Ba and my two aunts were never pregnant. They treated pregnancy like a task, not understanding that this event would change my life and body forever.

"Má, what am I supposed to do?" I asked into the dressing room mirror. My hands started to move. I waited, half expecting her to answer. But then my hands reached for my headphones and put them on my ears. I put on "Đợi Em Về" ("Waiting for You to Return"), the song that ended my solo show. It was sung by Khánh Hà, our Vietnamese diva who was a regular on *Paris by Night*. This song was the Vietnamese rendition of "Unchained Melody," the title song from the movie *Ghost*. I closed my eyes, wrapped my arms across my breasts and under the bulge of my drooping stomach. I began to slow dance.

And time goes by so slowly

And time can do so much

I held my body, Má's last gift to me. It had her DNA, my DNA, and my baby's DNA. She held me, and I held my baby. Three generations, swaying together to one rhythm. I was still terrified the baby would die, but I had to stop worst-case-scenario planning. I inhaled for four seconds and then took a deep six-second exhale. All I could control was this present moment. I was healthy, the baby was healthy, and no one could take that away from us—for now.

The stage manager popped her head in and gave me my five-minute call time.

"Thanks, five," I acknowledged with my eyes closed. When the song finished, I walked to the velvet curtain at the edge of the stage, waiting for my sound cue. Má, myself, and Cletus were all warmed up and ready now. We had work to do.

Call Me Má

Marv, what do you want the baby to call you? Appa, Ba, or something more mainstream, like . . . Daddy?"

Marvin's eyes were fixed on the road. He was driving our green Subaru Outback a little more carefully than usual. It was the last time it would be just the two of us. Faint stars and a still skyline watched us as we took the route we had taken the previous week to attend Baby 101 class. Marvin swaddled like a pro while I spent most of the class going back and forth to the restroom. I just hoped he remembered everything.

But one big question loomed over us. It was March 29, 2020, and COVID-19's first U.S. case had registered on the map two months before in Seattle. Our city was ground zero for the pandemic in the United States, and I wasn't sure if the hospital was going to let Marvin stay with me during delivery. The entire nation was trying to figure out if they should wash produce with soap, and here I was about to get induced at forty-one weeks. I had an army lined up to help us with postpartum care: my mother-in-law, Mrs. Kim; Dì Ngân; and Galaxy, a family friend. But now no one could travel to help us. Nobody understood how COVID was transmitted as body bags started to fill up at the assisted-living homes a few miles away. Marvin and I were on our own now. But Má and Ba were on their own too when they had driven to deliver me during their early days in America. So much was unknown to them. I tried to ignore that the roads were a little too empty. We drove.

"Appa sounds good," he said. It meant *father* in Korean.

I affirmed his choice.

"How about you?" he asked.

Of course the baby was going to call me *Má*. I tried to say it, but nothing came out. That was weird. I tried again. Nothing. For twenty-four years, I hadn't demanded, uttered, or cried it, because I knew she wouldn't come. I had called to her in the show, but that was Susan the character with Má the character. I was acting. But now this was real life, and I needed to reclaim her name, my new name, but I could not find the sound. Even though it was my first word into this world, I had lost it. I tried again. Nothing. I opened the glove box and blew my nose on scratchy fast-food napkins.

My vocal cords felt strained, but I kept trying until I sputtered out an em sound. This word had been dormant for so long, but I could hear it clearly in my mind. Without knowing the diacritic mark, "ma" could mean six different things: *ghost, tomb, but, mother, newborn rice seedling,* and *horse.* To know my mother, I had to uncover the ghosts that continued to haunt the living. I had to take pictures of tombs to understand that the supernatural was more mysterious and powerful than I could comprehend. I needed to make peace with the man closest to her, Ba, who is the year of the horse. I had to follow my calling for truth in the face of people's resistance when they tried to stop me with "but." And I needed to accept that my family might not have the capacity to be as vulnerable as I would like them to be, but they would always show me they cared through the newborn rice seedling, the symbol of sustenance and the number one Vietnamese love language. To know my mother was to overcome my shadow fears. To know my mother was to become one myself, with a little one I had been growing inside of me these past ten months. This sound, which had been bubbling in my throat for years, was ready to come out.

"Má," I croaked out with a bit more boldness. It was time to let it go. "Má," I said again, the strength in my own voice coming back. Marvin squeezed my hand twice and turned up our favorite Jack Johnson song. I wanted to feel calm, but I was not. When Má went into the hospital, she didn't come out alive. Everyone thought she was going to be fine. Her surgery was supposed to be routine. My child's birth should be routine. But what if it wasn't?

We rode up the elevator to the delivery floor. As the doors opened, my anxiety grew with a new wave of anticipation. I knew I had to be my own medical advocate. I started to speak with authority to protect my body, the only thing I have ever truly owned. I put every professional who worked with me through the wringer. I asked them point-blank if they were on probation. I checked their names on the medical board website to see if they ever had any disciplinary actions—especially with the anesthesiologist. After I cleared his credentials, I let him put the epidural in my spine. Once I did my due diligence, I placed my complete trust in the team at the hospital to shepherd me through the scariest procedure of my life. I finally felt more ease when one of my day nurses said she'd just come from a trip visiting her cousin in my hometown of Santa Rosa. Right then and there, I felt like Má was in the room. It was the sign I needed to know she was with me.

After forcing my ob-gyn to listen to Salt-N-Pepa's "Push It!" on repeat through an hour of active pushing, I became obsessed with a new weight that wasn't 140 pounds. This one was 8 pounds, 8 ounces. I had just given birth to a healthy baby boy. Finally, I could allow myself to love him. Once the nurses took him away for testing, I took a few selfies with my placenta, fascinated by the organ my body had created. Once I transferred to the recovery room, it was time for us to settle on a name. I thought back to the names that came before my son.

Ba was Liễu Trung Thu, his first name a nod to the mid-autumn moon festival because his parents couldn't remember the day he was born but were certain about the paper lanterns the children lit. Liễu stood for the weeping willow trees, and a part of me was proud to be so connected to my emotions. It was a badge of honor to connect deeply with the human experience, giving me an extremely rich life, even if I didn't come from money. Ba eventually changed his legal name to Tom Young Lieu. Tom because of Tom Cruise's role in *Top Gun*, the maverick Ba was to escape Việt Nam and to rebuild his life in a foreign world. And Young because of the song "Forever Young," a hope to be immortal and never forgotten.

When Má was born, she was Hà Thị Phường, then she changed it to Hà Thúy Phương, but the years in America weathered her to become Jennifer Ha. I never knew why she fell in love with the name *Jennifer*, but I know that was the last name she'd ever signed on her plastic surgery consent forms.

And my name was Susan Lieu, with no middle name. Whenever Vietnamese people asked me what my *real* Vietnamese name was, I felt a wave of complicated emotions when I replied, "I don't have one." Who had the time to listen that Má felt proud giving me an English first name because I was the first in the family to be born in America, the place she had dreamed about when she was hustling lotto tickets with two kids at twenty years old? When I was born, my skin reminded her of white lily flowers. The meaning of "Susan" is *lily flower*, one of the few plants that could grow easily in the dramatically different climates of the Mekong Delta and the Bay Area. Flouting Vietnamese tradition, I was without a single-syllable middle name, an even balance of both American and Vietnamese roots. A part of me thought she was being clever, choosing Susan because "USA" was wedged inside my first name, but I'll never know. So even though my name could appear as a loss of heritage, it was actually a celebration of everything Má had fought for.

And now as a mother, it was my turn to mark who I was at this moment by who I wanted my child to become—what I wanted the next generation to remember. When I performed my first solo show about my family in 2017, I just wanted to prove I wasn't a coward, that I wasn't living in fear. I thought, *then* I could become a mom. But after the first show, I never stopped; I just kept on going.

In the two and a half years of asking questions of my mother and playing out those answers in real time onstage, I now see how much I am like my mother. All the wonderful things about her, I wanted to pass on to my son. And all the trauma she'd had to endure, I wanted to check at the door. I knew parenting was going to be a wild ride and it was going to be far from easy, but I just wanted to be conscious of how intergenerational trauma would trigger me for the rest of my life. I had so much more work to do; processing emotions would be the crux of my healing. I had seen it happen night after night with my audience—*when we feel, we heal.*

I wanted to choose a name that captured all of that. Marvin and I settled on Art Lieu-Kim, a union of our two ethnic heritages, and no middle name like his mother and father. Artists are intentional creators, making meaning from the past and morphing it into something new. I did it for my family, and now my son could do it for his generation. Marvin had actually gone to art school to pursue his dream to be an architect. Marvin and I had also met in business school, and one of our favorite professors went by the name Art. Plus, I literally made and make art. It would be a pun—and I couldn't wait for my son's eye rolls. Not even a day old and I started to imagine the epic Halloween costumes I would make for Art to represent different art eras, like Duchamp's *Fountain* urinal or Munch's *The Scream*. Would it be too on the nose to start with an art palette and have him hold a paintbrush? I started to get excited about all the memories we would make together because now I was the má in charge.

Squeeze Back

Flying with a baby was a very different experience from flying on my own. I needed to account for a car seat, a foldable crib, and a will. I knew it was morbid to think like that, but Má's death was a legal mess ballooned with resentment and blaming on all sides. I wouldn't want to leave Marvin with that if anything happened to me. We finalized our advanced health care directives and got our COVID-19 vaccines, and then I immediately booked our tickets to California. I wanted Art to understand that our family wasn't just two adults who doted on him but dozens of people who would indiscriminately sniff-kiss and feed him. He wasn't just part of an American nuclear family, he was part of a Vietnamese clan. And I wouldn't just be introducing him, I was introducing my new self as a mother. I had romanticized our upcoming family reunion, looking forward to reconnecting with them until the moment they opened their mouths.

"You look like you gained forty pounds, Susan," Dì Ngân said. No welcome hug, how are you, or holding of my baby. Just some light body-shaming to kick off the barbecue.

"Do you mean before I was pregnant or since having the baby?" I tried to clarify. It wasn't like either one would be better than the other, but that was the only response I could come up with.

"You look fat," she said matter-of-factly.

This was the woman who was supposed to come take care of me after Art was born. She was supposed to be Má's proxy. I wanted her to make me all the medicinal Vietnamese postpartum soups. But here she was shoving impossible beauty standards down my throat, making all of us who were not size two and below feel like ugly monsters.

I wanted to smash her small, frail body to the kitchen floor with my gigantic, imperfect body. I wanted her to stop. And not just her but everyone. I was ready to suffocate the beauty industry complex right then and there.

My plan was interrupted by Wendy, who forced open the broken backyard screen door a few inches, asking for more melon. Dì Ngân filled a silver mixing bowl with fruit and gave it to me so I could make the handoff. As my cousin Thắng came into the kitchen to deal with the thawed durian, I made a dash out to the backyard patio.

Everything was happening now in slow motion. I was starting to feel the early swirls of a mental breakdown. I tried to make my exhales longer than my inhales. I consciously knew I was being triggered, but now I felt out of control. Kang's wife, Oriana, came up the patio steps, and I recounted what happened, hoping she could pull me out of it. Her reaction was less empathetic than I had hoped.

"You know, Susan, I just tell my kids no one owns their feelings but them. They can choose how they feel about things." She had three kids, and I could see how that was good advice. But this scenario— something about it didn't feel right. Yes, I could choose my reaction, but I was so tired of being complacent with hurtful behavior. I didn't want to be the family punching bag anymore, and I didn't want Art to think talking about bodies like this was okay.

"Also, they ask me every week if I'm pregnant," she said with a tinge of embarrassment.

I became annoyed for her. "But can't I ask them to not talk about just one topic? It's not like I talk about their bodies!" I said with exasperation.

"That's because they know you wouldn't dare," said Oriana. She was right, which made me even more furious. There was a reason why only men and children went into the swimming pool during the party. All the women were too ashamed of their bodies. If I really wanted to break the cycle of intergenerational trauma, I had to walk into the fire. It was time I stood up for myself.

I walked back into the kitchen, and Dì Ngân playfully touched my arm. I pulled back and looked her square in the eye. I had never been so frightened of a four-foot woman before, but she left me no choice. I wasn't an eleven-year-old girl anymore, I was a thirty-six-year-old mother. I told her I didn't like it when she talked about my weight. And then I went in for the kill with my broken Vietnamese.

"Má con chết vì mổ bụng. Dì Ngân có muốn con chết vì mổ bụng không?" *My mother died from a tummy tuck. Do you want me to die from a tummy tuck?*

Her happy-go-lucky face paled. My voice got louder as I reminded her I couldn't sit for a year because of my bruised tailbone from giving birth, so I had to be careful with exercise. But now I went to the gym three times a week. Dì Ngân looked surprised and now a little sympathetic. She never had kids. She definitely never went to the gym. Then I made a sacrilegious request of my mother's older sister.

"Don't *ever* talk about my body ever again," I boomed with my fists clenched tight. "Whether I'm skinny or if I'm fat, don't say anything. I don't want you, Dì Hiệp, and Dì Phương to say anything anymore!" I was yelling as loud as I possibly could, breathing fire into her tiny face. I wanted to make sure she heard every word and that I never had to repeat this ever again. I wanted everyone sitting out by the pool to hear me.

Dì Ngân was not fazed. She looked up into my eyes and squeezed my belly fat with both of her hands. This I was not prepared for.

"Sorry nhé. Đừng giận dì, okay?" *I'm sorry. Don't resent me, okay?*

I threw daggers back into her eyes and then squeezed her squishy stomach right back. I wanted to give her a taste of her own medicine.

"Okay," I said, holding on to her midsection. I took this as we had an understanding. She didn't flinch, and neither did I.

"Con có nghĩ Dì Ngân mập không?" *Do you think I'm fat?* Dì Ngân tried to make me smile.

I was stone-cold.

She let go of my fat and then grabbed my hand, insisting on me eating more of the vegetarian spring rolls, the one dish I'd asked for on special request. She brought a tray of prepped ingredients that could feed a small army. Of course she did. We laid out a station and then we began to make spring rolls together, acting as if nothing happened even though something major did happen. But now that I'd said my piece, we both could truly let it go. Bỏ qua đi, as the saying goes.

PART VI

MÃ

Horse

Persimmons

Three months after the barbecue, Marvin, Art, and I traveled to Texas so Ba could meet his newest grandson. The trip back to see Ba had been much better than I'd expected. It started a few days before we arrived with a text from Ba:

> Hey Susan what's special foods for you and Marvin favorite could you Send the list if you can.

I called him, chatting through the week's menu. When we were about to hang up, Ba asked if I wanted to visit Uncle #9.

"Of course! What day do you want to go?"

But his response was cryptic. He said it would be best if I went with my own family. A part of me missed that we wouldn't continue our little tradition together, but the other part of me felt like I was going through some form of graduation. It was innocent comments like these that continued to remind me that I wasn't just a daughter anymore. I had a family of my own now. And now as a wife and mother, I could see Ba as more than a father. He was once a son until he became an orphan. He was once a husband until he became a widower.

Over the years, Ba has shared his life story in bits and pieces. He was born in the year of the horse in 1954. The Battle of Điện Biên Phủ had occurred in May, ending French colonial rule in Việt Nam but also seeding the beginning of American aid to southern Việt Nam. The precise date of Ba's birth is unknown, but it certainly happened during Tết Trung Thu, the *mid-autumn moon festival*, when kids ran around in the dark with lit paper lanterns and vendors hawked salted duck egg yolk mooncakes in the market. His parents named him Trung Thu in honor of the auspicious season. He was the youngest of three growing up in rural Việt Nam. His sister, Hương, was the eldest, twelve years his senior, and his brother, Sịn, two years younger than Hương.

When Ba was not even one, his father died from an undiagnosed illness. The rural town didn't have doctors or medicine; it was a miracle whenever a nurse came into town. At age six, he lost his mother to a chronic cough, likely pneumonia. Since Ba was now orphaned, his aunt, whom we all called Lầu Ý, became his surrogate mother. Ba spent his childhood helping Lầu Ý by climbing banana trees, chopping off the fruit, so she could raise pigs. Every six months, she sold a pig to the butcher, but that barely made ends meet. Money was so tight, Tết was the rare time he would get one or two sets of new clothing for the whole year.

As long as I can remember, if we were in the Bay Area buying nail salon supplies and groceries on a Sunday, we visited Lầu Ý with a bag of nice fruit or pastries. On a rare occasion, he'd take her to play her favorite card game, blackjack. She didn't know a lick of English, but the old lady could play, outlasting her younger chaperones, returning to their hotel room at 2:00 a.m. and hitting the tables again at 7:00 a.m. When she finally passed in her nineties, Ba's one regret was that he didn't take his mother figure gambling enough. He lamented he was too fixated on chasing money. After Má's funeral, this was the only other time I had ever seen him so distraught.

Trung Thu, who went by the nickname Siêu, dropped out of

school in ninth grade for two reasons. The first was because he was male. Teenage boys were constantly recruited to go into the military. At a mere 110 pounds, the scrawny Siêu could barely lift a gun. If he dodged school, he could reduce his chance of getting enlisted. The second reason was because he had to make money. After leaving high school, Siêu enrolled in a vocational school learning how to fix scooters. He had an engineer's mind and enjoyed tinkering over talking. Undeterred from having to leave school, he continued learning in other ways, by spending time on his other passion: martial arts.

He was enamored with kung fu movies and sought out a gifted spirit-channeling teacher, who gave him his magical mantra. Siêu tattooed his word on his body using a fine-point needle, which activated his power. Whenever he lit incense and said his mantra, a martial arts warrior would jump into his body, ready to fight. His body vibrated as he practiced fight sequences with the teacher's many pupils. Their bodies transformed into invincible armor, and not even a sharp knife could shed blood.

In 1975, Sài Gòn fell, and Siêu married Phường. A year later, he had his first son, trading his mantra and cigarette habit to become a family man. As Communist rule intensified, all his time and money went toward finding a way out. His wife had wild ideas of escaping by boat with their two sons. Even though he was apprehensive, his nature was to be agreeable. And when he gave his consent, he was all in. Ba was governed by his sense of duty, and anything that got in the way of that was simply a distraction. The only direction he moved was forward.

Ba always had a neutral look, except for the one time he and I were driving down Fourth Street, the main artery in Santa Rosa that our shop and the mall was on. We passed by the Flamingo Hotel, and the radio started playing "The Lady in Red" by Chris de Burgh. Ba's face crumpled as he wiped his eyes, trying to drive with one hand. He and Má used to have dance class at the Flamingo, where they learned ballroom and the cha-cha. They would take lessons after work, one of the rare times they did something for fun, just the two of them. And this song was the big dance number they were practicing before she died. Whenever the radio played it, Ba would stop talking and just listen. His body was remembering hers. I would shut up and give him space. He didn't know that I knew it was their song.

When Marvin, Art, and I arrived at Ba's house, small bowls of steaming wonton soup were on the table. Ba showed me the menu for our five-day trip written on the last page of one of my old high school spiral notebooks. I made my own preparations with my therapist. I wrote out two mantras of my own. I needed them to ground me whenever I got inevitably triggered.

We have limited time, so I want quality time.
What he says is what he's been conditioned to say to survive. He's trying to show he cares and is trying to be helpful.

On the first day, we didn't have any major blowups. We were at our best when we had to complete tasks, like when I showed him how to reprogram his GPS or when we filled up the tires in his car. The next day was the big visit to Uncle #9. Marvin had to stay back to work, and Ba insisted I go without him.

"Con lớn rồi," he said. *You're old enough now.*

When I arrived at the dirt parking lot, the double temple doors were closed, but I heard commotion in the direction of the garden. I pushed Art's stroller over a bumpy, brick-laden path, passing statues of the monk covered in garlands of fake flowers. Then I found his new palace: a gaudy, two-story white building adorned with six giant red lotuses, golden angels all over the façade, and in bold red capital letters over the entrance archway "CẬU CHÍN." Dozens of Latin American people were milling about, carrying tote bags and pendants emblazoned with the man's face like he was the next Jesus. In the center of the dusty courtyard was a matching small building oper-ating an outdoor buffet with mock fish, vegetables, and powdered lemonade.

I approached a young man who looked Vietnamese and asked about the expansion. James, a new volunteer at Thầy's empire, told me Thầy's neighbor had benefited so much from the monk's teachings that he gifted the adjacent lot to the spiritual guru. James directed me to a stone bench in the new building foyer and said someone would come. There wasn't a sign-in sheet, since Thầy saw people based on feeling.

I opened up my phone to jot down my questions when another attendant politely directed me inside. I asked for five minutes, and the attendant quickly returned to repeat that Thầy was ready to see me. I gathered my things and lifted the stroller into what looked like a living room, where I bumped into Thầy standing nose to nose with me. He wore a draped knitted mustard shawl over his dark brown pajama set, his feet in white socks over Adidas slides. I had no time to take off my shoes when Thầy began firing at me.

"Could you relax? Could you take it easy? Learn to do your work. What time you eat, cook, watch TV, watch your baby. Activate your authentic power. Why are you here?" he asked. I bent down, trying to unbuckle Art as I racked my brain to recall my list of questions.

"How—how can I help heal my family?" I stuttered out.

"Could you heal yourself first? Could you take care of yourself first? When you die, who is going to take care of him? You don't know how to management. You are here, but your brain is somewhere else. He needs your love. If you don't love you, how you going to love him?"

I knew he was right, but loving myself was complicated. I couldn't divorce my feelings about me from my family's feelings about me.

"Anything else?" he asked with an upward drawl.

"Well—does my family actually love me?" I asked meekly.

"Of course they do," he said simply.

"Then why are they so angry at me?" I wondered aloud for the umpteenth time.

"You need to work on your own management of yourself. They're not angry at you." He said without wavering. He lifted his left eyebrow, waiting for my next question.

"This is my son," I began when Thầy cut me off.

"Could you let him be a man?" he asked with an accusing tone as he pulled a toy car and a lollipop out of a bag, handing them to my one-and-a-half-year-old son. "If you don't, he become a mommy boy later," he warned, followed by fake crying. Art was delighted with his new treasures, oblivious to the crash course I was getting in parenting. Thầy continued, snapping his fingers with every point. "Let him open, let him do what he love, and connect with him. Push him on the right path. Don't run the agenda. Let him be him. Let you be you. You get it? I don't want to see you trapped, and he trapped. I want to see you live your life," he said, his voice turning gentle. He carried on.

"Sometimes you don't listen. That's why you been hurt, that's why you been heartbroken, that's why you been depressed. And in the past, you walk one step, you fall back three steps. Money come in and go out too quick. Home not peaceful, relationship up and down. I watch you out there. The way you walk out, the way you get in—I know exactly who you are."

I tensed up, straightening my back. Were my shortcomings that obvious? He went on.

"What I want for you? I want you to walk higher, think higher, and dream bigger. And settle higher. But how am I going to do it? Turn on your spiritual GPS. Open your mind, learn to listen. Stay more in high consciousness. Stay more in now. Anything else, my dear?"

He struck a chord with all my yearnings over the years. I have struggled to be that person, and here he was saying it was in reach.

"You talk about activating my authentic power. Do you have any guidance?" I asked.

"I always draw my boundary. If something crazy come in, how am I going to react? Love. If something not quite right come in, how am I going to react? With compassion. That's your authentic power. Only two energies—one is fear, one is love. You get it now? Do what you love and you will get there. Believe in yourself."

I gave out a big sigh. If only it were so easy.

"How do you believe in yourself?" I asked in a tiny whisper.

"Practice," he whispered back, and then he went back to his singsong cadence. "Change your thought, you change your future. You know a lot, but you never cultivate. You bought a cooking book, but you never been cook! If you no cook, how you get food to eat? Look like you read a lot of book also, but never been cooking. Anything else?"

His analogy made me laugh. I bought a lot of pretty Asian cookbooks and dog-eared nearly every recipe but still hadn't mastered a single dish. The same went for my self-help books. I desperately wanted to mend my family, but they didn't budge. I came to the repeated realization that I could only control myself. And when I changed myself, it inevitably changed them.

Then Thầy informed me that I would have a baby girl. I moaned with dread. That wasn't part of the plan.

"Adopted, right?" I clarified. It could be a possibility in retirement age.

"Naturally," he fully enunciated, making my arm hairs stand up. He asked for my birth year and then, in quick succession, rattled off every lucky age from thirty-eight to my death at eighty-five. The numbers matched my visit with him from three years earlier. I had calculated he must have seen thirty thousand people since I'd last visited. His consistency was uncanny.

"You look just like your daddy, but your personality, you learn a lot from your mama," he said. He was right. My cheekbones were identical to Ba, but my fire came from Má.

"You copy a lot from your mama. And when you learn from mama, you learn your history. You learn to live, not learn to die," he said.

I brightened. Her epic return these past few years gave me the courage to pursue my dormant calling as a performer and the audacity to shift our family dynamics. Things were better than they had ever been. I just wished Ba and I could be closer.

"Does my mother have a message for me?" I asked.

"She's standing next to you. She say you copy worry from her. She say you not lost her. You gain another angel. She told you bớt lo." *Worry less.* "You worry for everybody, sometime you forget yourself. Could you divorce your worry and your stomach getting better."

I touched my poochy navel still covered in stretch marks. Could elders just get off my case already?

"And your mom told you to go to temple and do a little prayer. And she told me she love you a lot. Your mom is saying, 'Con gái tôi, bà thầy ơi, nó khùng khùng sao á.'" *My daughter, oh monk, she's crazy crazy.* "Sometimes you think a lot. Sometimes you confusing because your mind run too much. Slow down. Because a lot in your mind, that's not you. You the one watching. Learn to stay still and watching. Okay, my dear?"

I nodded and knew he was right. Meditation and exercise were the only surefire things that calmed my incessant mind.

I looked back at my list and felt content. I thanked him in Vietnamese and said my father sent his greetings. He shooed me away and turned back to a woman on the couch. As I wheeled the stroller away, I could hear him talking about me to the next visitor.

"Good lady, but a little hyper. You know hyper? Hay nghĩ lung tung." *She thinks all over the place.*

When I returned to Ba's house, he had me come out to the backyard, where he was grilling meat. The topic of work came up like usual.

But instead of motivating me to get a corporate job by calling me stupid, lazy, or disobedient, he took a different approach. He talked about his own regrets. As he flipped the pork chops with his tongs, he lamented about how doing nails meant he never saved for retirement. He wanted me to invest in myself, and I could do that with a securer job. He wanted me to have something better—for myself and for my family. He suggested I become a loan officer. This time, I wasn't offended. This time, I felt loved.

We stood there, staring at the meat as it cooked. His words landed gently on my heart. I didn't feel like I had to be on defense. Something inside of me shifted. Ba was fragile and imperfect, just like I was. Ba was sharing his regrets so I could be better off.

"I want that for me too, Ba."

We continued to stand there, waiting for the perfect char. I had nowhere to be but there, just existing in one of the few harmonious moments I had ever had with my father. When the meat was fully cooked, he told me a secret. He said with Má's plastic surgery, he was the last to know. Má spoke with her friend, her sisters, and the Vietnamese translator at the clinic before she even told him she scheduled the operation. He never told her to do it. He was the last to know. When he admitted that, I finally put my sword away. I didn't need to fight him anymore. He had told me everything he knew.

During the last morning together, I was trying my absolute best to stay calm so we could have a drama-free visit. I repeated my mantras while I brushed my teeth. Downstairs at the dining table, I watched Art play with scrambled eggs as I drank jasmine tea. I heard Ba holler from the other side of the house.

"Do you want to see some photos from when you first started selling chocolate?" Ba asked. I kept shooing away Gupta, Ba's eighty-pound dog who kept licking my baby's feet, waiting for food to drop to the floor. Art's expression kept shifting from ambivalence to danger.

"Okay!" I yelled back. Ba returned with a striped medium-size photo album and handed it to me. I opened it to the first page.

5/1/03 Dear Dad + Sonya—THANK YOU for letting me go to the East Coast :) so I could decide to go to Harvard. THANK YOU so much for making me curry on my birthday and canh chua on the day I got back from the East Coast. You two are the best parents I could ever have right now. I appreciate everything that you do but I'm too busy to ever let you know. Love, Susan :)

Wait. That wasn't how I remembered it. I turned the page and saw a postcard from Brown University.

Thank you for the airplane tickets! I'll be home soon before I make the BIG decision. I love you guys and miss you.—Susan

Why had I been so convinced that I had to do everything on my own? That Ba never supported my dreams? How did I come to distort my narrative over the years that I was so unloved? Ba and Dì Nhung were barely making any money at the nail salon, yet they bought me a cross-country ticket so I could choose between two Ivies. Ba made countless sacrifices for years so I could have that privilege.

On the next page, I saw a picture of me at seven years old at Susan's Nails. I was smiling in Má's customer chair with a red table lamp and silver hand dryer in the background. I probably didn't show my teeth because I had silver caps on all my decaying baby teeth. The story was I drank apple juice before I went to bed without brushing my teeth. My parents didn't know any better. I had a grill before it was cool.

6/14/07 Hey, Ba! Happy Father's Day! Cảm ơn Ba, vì những gì Ba đã làm, đã nhớ, và cười mỗi ngày. Cảm ơn Ba vì đã nuôi con. Cảm ơn Ba vì hôm qua, hôm nay, và ngày mai. Liễu Huệ Xuân.

Thank you, Ba, for all that you do, remember, and the laughter you give each day. Thank you, Ba, for raising me. Thank you for yesterday, today, and tomorrow. Liễu Huệ Xuân.

I laughed. That Vietnamese name was the one my Vietnamese language professor gave me in college. It meant *flower spring*, and I had so much trouble pronouncing it, I had to write it out for people to understand it when I lived in Việt Nam. The next card was a doodled flower with its brightness emanating with six dashes forming an aura around it.

Con muốn có hoa, mỗi ngày, mỗi ngày.
I want flowers, every day, every day.

I looked at the date and saw it was during my cult days. After all, I'd signed it from Suzen. I flipped through more pages. The time I was en route to work in a Zambian refugee camp, a picture when I visited the Taj Mahal in grad school, our quirky wedding save-the-date postcard, a postcard from our honeymoon in Spain, and every card I'd sent to Dì Nhung for Mother's Day. Most of the time, I addressed the mail to the nail salon. Sometimes I signed my name Susan, sometimes Liễu Huệ Xuân, and then I became Xuân An for a bit. By just my signature, I could pinpoint where I was living and what I was going through without looking at the date.

Then I saw the newspaper clippings. Wendy's and my first major newspaper article for Sôcôla, our chocolate company when I first moved back from Việt Nam. Black-and-white printouts of digital articles. And then I saw articles on my performances. Every article I sent him was carefully cut, folded, and displayed. He never mentioned them, so I thought he didn't care. I thought he threw them away. But here they all were, without a tear or wrinkle.

The rest of the pages were an odd assortment of things. A laminated copy of my original birth certificate. A black-and-white copy of my driver's license and passport. A card to Dì Nhung that read:

Chúc mừng sinh nhật! Ăn nhiều đồ hải sản nhé! Red Lobster! Xoxo, Susan + Marvin.

I guess I gave her birthday money to go get seafood that year. And a recent check I sent to Ba for his sixty-seventh birthday. It was the most money I had ever given to him at one time. A thousand dollars.

"Did you deposit this, Ba?" I asked.

"Bây giờ con có thể chuyển tiền bằng phone được mà!" he said. *Now you can deposit them on the phone!* He reached for his phone to show me.

"I know, Ba," I said, laughing. I closed the photo album and looked back at him. He was not the man I feared and resented anymore. Just as I could change, he could too.

"Con cảm tính quá," he said.

"What does that mean?"

"Ee-mo-shun-ul. Phải giảm lại," he instructed. *Emotional. You need to rein it in.* "Pull yur-sep out. Có đúng không?" He was searching for the right phrase.

"Oh. I think you mean 'pull yourself together.'"

"À, đúng rồi. Pull yur-sep to-geh-duh!" He looked at me for a response.

I knew the next thing I said was going to either get us to where we had been trying to get to for two decades or set us back from all the progress we had made. I remember Cậu Chín yelling at me about rock soup. This could be our moment to change course, to get back on the path together.

"Ba, if people don't have emotions, then it's not good either."

"Ờ, mà xúc động nhiều quá không tốt. Phải bớt lại," he tried with a compromise. *Yes, but too much isn't good. You need to lessen it.* I didn't concede. He tried another way. "Đối với đàn ông, không được xúc động quá đâu," he explained. *For men, you're not allowed to be too emotional.*

"That's Vietnamese culture. If people don't show emotion, then it's going to come out in drinking or hitting people." I wasn't exactly showing the complexity of the issue, but I wanted him to get my point, and that was the best my Vietlish could do.

"Nhưng mà giữ lại ở trong lòng còn khó hơn." *But it's even harder to hold it inside your soul.*

His comeback won the argument. I had never considered it that way. He just helped me wake up to what it was like to be him. With just one phrase, I finally got it. And I finally got him. He didn't want it to break me like it broke him. Every dagger he threw was what he learned to survive. It was what he had to do and all he ever knew. He thought shouldering the trauma himself would be better for everyone else. His ability to compartmentalize traumatized moments was perhaps a learned way to cope, but that meant a pileup of unresolved grief. He had been trying to protect me from his pain. I looked back up at Ba. We held an awkward gaze together, but this time, one of understanding.

Then he presented me a peace offering by asking if I wanted to eat persimmons. The day before, I'd mentioned I really liked them. Ba must have gone to the store that morning just to get them for me. He came back from the kitchen with a paring knife and a mesh bag of seven persimmons. There was still so much more I wanted to say and ask before the moment passed. But this could ruin the moment we'd worked so hard to get. I needed to be okay with doing what made Ba feel safe. And for now, that was him peeling, and me eating, ripe fruit together. Art started to play a game stacking the persimmons, shrieking when they toppled over. Ba joined in, and I took a video of them playing so I could remember that we did have good times. I knew all too well that sometimes memory had a way of distorting the truth.

Before we left for the airport, Ba showed me some new ab exercises he'd learned from YouTube that helped him lose three pounds.

His lower-back pain went away so he didn't have to wear a back belt when he slept anymore. I had no idea he was going through that type of pain. He demonstrated the moves on his yoga mat with a folded couch pillow and then made me do it too. Ba was always telling me the latest fat-burning exercise or device. I used to feel offended whenever he encouraged me to lose weight. This time, it felt different.

I brought up the fact that a relative with lower-back problems was considering surgery. Perhaps Ba's latest ab discovery could help.

"Sur-ge-ry?" asked Dì Nhung from the kitchen. She reminded me that my mother died from surgery and that it could be dangerous. The relative should try the exercises first before going through with surgery.

I was surprised that my stepmother brought up my mother. It seemed like now we were all a little more comfortable with learning from the past. Ba didn't react to what she said. He just kept showing me the techniques.

At the Departures gate, Ba and Dì Nhung extended their arms first with a hug for each of us. Art blew them a few kisses, and they sniff-kissed his face. I thanked them again for making us too much food. They patted my back two times and laughed.

"Ob couse!" Ba said with enthusiasm.

I'd taught him that phrase during the trip. He was trying to practice his English more, and I was trying to take things less personally. We were both trying to learn new things.

Inside the terminal, I got a text from Ba while my family was eating an overpriced burger and fries. It was a picture of him standing in front of his Toyota truck holding a Weedwacker with both hands. He was wearing a thick tan back support belt, a white face mask by his neck, and a dark pair of sunglasses with a baseball cap. The side of the truck visible in the photo had spray-painted stencil letters. All I could see in the photo was a cut-off DENING SERVICE with our home phone number on a two-by-four plank. The photo was from 1990, which meant he was thirty-six, my age at that moment. I had never seen this picture before. He followed it up with a text:

I think this picture may help for your book

I started nodding, with fries flopping outside my mouth in mid-bite. Marvin looked up from feeding Art.

"What's wrong? What's wrong?" he kept asking.

I felt a form of hopefulness for my family. Something big was happening. Something I had always longed for. I had started on this journey to deconstruct the myth of Má. But I realized where I went wrong. I became so obsessed with the past that I kept everyone else frozen in time too. I became attached to old stories of how we'd hurt one another and didn't allow my family to change even when they did.

For years, I fixated on all the things Ba didn't do or say. He could have been more empathetic with my need to know Má. He could have showed more concern for me than for my grades. He could have not defaulted to calling me "stupid" whenever he didn't have an answer himself.

But as much as I think Ba the Parent failed Susan the Child, I wasn't a child anymore. I had become a parent myself and knew, without a doubt, that parents love their children. For Ba, he had been deeply scarred as a young orphan, refugee, and then widower. Why did I keep penalizing him for something that wasn't his fault? Isn't that what I wanted my family to stop doing with me? All I had ever wanted was Ba's unconditional love. Whenever I went to a meditation retreat or even during my cult days, all roads would lead to my deep understanding that my essence was love and my purpose was to be and give love. My relationship with Ba was the ultimate test of those beliefs because he still had the ability to make comments that cut me off at the knees. How I responded was a reflection of where I was in my own spiritual growth.

Why couldn't I apply a lens of curiosity onto his life like I did to

Má's? Maybe it was safer to do it with the dead. They were more forgiving and less threatening than the living. But from the look of Ba's text, I guess people could change. But maybe I could see it only now that I'd let go of my expectations. For years, I expected him to be someone he just didn't have the capacity to be. It wasn't because of his lack of love, it was because how he tried to show it went through his own sieve, a life scarred by trauma.

After years of searching, I finally knew Má and inevitably came to know Ba too. There could not have been any Má without Ba. Since that refugee escape, Ba had been by Má's side, supporting her in the background. He was so reserved and had so much humility, I didn't appreciate his consistency. The photo album, the persimmons, his gardening photo. He was trying to show he cared, in his own way. This was his peace offering. A gesture so subtle, I could have missed it.

Humans were capable of healing. Ba could change. I could change. This past week, something magical happened when I stopped doubting him—he stopped doubting me too. We didn't have to keep reliving our trauma over and over again. There could be another way. I texted Ba right back:

I love it! This is perfect.

One of the few objects I have left from Má is a gold ankle bracelet with a small horse head dangling from it. Ba's zodiac sign is the horse. When she walked the earth as a mother, he was with her every step of the way. During a reburial, a paper horse is burned so the spirit can ride on it, finally free to live its afterlife. This text from Ba was that burning of the paper horse, the closure I had been seeking on this wild quest to know Má. All three of us were now free.

For the longest time, I felt too Vietnamese to be American and too American to be Vietnamese. My nose was too flat, my body too chubby, and my mother tongue too broken. But knowing everything I knew now, I am honored to be the child of refugees. My ancestors were resilient and resourceful, which I inherited. They are the wind at my back, the impulses I feel, the tenacity to say the unspoken. Bỏ qua đi, they say. *Let it go.* I found so much denial in that phrase, and now, I see its liberation. It also means *to forgive.* Bỏ qua đi. I have, I do, and I will.

My name is Susan Liễu. I come from a line of courageous nail salon workers who are my heroes. Má was a manicurist, and Ba was a manicurist too. I am the *manicurists'* daughter and, this is just the beginning.

Acknowledgments

To my husband, Marvin, you are the yin to my yang, my Bette Midler wind-beneath-my-wings. You have been there for every scribbled dream, every family setback, every show, and every time I was in a pit of despair. Thank you for choo-choo-choosing me and helping me fly.

To my son, Art, you inspired all of this. If I was going to do the whole mothering thing, I had to face my fears around my calling and finally get closure around my mother's death. YOU gave me the courage to do it. And once you came into the picture, my personal and artistic focus shifted from intergenerational trauma to healing. I hope our family story inspires you to realize your biggest, hairiest, most audacious dreams. Má is by your side and rooting for you.

To my sister, Wendy, I can still remember us as teenagers in the early 2000s, speeding to the farmers market with freshly made chocolates while blasting "Your Body Is a Wonderland" out of your white two-door Integra rice rocket. There is only one person in the world who knows exactly what I am thinking, and that's you. Thank you for your loyal commitment to healing our relationship, for always being there to save my ass, and for your instrumental help during this memoir writing process. You have been a critical bridge for other family members to come on board. Thank you for being my best friend through all the good and the bad.

To Má and Ba, I am in deep gratitude for your courage, perseverance, and unwavering love for our family. I attribute my grit, unreasonable expectations, and zest for gatherings from you two. I stand on your shoulders and can touch the stars. I feel incredibly blessed to be the manicurists' daughter.

To my siblings, the Liễu Crew. Wendy and Kang, thank you for your support around my research requests, coming to shows, housing and feeding me—actually, thank you for doing that for me my entire life. And Hang, thank you for your honesty—I know you wouldn't say the things you did unless you cared. I hope all of you see this memoir as an honorable homage to Má and hold it as an artifact for us to remember the past, so that we can forge better futures—for ourselves and the generations that come after us. To all the spouses of my siblings—Gaina, Oriana, and Sameer—I love how our clan has grown with you in it. I'll see you all at the next Extreme Indulgence?

To my extended family in America and Vietnam—Dì Phương, Dì Ngân, Dì Hiệp, Dì Ngọc, Minh Tâm, Thắng, Thy, Ái, Thanh, and so many other family members—thank you for going on this wild goose chase with me so I could remember my mother. Dì Phương, you have been the steward of my mother's memory, and I want to thank you for answering every single phone call. Thank you all for sharing stories, letter scans, photos, even her last remaining pieces of clothing. Because of you all, I have an actual relationship with our motherland. You have generously laughed at and with me (I know the difference!), acted as tour guide and translator, and shared your culinary genius with me. Thank you for helping keep her alive for me with your lighthearted humor and overabundance of food. I know she continues to exist within all of us because we make it so. And to my mother-in-law, Mrs. Kim, thank you for taking care of Art all the times I had to go away to write. He has the best Halmoni ever.

To my book team—holy shit—it happened! To my literary agent, Monika Verma, who took a chance and attended my *140 LBS* New York premiere. You have been a calming and encouraging shepherd through every draft and step in this publishing process. Thank you for holding me through all the highs and lows with wacky memes, crunchy snacks, and your reassuring advice. To my book doctor Alexis Gargagliano, thank you for performing triple bypass surgery on me as a writer. Your insight, patience, and scrutinizing mind helped me break through all the blockages I encountered, to find the throughline and to find my voice. Your wizardry helped me find the heartbeat of the book. Thank you, thank you, thank you.

And to my editor, Deb Futter, and assistant editor Randi Kramer at Celadon, you were right all along. "No wine before it's time," said Deb. How I loathed that line during my two years of writing and how I now see the wisdom in it all. Fermentation is a process! Thank you for your guidance, honesty, and faith in me so we could manifest this book together. To everyone at Celadon who touched this book with so much care, thank you. She is now ready to travel the world.

To my early readers who read messy book proposals, gave me a gut check on sections, checked all things Vietnamese, thank you for holding this book as it grew from fetus to baby: Becca Chase-Chen, Jondou Chase-Chen, Evyn Lê Espiritu Gandhi, Marvin Kim, and Wendy Liễu. To my Circle Rock Sisters, Mónica Guzmán and Julie Phạm, thank you for coming to my first-ever show, hosting numerous postshow talkbacks, listening to my raw work at all of our writers' retreats, making connections, and dreaming with me over all the hot pots. Our circle has no beginning and it has no end. And finally, to my Vietnamese translators, Nguyễn Thị Minh and Bích-Ngọc Turner, I bow down to your mastery of this poetic and nuanced language!

To Hedgebrook, where I completed my first draft; to Vashon Artist Residency, where I broke through walls to finish my last draft; and to Mineral School, where I am sketching out the bones of my next project—thank you for holding space for a tired mother to rest, write, and replenish. In your sacred space, I was able to bloom. I am so grateful for the golden ticket each of your organizations bestowed upon me so I could birth the darn thing! And to Flow Club, thank you for creating an accountability platform for an extrovert like me to claw my way to the finish line.

This book would not exist without the theatrical journey I took to produce my debut solo show, *140 LBS*. Jenny Crooks, I think you are the first white girl I ever sniff-kissed. You have been indispensable as a confidante, stage manager, assistant director, tour schlepper, photographer, and clairvoyant systems-thinker that transforms my blubbering ideas into reality. Thank you for always being down to clown. To my directors Paul Budraitis and Sara Porkalob, thank you for bringing your superpowers to the table so I could evolve into the storyteller I am today. To the four souls who cradled my idea and helped me realize my first-ever show *Dr. X: How I Avenged My Mother's Death*: Haewon Baik, Charles Felix, Ashlen Hodge, and Sarah McKinley. To Stacy Nguyen, who created the most iconic artwork for *140 LBS* and *OVER 140 LBS*, I am amazed by your brilliance. Thank you all for holding my delicate story with such care.

To every "stage" and cultural institution that helped me "find my light": 18th & Union, ACRS, ACT Theatre, Book-It Repertory Theatre, Bumbershoot, Carolines on Broadway, Center for Asian American Media, Consortium of Asian American Theaters & Artists, Dent the Future Conference, Diasporic Vietnamese Artists Network, Freehold Theatre, Friends of Little Saigon Seattle, Jean Cocteau Cinema, Jet City Improv, Joe's Movement Emporium, Người Việt Community Center, Oakland Asian Cultural Center, On The Boards, Pao Arts Center, Phở Bắc Súp Shop, Pocket Theatre, Purple Onion, Reimagine, RISK!, San Francisco Columbarium, Seattle Public Library, She Is Fierce, She Who Has No Master, Theatre Mu, The Brainwash, The Collective Seattle, The Magic Hat, The Marsh, The Moth Mainstage, Vietnamese American Arts and Letters Association, and Wing Luke Museum.

To my artistic home, Theatre Off Jackson, thank you for believing and supporting me since day one. The woman behind this historic institution is Patti West, a die-hard arts advocate and incredible collaborator. Thank you, Patti, for all your nudges and all the creative ways we have been able to support each other over the years. To my theatre angels—Kathy Hsieh, Martin Sepulveda, Roger Guenveur Smith, Roger Tang, and Kristina Wong—thank you for waving your wand every time I asked, and more importantly, every time I didn't ask. And finally, to my benefactors, thank you for believing in my work, cutting checks, and supporting emerging artists! Hats off to 4Culture of King County, Artist Trust, Seattle Office of Arts & Culture, and STG. And to Julz Amidala, Susan Berresford, Mike Calcagno, the Cheng-Belys, Aaron Coe, Joe Garvey, Richard Harris, the Hassans, the Haylers, Greg Kisor, Keiko Koizumi, Tom Layton, Susie Lee, Stephanie Lim, the Lippmans, the Lockards, Doug McGray, Tom Speer, Garry Tan, and Deb Wetherby. Thank you for seeding me so I could bloom.

Over the years, there have been some very special people who have taken the time to hold up a mirror to me, reflecting back what I've struggled for so long to believe. I would like to recognize my greater tribe who have made me whole, who I see as family.

First is my surrogate mother, Galaxy Hasley. For two decades you have listened fiercely and nonjudgmentally. Your unconditional love nurtured me when I was broken. I am so grateful for that afternoon when you pulled me aside when I wanted to let go. You reminded me that it could get better, and it did. Thank you, Gigi, for helping heal my family in a mosaic of ways. Always, all ways.

There are an army of women who have mothered me over the years by looking out for me, letting me stay way too long after dinner because I didn't want to go back home, giving me life-changing opportunities, reminding me to take care of myself, and just taking the time to hug me while I cried. Please note that more than half of these women dedicate their lives as educators! Here they are in chronological order of my life: Mrs. Kirby, Vivian Huong, Peggy Mulhall, Lois Aiello, Nancy Watson, Cindy Tillitz, Ola King-Claye, Lynn Ashmore, Holly

White-Wolfe, Mary Jo Renzi, Azalia Fernandez, Carol Millikan, Natasha Deakins, Christie Rose, Jessica Reynolds, Tracey Pugh, Claudine Latchaw, Alice Waco, Sonja Bedford, Catherine Borchert, Pam Devlin, Nancy Vogl, Laurie Fong, Yvonne St. John-Dutra, Sheryl Barnes, Tunie Hamlen, Varsha Ghosh, Maria Dominguez-Gray, Barbara Uliel, Nancy Poon Lue, Minden Beach, Judith Brown Morrow, and Christine Martin.

And then there are the paternal figures who have been my endearing cheerleaders: Rich St. John-Dutra, Jim Holly, Tom Low, Denis Ring, and Ben Dehghan. Joe Garvey, you're not the dad type, but you have believed in my creative potential since day one. Thank you for pretending to laugh at my first stand-up show at that laundromat years ago—you're just a gem. Daniel Tam-Claiborne, your kindness and enthusiasm for lunch is a bright light in my life. Thank you to you all for folding me into your lives with your time and hearts.

And where would I be without my sisterhood? I savor every moment we get to laugh, cry, rage, and wish together. My WRIT LARGE soul sisters, Danielle Scaramellino, Diana Essex-Lettieri, Esther Chou, and Holly Hickling, I feel so honored to walk this life with you.

To the many women in my life whose friendship fuels me, I love you all so much. Thank you for helping in all the ways you have as I metamorphosized into an artist: Erika Carlsen, JC Cassis, Nikki Châu, Amy Dotts, Justine Ang Fonte, Irina Gummeik, Sinae Hong, Marissa Iannarone, Sarah Lafleur, Terri Lê, Chelsea Lê, Brittany Lobo, Vy Nguyễn, Natasha Wasinski Nudel, Jeanette Park, Chelsea Acosta Patel, Michelle Phạm, Gina Phillips, Catherine Thurner Ross, Chinara Satkeeva, Katia Savchuk, Lara Schweller, Rani Shah, Sophia Trịnh, Kate Wang, Nancy Nguyễn Watiker, Martina Welkoff, and Jenny Yang. To every woman at Earth Mothers Circle and Juicy Healing Circle, I continue to howl with you.

To our Seattle "couple friends" who fanned my artistic embers. Thank you for listening, brainstorming, showing up, helping us navigate parenthood, and breaking *very delicious* bread: Becca & Jondou Chase-Chen (and Ruth and Sunny too!), Abby Cullinan & David Diaz,

Sarah Greenwalt & Kevin Sherman. You are our Pacific Northwest family, and we are so lucky for your friendship.

To all my therapists, psychics, spirit channelers, and personal growth workshop facilitators over the years, I know you legally probably can't accept my classification of you as "family," but know that I appreciate your holding space over the years for me to work through my mess. You have been pivotal in my growth to who I am today.

And finally, to my wonderful community of fans! You give me meaning and encourage me to keep going. Thank you for coming to my shows (especially the weird experimental ones!) and getting tickets for your friends around the country, helping me realize my wild ideas with practical connections, hugging me, sharing your own quest for healing, supporting my crowdfunding campaigns, hanging up posters around the country, and (of course) feeding me while I was on tour. This journey to becoming an artist has been deeply healing and hilarious—and none of this would have been possible without you. I give you all an unironic "Namaste" bow. The Divine in me sees the Divine in you, truly. I am forever grateful for your support and look forward to seeing more of you. Remember, *when we feel, we heal.*

About the Author

Susan Lieu is a Vietnamese American author, playwright, and performer who tells stories that refuse to be forgotten. A daughter of nail salon workers, she took her award-winning autobiographical solo show *140 LBS: How Beauty Killed My Mother* on a ten-city national tour, with sold-out premieres and accolades from the *Los Angeles Times*, NPR, and *American Theatre*. Eight months pregnant, she premiered her sequel, *OVER 140 LBS*, at ACT Theatre. She is a proud alumna of Harvard College, Yale School of Management, Coro, Hedgebrook, and Vashon Artist Residency. She is also the cofounder of Sôcôla Chocolatier, an artisanal chocolate company based in San Francisco. Susan lives with her husband and son in Seattle, where they enjoy mushroom hunting, croissants, and big family gatherings. *The Manicurist's Daughter* is her first book.

CELADON
BOOKS

Founded in 2017, Celadon Books, a division of
Macmillan Publishers, publishes a highly curated list
of twenty to twenty-five new titles a year. The list of
both fiction and nonfiction is eclectic and focuses
on publishing commercial and literary books and
discovering and nurturing talent.